the
demographic
cliff

the demographic cliff

HOW TO SURVIVE AND
PROSPER DURING THE GREAT
DEFLATION OF 2014–2019

Harry S. Dent, Jr.

PORTFOLIO / PENGUIN

PORTFOLIO / PENGUIN
Published by the Penguin Group
Penguin Group (USA) LLC
375 Hudson Street
New York, New York 10014

USA | Canada | UK | Ireland | Australia | New Zealand | India | South Africa | China
penguin.com
A Penguin Random House Company

First published by Portfolio / Penguin, a member of Penguin Group (USA) LLC, 2014

Illustration credits
Pages 111 and 113: Hoisington Investment Management Co.
Pages 147, 148, 150, 151, and 341: Courtesy Robert Prechter, © Elliott Wave International
Other graphs by the author

ISBN 9781591847274

Printed in the United States of America
1 3 5 7 9 10 8 6 4 2

Set in Janson MT Std
Designed by Alissa Amell

CONTENTS

the demographic cliff

INTRODUCTION

I'm not usually on the bearish side of predictions, having been an outspoken bull since the late 1980s. I was watching the rise of the massive Baby Boom and thinking optimistically when most economists saw the United States declining after the first financial peaks of the 1980s. I anticipated the decline of Japan in the 1990s when economists were proclaiming it would overtake the U.S. economy. Now people are saying the same thing about China's growth in the next decade, despite the fact that Japan's economy remains virtually comatose two decades later.

At Dent Research we have a not-so-secret weapon: *demographics*. It is the ultimate indicator that allows you to see around corners, to predict the most fundamental economic trends not just years but decades in advance. Demographic data can help identify macro and micro trends. On the small side, I can tell you when people spend the most on potato chips—age forty-two. Thinking bigger, I can point out to you how our economy has boomed and gone bust on a forty-six-year lag tied to the birth index for peak spending of the average family since 1983.

I believe, in short, that if you understand the demographic data, using it to your advantage just isn't that difficult.

Inflation rises with younger people entering the workforce, then wanes after they become most productive in their forties. Deflation can set in when more people retire than enter the workforce (that's happened in Japan). Younger people drive innovation cycles, older ones don't (there are more adult diaper sales in Japan today than sales of baby diapers!). Demographics are the key to the future: if you don't understand such trends, from the trivial to the tremendous, you will miss many things that you should have seen coming.

Many economists refuse to see beyond the next election. They see political factors as central, but I disagree. The key to the future is the predictable things people do—and, for the most part, politicians are merely reacting on a lag. By understanding the demographics, we can identify the key economic trends that will affect our lives, businesses, and investments during our lifetime.

The Debt Drug and Other Problems

In response to the global economic panic in 2008, governments around the world pulled out all the stops, stimulating beyond anything imaginable years ago. Governments and central banks employed quantitative easing (QE), a new "debt drug" that involves buying financial assets to increase the monetary base—$11 trillion and rising globally. The goal was to prevent a continuing global slowdown by deleveraging the greatest debt and financial asset bubble in history.

But this practice perverts markets, interrupting the free market's natural mechanisms for rebalancing and fostering innovation. This messing with Adam Smith's "invisible hand" means you need to prepare for the worst downturn and crash of your lifetime, which I predict will arrive in early to mid-2014. Governments are going to keep drugging themselves with QE until they fail and the economy corrects itself between 2014 and 2019, when all of my key cycles point down together—I've never seen a cycle alignment like this before. Since 1983 the private sector of the United States alone has accumulated $42 trillion in private debt (it grew at 2.7 times GDP for twenty-five years), but we can't keep growing government debt forever in the name of supporting the now slowing private economy. When the economy corrects itself—and it will—there'll be a sudden deflation in prices. Financial asset bubbles will burst all around us, just as we saw in late 2008 before government stimuli brought it to a halt.

Let's take another demographic angle. Record real estate prices around the world aren't good for the economy because they raise the cost of living and the cost of business. When you look closely at the numbers, it's apparent that older households benefited the most from the 2000–2005 bubble. But if we want the younger generation to invest for the future, we need real estate and stock prices to come back down to reality. We need debt levels to be written down so households and businesses can free up cash flow and afford to expand again.

Speaking of our aging population, we also need to get real about the simple fact that our life expectancies have risen dramatically over the last several decades. Too many of us still aspire to retire in our early sixties when we should be thinking of retiring in our early seventies. If we accept the truth of that, we solve much of the massive entitlement crisis we face with fewer and fewer workers and more and more retirees. In fact, retirement is a myth created in the last several decades. Unless your health is failing, why retire and do nothing? Contributing and serving people is what we humans are all about, not sipping martinis at the pool!

We have seen an unprecedented boom for the last three-quarters of a century. Special interests have created all types of tax loopholes and health care inefficiencies that need to be revolutionized, not changed by increments. Then there's education, the highest inflation sector of our economy. There is no way to fix our unbelievably complex tax code or health care or education systems with incremental political change. The only way we get such a revolution is a breakdown of the system that has worked so well for decades and even centuries. How do we get there?

The Four Seasons

Demographics and the pace of technological innovation can be used to predict what is to come. In the pages that follow, I'll outline a simple, four-season cycle with a duration roughly that of the human lifetime of about eighty years.

New technologies and generational boom-and-bust cycles create a sustained boom that starts in the spring, hits speed bumps in summer with high inflation (think high temperatures) and falling generational spending that then descends into an autumn bubble boom with rising generational spending and productivity, falling inflation and interest rates. That final boom creates bubbles in financial assets and new technologies and business models that, like after the fallow season of winter, will pay off for many decades to follow, but must first get more efficient by means of the deleveraging of debt bubbles and financial assets (as happened in the 1930s and will occur in the decade ahead).

This is a natural cycle of boom and bust, inflation and deflation, innovation and creative destruction that is the invisible hand of the free market system that has driven us to unprecedented wealth and incomes, especially in the last century. But, as we've seen, governments taking more and more of the debt drug have stopped the rebalancing of our economy after a glorious fall bubble boom. That means we won't get to spring and long-term growth again unless we allow the rebalancing and deleveraging to happen.

In the chapters that follow, we'll visit the challenges we face and the opportunities that will be on offer. In chapter 1, I show how demographics drive our economy predictably, and how you can see economic trends decades in advance. I predicted twenty-four years ago that the U.S. economy was likely to peak around 2007. But Japan peaked before the United States in the early to mid-1990s, and Europe will see declining demographic trends starting in 2014. Even China will see plateauing demographic trends ahead and then fall after 2025. More countries will go off the Demographic Cliff in the years ahead, making stimulus plans from governments less and less effective.

In chapter 2, I will show how Japan is in a "coma economy" due to endless QE and a failure to face and restructure its massive debt. QE should be a brief tool to stem a short-term crisis and shouldn't be mushrooming into a longer-term policy—as we've seen happen. Europe's large-scale QE and bailouts into early 2012 finally failed with a recession in mid-2012 that the European countries can't seem to shake. How will Europe fare when demographic trends are adverse, given how much trouble it's in already due to colossal debt and imbalances created by the euro dating back to 1998?

In chapter 3, you'll learn how the real estate bubble around the world started with the middle-class generation buying homes after World War II, and then got a booster shot arriving with the huge Baby Boom generation from the 1980s forward. But today the buyers will be increasingly outnumbered by the dyers in most wealthy countries. That conveys a painful truth: under such circumstances, there will be a zero net return adjusted for inflation because in developed countries, a smaller generation is following a larger one for the first time in modern history. Prices will fall, or, at best, adjusted for inflation, remain flat for a long time to come (recall that Japan's real estate fell 60 percent in the 1990s and has yet to rebound, nearly a quarter century later). We need to go back to the lessons of Monopoly, where you buy real estate for the rents, not the appreciation.

During 2013, the U.S. economy appeared to be on a path to sustainable growth again. But the recovery in stocks, real estate, and the overall economy resulted only from that endless government stimulus thus far. That's another of those bubbles, and I'll tell you about the unprecedented debt bubble in chapter 4 and then look at the history of debt and financial bubbles in chapter 5. I have studied every major bubble for hundreds of years and they are all the same. Trends get very favorable and then everyone wants to retire on them through speculation. China is the greatest bubble I have ever seen, as its government has driven its economy for decades solely through massive overbuilding. Its real estate bubble is beyond anything in the developed world. China will be the last and greatest bubble to burst—look out below when that happens—but all bubbles share the same fundamentals, one of which is that they all burst, and then they go back down to where they started or lower. We're not there yet!

In chapter 6, I'll talk about commodity prices. Many economists say that China and the emerging world will save us from a global slowdown. But that doesn't align with the fact that emerging-country stocks have been declining since April 2011, and China's since February 2010. That represents another early warning system that something is wrong. I'll show you how commodity prices peak every thirty years—and they peaked in mid-2008. When commodity prices go down, the emerging countries that export them go down, and China now exports more to them than to developed countries. You'll see why I call commodity prices the Achilles' heel of emerging economies.

The Upside to the Downside

What's the upside to the downside here? The world and almost all financial assets will be on sale. In practice, that can have some very positive ramifications for you.

In chapters 7, 8, and 9, I'll reverse my field and look not at the bad news but at strategies for prospering in this inevitable, challenging, and most productive winter season for investors, businesses, and governments. If you have the common sense to understand that you can't fight a debt crisis with more debt, and that the massive Baby Boom generation around the world will only spend less as they age, not more, then you will listen to what I have to say and prepare your investments, your business, and your family and kids for this inevitable and necessary crisis ahead—especially between 2014 and 2019. The worst is likely to come in 2014 to 2015 and 2018 to 2019, as I explain through our many cycles in chapter 7.

You need to take some steps and recognize that these are once-in-a-lifetime possibilities for profiting, as did Joseph Kennedy in investing and General Motors in business during the Great Depression.

First: Understand that investors who protect their capital after the most recent and most artificial bubble will be able to buy everything from stocks to gold to beachfront property at the lowest prices of their lifetimes.

Second: Your children will be able to buy houses at affordable prices and get the lowest mortgage rates of a lifetime, as will you for a vacation home.

Third: Businesses will be able to gain market share that will pay off for decades and buy the most valuable assets of your failing competitors at cents on the dollar.

Fourth: Governments will be able to restructure debt and entitlements in a crisis that will force their citizens to be realistic, and bring common cause to the most polarized politics in modern history.

Underlying all this is the fact that growth throughout all of history—human and not—is exponential and cyclical. The two best experts on exponential progress I see in technology and economics are George Gilder and Ray Kurzweil, while my expertise is more in the cyclicality of such progress. I study population demographics, which have grown exponentially since the dawn of man, as have our technologies. I also study technology cycles: how they grow exponentially and also go through four predictable stages where business and investment strategies have to change for continued success. But there are longer-term cycles in demographics and technology. We have seen massive down cycles from the ice ages every 100,000 years or so, to the Dark Ages from A.D. 450 to 950, and then an on-and-off depression cycle from most of the early 1800s into the Great Depression of the 1930s.

There is much to see here from demographics, technology trends, and history—and from a thirty-thousand-foot view it's not that complicated. So my advice is to not rush to judgment when I say something that runs counter to what you think or have heard. I think you will find good sense in the simpler and more human nature of my approach to economics, in understanding longer-term trends by understanding what people like you do as they age. People matter in our high-tech, middle-class age. We can measure what people will do as they age and project economic trends no one would think possible—more long-term than short-term.

Don't you want to know what is likely to occur over your and your kids' lifetimes to prepare for the future? Let's look more closely at demographics. After all, "Demography is Destiny," as the nineteenth-century social scientist Auguste Comte is said to have stated, decades after Adam Smith came up with the free-market concept of the "invisible hand."

CHAPTER 1

THE DEMOGRAPHIC CLIFF AROUND THE WORLD

One simple indicator warned of the crashes in Japan from late 1989 forward and in the United States in 2008. It's called the Spending Wave.

The wave is not a function of stock valuations, but of consumer spending patterns over the course of their life cycle. It's about the predictable things people do as they age.

Demographics tell us a typical household spends the most money when the head of the household is age forty-six—when, on average, the parents see their kids leaving the nest. Reading these numbers is no different from life insurance actuaries predicting when the average person will die and, based on that, making projections decades ahead.

Essential to understanding broad economic trends is the recognition that new generations of consumers enter the workforce around age twenty and spend more money as they raise their families, buy houses and cars, borrow, and so on. You may peak at a different age, likely in your early fifties if you are more affluent and went to school longer (as your kids probably did or will, too). The demographic climaxes in average peak spending led to the rising boom from 1983 to 2007, then the slowdown in 2008 that will carry on until 2020 until trends bottom out and 2023 before trends turn up again. These numbers won't predict stock crashes and swings in the markets in between, but the big picture is undeniable.

In 1989, stocks in Japan peaked dramatically at 38,957 on the Nikkei. A major real estate peak followed in 1991. Despite unprecedented monetary stimulus since 1997 (there's that QE—quantitative easing—again), more than two decades later stocks remained down 80 percent in late 2012. Likewise, twenty-two years later, real estate is still down 60 percent from the peak, and commercial real estate by even more. Real estate has never bounced back significantly, even though, from 1999 forward, a new—but significantly smaller—generation began to reach the right age to buy houses.

Did you know that almost all of the money spent on housing occurs between ages twenty-seven and forty-one? In *Our Power to Predict* in 1989, I predicted Japan would see a twelve-to-fourteen-year downturn, while the United States and Europe would see their strongest decade in history. Only demographic indicators could anticipate such a powerful shift in the global economy.

After two lost decades in a coma economy, in early 2013 the Japanese government announced that it would implement the most aggressive stimulus program in history to turn things around. Stocks advanced dramatically in response into mid-2013, but we can't know for how long, given that the advance is based on a desperate monetary policy meant to fight dire debt ratios and demographic trends. Since Japan's first demographic slowdown was over in 2003, why wasn't the last decade more prosperous?

The world's economists simply have not come to terms with not only what happens when the largest generation in history reaches its spending peak, but also what it means when that generation is followed by a smaller one. We need to consider hard questions, such as what happens when Japan, most of the countries in Europe, the North American countries, and even China face shrinking workforces and reduced population growth. And what happens as more people retire than are entering the workforce? How does that affect economic growth and commercial real estate? What happens when more homes go onto the market as people die than there are younger buyers to buy them? Such a situation has not occurred before in modern history, and it will have a powerful effect on economics. We've seen it already in Japan, which I will cover in chapter 2.

The Best Leading Indicator

The best indicator? *People do predictable things as they age.* That's it in a nutshell. So, let's look at how demographics drive economic trends, from the macro to the micro, in modern middle-class economies.

Only since 1980 have we had clear and detailed annual surveys from the U.S. government on how consumers spend, borrow, and invest over their life cycle, down to very small sectors (remember my reference to potato chips? Sales of those peak at age forty-two for the average household). But with great volumes of such data, it is possible to forecast the most fundamental economic trends.

Consider that the Consumer Expenditure Survey (CE) from the U.S. Bureau of Labor Statistics measures more than six hundred categories of spending by age—and spending really changes in different areas according to age. The average family borrows the most when the parents are age forty-one, typically the time of their largest home purchase. They spend the most at age forty-six, although more affluent households reach that peak later, between age fifty-one (top 10 percent) and fifty-three to fifty-four (top 1 percent). People save the most at age fifty-four and have the highest net worth at age sixty-four (and later for more affluent households). Predictably, as we live longer these peaks slowly move up in age. The Bob Hope generation, born in increasing numbers from around 1897 to 1924, reached their spending peak at age forty-four in 1968, meaning their boom was a forty-four-year lag on the birth index from 1942 to 1968.

The average person enters the workforce at age twenty, an average of those who complete their education with a high school degree at age eighteen and those who graduate from college at age twenty-two. Typical Baby Boom couples got married at age twenty-six (though that age is rising, presently hovering around twenty-seven-plus). That's when apartment rentals peak, too, and the average kid arrives when his or her parents are ages twenty-eight to twenty-nine. That stimulates the first home purchase at about age thirty-one—as soon as people can afford it! As the kids first become teenagers, parents buy their largest house, between ages thirty-seven

Figure 1-1: Consumer Life Cycle

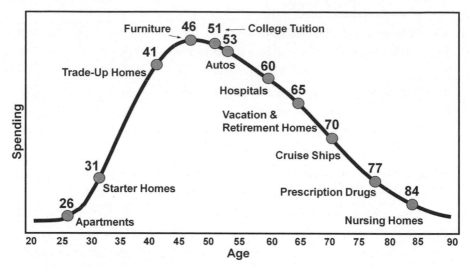

Data Source: U.S. Census Bureau, Dent Research

A sample of some key areas of consumer spending out of the broad survey. Does this resemble your life pattern? If not, it's likely because you are more affluent and peak a bit later in these areas.

and forty-one. (Why? Parents and kids both need more space in this difficult period of adolescence. You want the kids to be way over there and you way over here—and the kids agree!) We continue to furnish our houses, and thus spending on furniture overall peaks around age forty-six, which, again, is also the peak in spending for the average household.

In the downward phase of spending, some sectors continue to grow and peak. College tuition peaks around age fifty-one. Automobiles are the last major durable good to peak (that's around age fifty-three), as parents buy their best luxury car after the kids have left the nest and they don't need a boring minivan anymore. Some get fancy sports cars. Some get big pickup trucks. These are in fact the sectors doing the best in 2013 before they peak after 2014. But then their vehicles last much longer as they have nowhere to drive without the kids, so car spending plummets thereafter.

Savings rise most from age forty-six to fifty-four and continue to grow, though more slowly, toward a net worth that peaks at age sixty-four, one year after the average person retires at age sixty-three. Spending on hospitals and doctors peaks between age fifty-eight and sixty. Vacation and retirement home purchases peak around age sixty-five. People travel more from age forty-six to sixty, after their kids leave the nest, but then they begin to find it too stressful. They finally choose to just go on cruise ships and be stuffed with food and booze with no jet lag or customs hassles. That peaks around age seventy. Then there are the peak years for prescription drugs (age seventy-seven) and nursing homes (age eighty-four).

I have highlighted only some key areas: the data can tell you much more, such as when consumers spend the most on camping equipment, babysitting, or life insurance.

(I have a special research report, *Spending Waves*, that looks at more detailed spending patterns by age across many sectors. You can find more information on that at www.harrydent.com/spendingwaves.)

The peak in overall spending in Figure 1-2 is at age forty-six and revolves around kids' getting out of school and the need for spending dropping for parents so that they can both enjoy life more and save for retirement. Spending on furniture peaks here as well. But note that there is a plateau between age thirty-nine, when home buying starts to peak, and age fifty-three, when auto spending peaks. Then spending drops like a rock all the way into death! This is a big deal that governments, businesses, and investors are not anticipating as the massive Baby Boom generation ages in one country after the next.

The difference in spending patterns between a nineteen-year-old, a forty-six-year-old, and a seventy-five-year-old is huge. How much did you earn and spend yourself at age eighteen or nineteen? How much did you earn and spend when you bought your largest house and then furnished it in the years to follow? How much do seventy-five-year-olds spend . . . and do they borrow money? Consumers are anything but a constant when generational cycles are shifting the age concentrations significantly—especially the unusually large generations like the Baby Boomers. Note that some individual spending sectors can be very volatile, such as in acquiring items like

Figure 1-2: Total Consumer Expenditure by Age

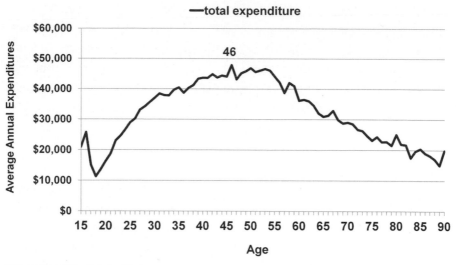

Data Source: U.S. Census Bureau

If you want to reduce middle-class economies down to one important factor, this is it: *consumer spending by age.* **Most economists assume consumers are more like a constant and that business and government swings drive our economy. In fact, consumers are 70 percent of the GDP, and business investment only expands if consumer spending is growing and the government taxes businesses and consumers for its revenues; hence, it follows consumer spending indirectly as well.**

motorcycles, which are largely purchased during the male midlife crisis years between forty-five and forty-nine, or RVs (recreational vehicles) that are largely bought between age fifty-three and sixty.

In the big picture, what makes this consumer spending cycle so powerful is the fact that people are born (and immigrate) in clear generational waves. These are the two ways that you become a worker and consumer in a country like the United States—workers represent "supply" of goods and the same people as consumers represent "demand." Hence, new generations drive both as they age into their peak spending years—and that's precisely what causes a broad boom in our economy, which happened from 1942 to 1968 and from 1983 to 2007.

A century ago, immigration was the largest driver in the U.S. economy. New arrivals were the biggest factor in what I call the Henry Ford generation, which powered the economic boom that bubbled into the Roaring Twenties. More recently, we have for two decades predicted that immigration will fall sharply again from 2008 forward, when declining spending by Baby Boomers was also pushing us toward the next great depression between 2008 and 2023. We've seen that happening, with the drop-off from Mexico especially apparent. Along with declining births since 2007, U.S. population is

Figure 1-3: U.S. Immigration, 1820-2012

Data Source: Department of Homeland Security, 2013

Looking back to the late 1800s, you can see that immigration is anything but constant. There were two major peaks in immigration: the first in 1907 with a major drop-off after 1914; the second was around 1991 with a major drop-off beginning after 2008. Note that immigration dropped to near zero in the 1930s after the greatest surge in American history.

simply not going to grow as fast as economists forecast by extrapolating past trends.

In the recent immigration surge from the 1970s into the 2000s, which peaked in 1991, the immigrants added more to the Baby Boom generation (born from 1934 to 1961) than to the Echo Boom (born from 1976 to 2007) to follow. The highest numbers of immigrants arrive around age twenty-three (what is called the *mode* in statistics), with the average age at thirty. The new arrival usually enters the workforce and starts producing and consuming. Hence, immigration has an immediate impact on the economy, unlike new births (the latter arrivals require eighteen to twenty-two years to enter the workforce and become productive).

When my outlandish forecasts back in the late 1980s for a Dow of 10,000 by 2000 started to look a bit too conservative, I realized that I wasn't adjusting for immigrants, which I did in 1996. I developed a bell curve for the age of immigrants over decades of data using a computer model to determine when immigrants were actually born on average so I could add them to the birth index as if they were born here. And at Dent Research we make our

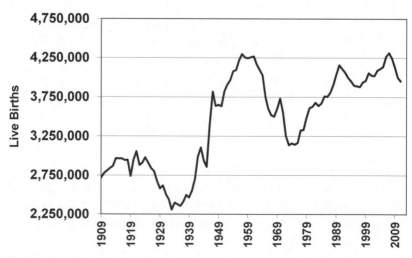

Figure 1-4: U.S. Birth Index, United States 1909-2011

Data Source: U.S. Census Bureau

Figure 1-5: Immigration-adjusted Birth Index, U.S.,1909-2009

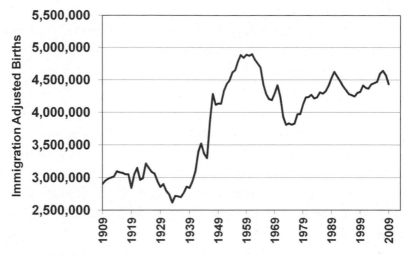

Data Source: U.S. Census Bureau

Note how much larger the Baby Boom was than the Bob Hope generation before it. The Echo Boom hit similar levels of births at its peak in 2007. But the last is a smaller wave as a generation, and from 2008 into the early 2020s, births are going to tend to fall more than rise due to a bad economy, just as they did in the 1930s and the 1970s. Note that it's also necessary to adjust the birth index for immigrants to get the total size of each generation. When legal and illegal immigration during the Baby Boom generation is added, the Baby Boom towers higher still.

own future forecasts for immigration taking into account the business cycle instead of the normal straight-line projections of economists.

We found that, when adjusted for immigrants, the Echo Boom generation never reaches the growth numbers of the Baby Boom generation. Hence, it is the first generation to be smaller than the one before it. This pattern is consistent throughout the developed world, with the exception of Australia and the Scandinavian countries. Many European and East Asian countries have no Echo Boom generation at all.

Not everyone recognizes the subtleties of this. In print and broadcast journalism—a May 2013 article in *Barron's,* for example, and on air at CNBC—we're told that the millennial or Echo Boom generation is larger than the Baby Boom generation. By habit, I cringe when I hear broad statements concerning demographics (too often the speaker hasn't done in-depth research and reaches wrong conclusions). In this case, the statement is partly true, partly not.

The easy part—and the one that economists usually get right about demographics—is that the populations of most developed countries are aging and that rising entitlement burdens will fall on the younger generations. How will the lower spending and earnings levels of a smaller generation affect the economy? Take a good look at the Japanese economy, which went into a coma after Japan fell off the Demographic Cliff between 1989 and 1996: Japan has had zero inflation and GDP growth for the last two decades (see chapter 2).

Taking a close look at the data, it's clear that the Echo Boom generation does exceed the Baby Boom generation in sheer numbers. In the United States, the birth rate for the Echo Boom group started at a higher level, and its rising birth span of thirty-two years (1976–2007) was longer than that of the Baby Boom group, at twenty-eight years (1934–61), as Figure 1-6 shows. Baby Boomers total 108.5 million adjusted for immigration, compared with 138.4 million Echo Boomers. But the more important point from my research: the peak immigration-adjusted births of the Baby Boom generation are still substantially higher and have a bigger overall wave.

In the next boom, from about 2023 forward, the number of households needed to keep the economy going by spending and borrowing money, buying homes, investing, and other economic activity simply will not grow as fast or to the same levels. Yes, many (but not all) developed countries will experience a boom driven by demographics about a decade from now, but it will not be as strong as that precipitated by the rising spending and borrowing of the Baby Boomers.

Growth is more likely to come as a result of technological advances, especially those that will increase longevity and working years, which could help compensate for the lower number of workers. Such areas as biotechnology, robotics, nanotechnology, and new energy sources that are cleaner will be the drivers, but it will be a long time before they affect the economy

Figure 1-6: Generation Population Size, U.S.

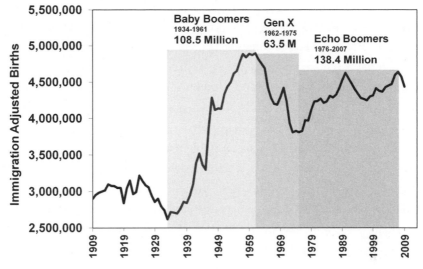

Data Source: U.S. Census Bureau, Dent Research

The key to demographic trends and forecasting is reading the wave—namely, the rising wave of births and growth—and distinguishing the relative size of the acceleration of each generation. The Baby Boom is like a ten-foot-tall wave coming onto the beach, whereas the Echo Boom is a five-foot-tall wave. A surfer can instantly tell you the difference! Although the Echo Boom wave is wider in its scope, the Baby Boom wave is taller and greater in magnitude and peak numbers.

broadly, because it takes decades for new innovations to gain momentum. For example, the automobile was invented in 1886, but only began to move into the mainstream U.S. economy from 1914 to 1928.

The Spending Wave

Now for our most powerful single economic indicator for projecting fundamental economic and spending trends decades in advance: the Spending

Wave. Here we simply take the immigration-adjusted birth index and move it forward forty-six years for the predictable peak in spending of the average American household. How simple is that? Look at the broad correlation with the S&P 500 adjusted for inflation over time. It is in the short-term swings that there is so much volatility, whether in boom or bust. Demographics can accurately project long-term trends in booms and busts in our economy, but cannot predict short-term swings in our economy that come from all types of geopolitical and other human impacts.

To review: The birth trends for Baby Boomers started in 1934 but accelerated in 1937 and peaked in 1961. A forty-six-year lag for its peak in spending would project a strong boom from 1983 through 2007. Is that not what happened, despite some big swings due to stock and real estate bubbles that burst along the way? The preceding Bob Hope generation boom had a forty-four-year lag on rising births between 1897 (estimated) and 1924, or 1942 to 1968. Then that generation saw a slowdown from 1969 through 1982. This is

Figure 1-7: The Spending Wave

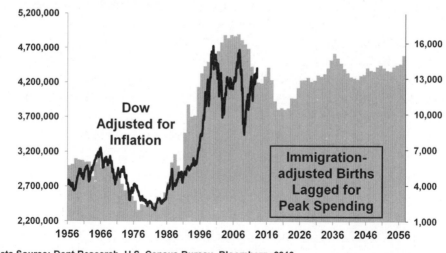

Data Source: Dent Research, U.S. Census Bureau, Bloomberg, 2013

This simple indicator told me twenty-five years ago that the U.S. economy would expand around 2007 and then slow between 2008 and 2020–23.

not a short-term indicator, but it is the best long-term leading indicator in history.

Economists think no one can predict longer-term trends because the world and technologies are changing faster than ever. The truth is we have new information on demographics that we never had before, which makes predicting the long-term economic trends easier than predicting shorter-term trends, given the impact of political events and business and stock market swings that occur due to human nature. Looking at the broader picture, we see the predictable things we do as we age as key to the economy, including innovation and inflation, which comes in our younger years; spending and borrowing into midlife; and saving, investing, and exercising political power into our elder years.

The coming boom from 2024 into 2036 and beyond will not be as dynamic in developed countries like the United States as the boom from 1983 to 2007, when the Baby Boom generation drove dramatic earning, spending, and borrowing trends, innovation (in the 1970s) of new technologies, and their adoption. That next boom will focus on emerging countries, including India, Southeast Asia, Latin America, and to a lesser extent China, because its population is aging rapidly.

The more we dig into demographics, the more we find how pervasive an effect it has on modern economies with high-income, middle-class populations and unprecedented levels of upper-end affluence. But let's look at another major factor in our economy: inflation, which is not largely a monetary phenomenon (sorry, Milton Friedman). It is driven more by people.

Consider this logic: Young people cause inflation. Why? They cost everything and produce nothing. That's because, quite rightly, they are in a learning stage until ages eighteen to twenty-two or so in our affluent modern economy. It costs on average about $250,000 for parents to raise a child, not counting college costs if they go. It costs governments a big portion of their budgets for education. And just as a new generation enters the workforce, businesses have to invest in workspace, equipment, and training. In effect, young people are an investment in the future for all sectors of our economy. They begin to pay off when they enter the workforce and become productive new workers (supply) and higher-spending consumers (demand).

Conversely, older people tend to be more deflationary. They spend less, downsize in major durable goods, borrow less, and save more. They don't require investments in new infrastructures like offices or larger homes, or in major education; they ultimately leave the workforce and downsize to smaller homes or even nursing homes. This stands in contrast to young people, who require massive investments in education, office space, and technology as they prepare for and then enter the workforce.

In 1989, one year after I discovered the Spending Wave, I discovered a surprisingly strong correlation between inflation rates and a 2.5-year lag on workforce growth (see Figure 1-8). This is an amazing short-term correlation, given how many factors affect inflation: food and gas prices, monetary policy, swings in economic cycles, currency exchange rates, and others. And there are swings against this indicator in real life from such variables. But the long-term trend follows very accurately, just like the Spending Wave, despite such short-term volatility for so many other reasons that are very hard to predict and determine.

Workforce growth over time is simply a function of younger people entering on average at age twenty (and rising slowly over time) and older

Figure 1-8: Inflation Indicator, 1953-2015

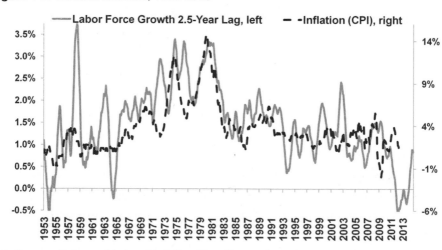

Data Source: Bureau of Labor Statistics, Dent Research, 2013

people retiring at age sixty-three on average. Retirement age is likely to rise more rapidly in the next decade as many Baby Boomers will not be able to afford to retire in a bad economy, given that they have little savings, having expected good times to last forever. The Bob Hope generation saved a lot more, as they grew up in the Great Depression and World War II, a sobering experience that made them more conservative even in the good times. Baby Boomers also express a desire not to retire as early as their parents did, although actions speak louder than words. The average retirement age has been pretty steady between sixty-two and sixty-three for the last two decades, and that includes Baby Boomers who started to retire from 2000 forward and will continue to do so until at least 2024.

The Inflation Indicator can only give us a 2.5-year window on inflation trends, but, because we can predict the number of twenty-year-olds who will enter the workforce on average and the sixty-three-year-olds who will exit, we can roughly project workforce growth and inflation two decades in advance (see Figure 1-9). Back in the late 1980s when I was predicting the greatest boom in history into 2007 or so, I also saw inflation falling to near zero by 2010. That's what happened.

Workforce growth has gone from a high of 4 percent in the late 1970s to 3 percent in the late 1980s to 2 percent in the late 1990s, stands at around 1 percent currently, and will be 0 percent by 2020–23. The greatest inflation in modern history was not caused by central bankers, nor was high workforce growth in the 1970s caused by politicians. Who would want to create 16 percent inflation and mortgage rates and upset everybody? The weak workforce growth currently even with massive stimulus is actually consistent with where this model says we should be, again about 1 percent a year or 125,000 to 150,000 jobs a month. That was a bit higher in 2013 due to strong stimulus and a recovery of past lost jobs, but still has not brought us back to the level of employment in 2007 at the peak.

In this unique time period wherein a great depression actually started to unfold in late 2008, governments have gone to unprecedented extremes to stimulate and prevent a depression, deflation in prices, and debt deleveraging. They are going against the grain of the natural forces of the economy . . . and this won't end well, as occurs with any drug addict in denial. The

Figure 1-9: Inflation Forecast, 1950-2030

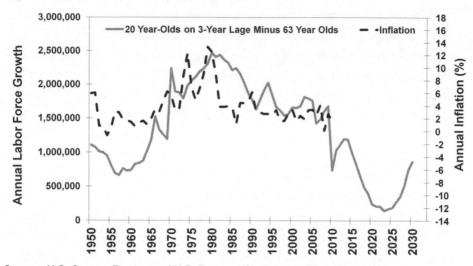

Source: U.S. Census Bureau and U.S. Bureau of Labor and Statistics

The most important trend to note from the Inflation Forecast model is that the model points toward deflation in prices between 2010 and 2023 without any impacts from debt deleveraging or commodity prices collapsing, which I also see ahead.

economy's natural forces and fundamental trends will win in the end, not central bankers and governments.

If you want to see the future, watch demographic trends, as they are the ultimate leading indicators. Even better: most economists, investors, and businesspeople don't understand this, so it creates a unique advantage for you as an investor or business.

The Ultimate Economic Model

I call it the Eighty-Year, Four-Season Economic Cycle.

Everything I have studied in life seems to run in four seasons or stages. Our annual weather cycle is one obvious example: spring, summer, fall, and winter. Not so different are the four stages of our life: youth, adulthood, midlife, and retirement. There are four stages of the business cycle, too: innovation, growth, shakeout, and maturity. Just as there are four weeks in a month and four phases of the moon, I've found our economy evolves in four-season cycles as well, one that assumes the approximate duration of a human lifetime, currently about eighty years.

The first credible economic cycle I studied in the early 1980s was the Kondratieff Wave, revealed by the Russian economist Nikolai Kondratieff in 1925. Back then this was a fifty- to sixty-year cycle (when we didn't live as long) that saw peaks in inflation rates in 1814, 1864, 1920, and more recently 1980. This cycle of inflation and deflation was characterized as having four seasons: a spring boom with mildly rising inflation; a summer recession with inflation rising to a long-term peak with major wars; a fall boom with falling inflation, powerful new technologies moving into the mainstream, and a credit bubble that leads to high speculation and financial bubbles; and then finally the winter season with the bursting of the bubbles, debt deleveraging, deflation in prices, and depression (and wars can occur here as well, such as World War II).

This cycle seemed to lose its generally predictable pattern decades ago for two reasons: First, after World War II the cycle got very exaggerated, with massively higher inflation trends from the entry of the supersized Baby Boom generation into the workforce, which is inflationary; and second, when the next winter season to follow the Great Depression was due in the 1990s on that old sixty-year cycle, we got the greatest boom in history instead. That's why there was a rash of books in the late 1980s and early 1990s calling for a great depression: Ravi Batra, Robert Prechter, James Dale Davidson, and Harry Figgie wrote them, and they all sold boatloads of books. I respect most of these authors and read their books thoroughly, as they had a much greater perspective of history and cycles than most economists.

At the same time, however, I was studying demographics and the Baby Boom. I understood that there was no way we could have a great depression when the largest generation by far was in its sweet spot for spending and borrowing in the 1990s. I came out with a book in late 1992 called *The Great Boom Ahead*. I presented my thoughts on a new, four-season economic cycle that spanned approximately eighty years. I saw that the Baby Boom simply exaggerated the cycle in terms of the magnitude of inflation and booms, and our life expectancies took a big leap in the last century, extending all human-related cycles, including the length of booms and busts.

The point is that the Kondratieff four-season cycle is still very much valid, but it has been stretched and magnified. If we just project cycles in spending and inflation through demographics, we can more accurately time this powerful and overarching, four-season economic cycle into the future.

One explanation for the shift from a near sixty-year to an eighty-year cycle is that our economy changed dramatically in the last century. Up until the early 1900s, the United States was still an agrarian nation with 80 percent of its population involved in agriculture, mining, and even trapping. Commodity cycles follow a very consistent thirty-year cycle (see chapter 6), and generational and demographic cycles followed closer to a forty-year cycle. Cycles that revolved more around the commodity cycle meant booms and busts about every twenty-nine or thirty years because agrarian consumers didn't have nearly the effect on the economy that the urban, much more affluent middle-class ones do today. Rural consumers even today in China and India have little economic impact as they are mostly self-sufficient farmers. In contrast, in the twentieth century, major long-term stock peaks in this country came in 1929, 1968, and 2007 when adjusted for inflation. Those were thirty-nine years apart, and also coincided with the peak spending of the last three generations.

Two boom-and-bust cycles make the four-season cycle, so two commodity cycles would come to fifty-eight to sixty years on average, in line with the Kondratieff cycles up to the early 1900s. After the Roaring Twenties we saw the first mass affluent middle-class society in history. Their spending cycles started dominating instead of the commodity cycle. Hence booms and busts came every thirty-nine to forty years, adding up to two boom-and-bust cycles over seventy-eight to eighty years.

The magnitude of the Baby Boom generation stretched the heights of inflation and economic/stock booms, while rapidly rising life expectancies and a shift from a commodity-based economy to a mass-consumption, consumer economy also factored into the lengthening of the boom-and-bust cycles from thirty to forty years. All of that explains why most Kondratieff proponents were wrong about a depression in the 1990s. On the new cycle, that depression would come twenty years later—and thus was slated for this decade, the 2010s.

In Figure 1-10, the second line represents the Spending Waves of each generation and the boom in the economy and stocks that accompanies it. The Bob Hope generation had its rising Spending Wave on a forty-four-year

Figure 1-10: 80-Year Four-Season Economic Cycle

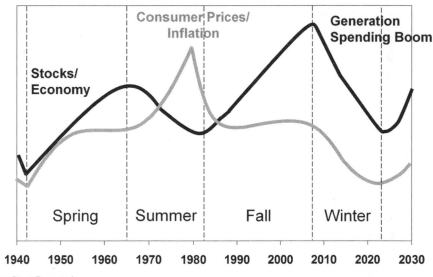

Source: Dent Research

The new eighty-year cycle summarizes the current cycle that started in 1942 after the Great Depression, or the last winter season. The inflation index in the chart follows the traditional pattern of the Kondratieff Wave: moderate and rising inflation in spring, high and peaking inflation in summer, falling inflation in fall, and deflation in winter. Think of inflation like temperatures in our annual weather cycle. High temperatures are like high inflation and low temperatures are like deflation. Both are uncomfortable and present challenges for the economy and stock markets.

lag to births from 1942 to 1968, and that represented the last great bull market in stocks. The S&P 500 peaked in 1968 when you adjust for inflation. Then there was an on-and-off recession from 1969 through 1982 in its downward Spending Wave. Then the Baby Boom had its Spending Wave on a forty-six-year lag from 1983 to 2007, again with the greatest stock boom in history following almost exactly—from August 1982 to October 2007. From the great recession of 2008, Baby Boom spending trends point down into around 2020, then flatten out and don't turn up with the Echo Boom until 2023 or 2024. This is how I roughly predicted the next winter, depression season way back in the early 1990s, including the peak around 2007.

How do you put these to use? Investment, business, and personal strategies have to be different for each season, just as you prepare differently and dress differently for seasonal changes in weather. If you see the change of season coming, it's no problem to adapt. If you don't, you're in trouble.

I will look at how the seasons are different and how strategies need to change in this winter season ahead for investors in chapter 7, businesses in chapter 8, and governments in chapter 9. But first, given the building blocks of how demographics drive modern middle-class economies in developed countries, let's look more closely at the Demographic Cliff and how it will continue to affect the world in the coming years.

The Demographic Cliff Around the Developed World

The Spending Wave indicator applies to any major country or region of the world. The only difference is that for most countries data on demographics tend to be in five-year cohorts by age instead of one-year increments. But let's take a country-by-country look at the data.

Japan peaked in births after two final baby booms into 1942 and 1949. On a forty-seven-year lag (Japan peaks a year later due to lower immigration and higher schooling), the Japanese Spending Wave then peaked twice, in late 1989 and late 1996—and stocks in Japan have been down off and on ever since. This compares with the United States peak in births to follow, between 1957 and 1961, and Canada's in 1960. So the Spending Wave for North

Figure 1-11: Demographic Peaks around the World

Country	Peak Spending
Japan	1989-1996
United States	2003-2007
Germany	2010-2013
United Kingdom	2010-2013
France	2010-2020
Italy	2013-2018
South Korea	2010-2018
Spain	2025
China	2015-2025

Source: Dent Research

When the Spending Wave peaks among major countries and regions around the world.

America peaked around 2007 and then started falling off the cliff toward slower spending. Spending in Europe will begin to peak next, only more broadly, but plateaus roughly into 2013–14, and then spending will fall off the cliff in one country after the next there, most by 2018.

Germany will be the first major European country to fall off the cliff after 2013, along with England, Switzerland, and Austria. South Korea's spending will plateau from 2010 to 2018, then fall as dramatically as in Japan for decades and decades to follow. Even workforce growth in China will plateau, between 2015 and 2025, after which Chinese demographic growth will decline indefinitely. China will be the first emerging country to go off the Demographic Cliff, although it still has further urbanization trends in the future to create a more moderate level of growth for a few decades.

If Europe is already in a recession and has major debt problems now, how will it fare when spending goes off the Demographic Cliff after 2013 or 2014?

In fact, there is no chance that a major global crisis won't happen by the end of this decade. Even South Korea will fall off the Demographic Cliff after 2018, the last such country in the wealthy region of East Asia. The second half of this decade clearly is going to be economically worse than the Great Recession of 2008–09, with the worst of our demographic and geopolitical cycles hitting between 2014 and late 2019.

Spending for the United Kingdom plateaued between 2010 and 2013, but then will begin to fall off the cliff; France's plateau is the longest, from 2010 to 2020. The plateau for Italy lasts from 2010 to 2018. Spain is the last to peak around 2025, but it is already in a depression after the bursting of the greatest real estate bubble in Europe. Note that the drop-off after the peak in spending is the steepest in the southern and central European countries: Greece, Spain, Portugal, Italy, Germany, Austria, and Switzerland—and Germany is supposed to hold up the euro zone?.

As mentioned above, the Spending Wave peaked in the United States in late 2007, but will move forward to a second Demographic Cliff by around 2014 or so, because the wealthiest 1 percent to 10 percent of the population will peak in spending by that time. In the United States, income inequality is stronger than in Canada or Europe, as the top 10 percent controls nearly 50 percent of income and spending and the top 1 percent in income alone accounts for nearly 20 percent. Also, the top 10 percent controls over 90 percent of financial assets (outside of personal residences), which the Fed has only exaggerated with endless QE and monetary stimulus.

So who is the Fed going to get to spend once the rich people go off the Demographic Cliff as their late-stage kids finally leave the nest? Who will be hit the worst in the next financial meltdown and bubble burst? Not Homer Simpson, the common man. He already is experiencing lower real wages, fewer and worse job opportunities, and often an underwater mortgage. It will be the most affluent that suffer massive losses in net worth as financial assets crash again once reality sets in after years of stimulus.

Our best long-term and intermediate cycles (see chapter 7) suggest another slowdown and stock crash accelerating between very early 2014 and early 2015, and possibly lasting well into 2015 or even 2016. The worst economic trends due to demographics will hit between 2014 and 2019. The U.S.

economy is likely to suffer a minor or major crash by early 2015 and another between late 2017 and late 2019 or early 2020 at the latest. The Dow could fall to 5,800 to 6,000 by mid-2015 or a bit later, and to as low as 3,300 to 3,800 by early 2020, which would simply erase the greatest bubble in stocks that started in late 1994.

The United States and the euro zone now are the two largest economies in the world. The U.S. Spending Wave moves more sideways for decades to come. The euro zone as a whole (Figure 1-12) has no Echo Boom generation, unlike in the United States, but southern Europe has the highest youth un-employment in history, and more young people are dropping out of the workforce or leaving every day, as there simply are no jobs, and the older

Figure 1-12: Spending Wave, Europe, 1950-2100

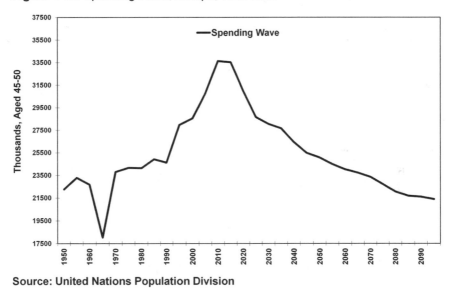

Source: United Nations Population Division

Look at the spending peaks and falls ahead among the entire euro zone. The broader picture of Europe is dismal: a plateau from 2010 to 2013 or 2014 will be followed by a very deep cliff and spending declines to follow. Workforce and population will actually shrink for decades in many countries, especially in southern and central Europe.

Figure 1-13: Spending Wave, Germany, 1950-2100

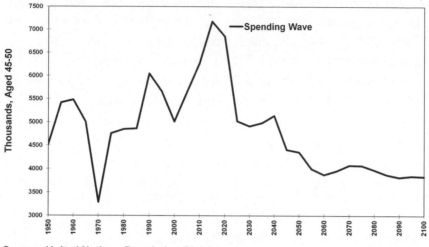

Source: United Nations Population Division

Germany is critical for holding the euro zone together, but spending there will go off the cliff after this year. Germany, Switzerland, and Austria, which all face steeper drop-offs in the decades ahead, have no real Echo Boom generation to come, much like the southern European countries.

generation is staying in the workforce longer. How will Europe recover? Recovery is unlikely in southern and central Europe (especially in Germany; see Figure 1-13), even in the next global boom from around 2023 forward, unless these countries attract strong immigration, and that is not likely.

In looking at each country specifically, it is true that economic trends due to demographics in Norway, Sweden, Finland, and Denmark hold up better in the next decade and grow mildly again from the 2020s forward. The Netherlands, Belgium, France, and the United Kingdom should head more sideways in the decades ahead, more like the United States. However, the trends for Germany, Switzerland, Austria, Greece, Spain, Portugal, and Italy should move strongly downward for an indefinite period. Why do the more northern European countries have higher birth rates? They offer women who work strong maternity leave and support. This is the best investment a country can make for the future. Demographics dictate that the economic disparity between the northern and the central and southern countries will only grow. How will the euro fare under these conditions over time?

You might think, "Oh, Asia will bail the global economy out with its growth." But emerging markets are already slowing and underperforming due to falling commodities prices since April 2011. We predict that commodities prices will fall for roughly another decade (see chapter 6). East Asia, including China, is the most dynamic sector of the global economy, but its populations are aging rapidly. Look at South Korea's Spending Wave (see Figure 1-14). South Korea has had a "miracle economy," much as Japan did twenty-two years ago. But South Korea's spending will plateau from 2010 into 2018 and then fall off the Demographic Cliff on a twenty-two-year lag from Japan. South Korea has almost no Echo Boom generation, worse than Japan. The story is similar for Singapore, which peaks around 2010, followed by Taiwan.

Figure 1-14: Spending Wave, South Korea, 1950-2100

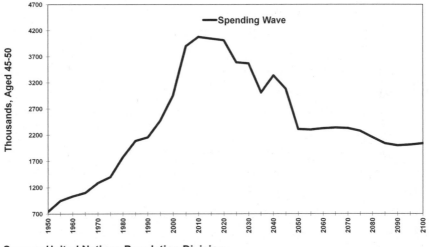

Source: United Nations Population Division

This emerging country became a rich country in just three decades, from the 1980s to the 2000s.

Figure 1-15: Spending Wave, Spain, 1950-2100

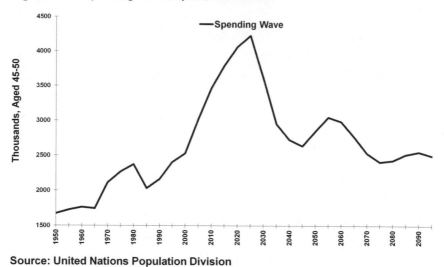

Source: United Nations Population Division

Spending in Spain should continue to edge up into 2025 (see Figure 1-15). This continued rise is not consistent with actual birth rates and hence must be the result of high immigration, fueled by the massive construction boom and real estate bubble in Spain. The bursting of that bubble is the main reason that Spain is in a deep economic slump, with youth unemployment at 57 percent and total unemployment at 27 percent as of mid-2013, similar to Greece. That also means many of those immigrant workers will migrate back to their home countries, erasing more of Spain's demographic advantage.

In Spain, construction alone accounted for 13 percent of the employment, versus just 6 percent for the United States at the top of its real estate bubble. Home prices are still falling, which weighs on the banks. If Spain is in this much trouble now, how bad will things be once spending falls off the cliff after 2025, given a projected steep decline in spending due to demographics and no Echo Boom generation to follow? This situation is echoed in the rest of southern Europe.

"Oh," you say, "but China is now the second-largest economy in the

Figure 1-16: Overcapacity in Major Chinese Industries

- Electrolytic Capacitors   50%

- Cement   40%

- Solar Batteries   40%

- Steel   35%

- Flat Screens   32%

- Copper   17%

Source: Larry Lang, Chair Professor of Finance, The Chinese University of Hong Kong

Larry Lang's estimates of overcapacity in major industries, which confirm the findings of other researchers, including Pivot Capital Management Ltd. in the past.

world and growing at 8 percent plus and will save world economic growth!" We have said for the last three years that China's economy, driven by a top-down Communist government, will ultimately discredit the notion that a government-driven economy is better than an economy driven by capitalism and democracy. China is overbuilding infrastructures, real estate, and industrial capacity at unprecedented rates.

Professor Larry Lang from the Chinese University of Hong Kong has clearly stated that Chinese economic statistics are not what they seem. Growth in GDP is wildly overstated (as confirmed by basic statistics like electricity use in new homes). Lang thinks that GDP growth is around 4 percent at best, not 8 percent, and that inflation is much higher than 3 percent and rising.

Others estimates find that 24 percent of completed homes or condos are empty, as they are not using electricity. Major Chinese cities, including

Hong Kong, Shanghai, and Beijing, have the highest ratios of real estate to income in the world by far, typically with real estate prices of twenty to thirty-five times income versus the ten times income in San Francisco at the peak of the U.S. real estate bubble. China's private credit bubble is accelerating, whereas most countries are slowing down in credit generation. Of $1.5 trillion in global credit created in the first quarter of 2013, China created $1 trillion. Thus, private credit is likely to be growing at $4 trillion a year, or 50 percent of GDP, probably higher if GDP is overstated.

Although it is the emerging country with the greatest and fastest economic growth in the world, China's workforce growth will plateau and decline a bit between 2015 and 2025. What this adds up to is that, after 2025, the early stage of the next global boom, the economy of China will fall off the Demographic Cliff (see Figure 1-17). Workforce growth is even more critical economically than the forty-six-year Spending Wave among emerging countries, where earning and spending waves are not as steep.

I've said it before but it's true: urbanization is the key trend for emerging countries. Yes, China will continue to grow as it moves from just over 50 percent urban toward 70 percent to 80 percent in the decades ahead. However, migration from rural to urban areas is driven by young families, which China is running out of quickly. The Chinese population is aging faster than that of the United States. China's government knows this and is now planning to move its urban population from 53 percent to 72 percent by 2025. That will mean 250 million unskilled rural farmers will be moved into more urban areas. Does that sound feasible to you?

China has already overbuilt its infrastructures over the last decade with the fastest urbanization in history and is now planning to double down on that bet. It is likely to land hard once the global growth train stops in the coming years, likely between 2014 and 2019. It will have moved hundreds of millions of farmers into high-rises with no way to support them unless the jobs gravy train keeps rolling—which it likely will not. Does that sound like massive civil unrest to you? I see a potential urban disaster in China in the decade ahead, which I will cover more in Chapter 6.

From the early 2020s forward, the Chinese economy could grow at 3 to 4 percent—or less—after it finally works off its overexpansion hangover, as

Figure 1-17: Workforce Growth, China, 1950-2050

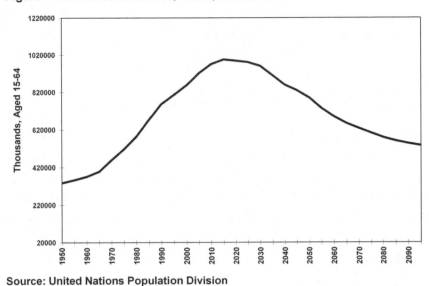

Source: United Nations Population Division

In 2012, China's workforce fell slightly for the first time in decades. It will plateau at best in the next decade and then fall dramatically for decades ahead.

Southeast Asian economies had to do between 1997 and 2002 following government-driven expansions that were not even half the magnitude or half the duration of what China has done. India is likely to be the next large-growth economy to eclipse China in growth after what has, thus far, been an inept pattern of urbanization and underinvestment in infrastructures. Mexico is already taking market share from China in manufacturing industries, especially those that market to North America, and its economy should grow faster than those of Europe or East Asia in the next boom.

There's much to be found in those numbers, including that India's demographic spending trends will not peak until around 2065 to 2070; in the same way, Mexico's and most of Latin America's point upward until 2040. In the next great crash ahead, then, for investing we will focus on India, Mexico, Turkey, and the Southeast Asian countries (Cambodia, Vietnam, Thailand,

Malaysia, Indonesia, and Myanmar; see chapter 7), and on health care–oriented sectors like biotech, medical devices, and pharmaceuticals in the United States and developed countries.

The Second Demographic Cliff in the United States

There's an affluent drop-off ahead. The United States has had a much more buoyant economy than Europe, despite the fact that Europe has actually seen more monetary stimulus, or QE, and its collective economic size is slightly larger. A big reason is the greater income inequality in the United States, where the top 1 percent and 10 percent control much more of the wealth and income than in most European countries, or in Japan or South Korea, or even than in Australia and New Zealand. These more affluent people have kept the U.S. economy chugging along, since they are the ones who benefit from the QE and monetary policies that are pushing up stocks and financial assets that they dominate.

One key insight into these very high income households is they do best in bubble booms, like the 1920s where they controlled up to 45 percent of net worth, and the 1990s and 2000s, where they reached closer to 40 percent (although some studies found their assets reaching as high as 45 to 47 percent in recent peak years). (See Figure 1-18.)

In part, this is made possible by the fact that the top 10 percent recently controlled as much as 80 percent of the nation's financial assets, the top 20 percent over 90 percent. The greatest impact of the Fed's money printing and QE has been to drive money into higher-yield investments like stocks, junk bonds, and commodities. Into late 2012 interest rates got extremely low after QE3, and commodities started to fall due to slowing emerging markets, which are the biggest consumers and exporters. That left stocks to bubble the most.

It is clear that the top 10 to 20 percent benefit most from the Fed-created bubble in financial assets, especially stocks (see Figures 1-19 and 1-20). Homer Simpson owns few equities; he has more stake in his home, which has not bounced very much. In contrast, their asset positions permit the affluent

Figure 1-18: Share of Wealth by the Top 1%

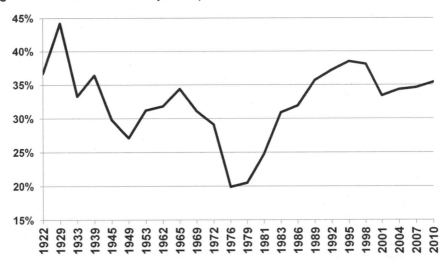

Data Source: Edward Wolff, as printed in *Wealth and Democracy and New York University, 2010*

The affluent are more entrepreneurial and make huge gains in equity and investments when financial assets bubble up and when many new technologies move mainstream for the first time, as in the Roaring Twenties.

to spend strongly, as the top 20 percent drives over 50 percent of consumer spending.

Surveys in early 2013 have shown that about 20 percent of people think the economy is better than ever, while 78 percent say we never came out of the great recession. We know who's in the first group: that's the top 20 percent who face no unemployment challenges, are less likely underwater in their mortgage, and are benefiting from the meteoric rise in stocks and financial assets, as they own almost all of them.

If the top 20 percent that controls over 50 percent of spending decides to spend less for all these reasons (and as demographics alone dictates that they will), then how is the Federal Reserve going to keep stimulating the economy? The everyday consumer never came out of the last recession. People in the top 20 percent are the only ones still feeling flush and spending, as

Figure 1-19: Share of Income, Top 1% and Top 10%

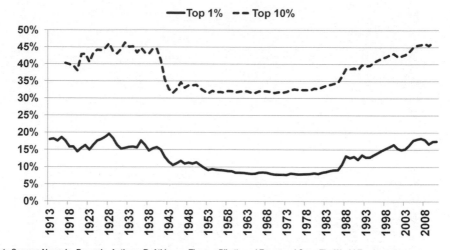

Data Source: Alvaredo, Facundo, Anthony B. Atkinson, Thomas Piketty and Emmanuel Saez, The World Top Incomes Database, http://g-mond.parisschoolofeconomics.eu/topincomes, 2013

If you add the second 10 percent, the top 20 percent likely dominates 55 percent to 60 percent of consumer income, and likely 50 percent plus of spending,
because they save a bit more. This top 20 percent tends to be college graduates, and they are not experiencing the unemployment challenges that the
other 80 percent are.

Figures 1-20 to 1-22 show. They will ultimately cave as well, which is why
endless stimulus cannot return our economy to normal growth rates and job
creation.

Another issue is that other cliff, namely Washington's fiscal cliff. To avoid
it, the U.S. Congress reached a last-minute resolution in early January 2013.
The Republicans held out for repeal of the tax cuts to be effective for the top
1 percent of earners, those making less than $400,000 per year ($450,000 for
joint filers) in income, rather than the top 2 percent of earners, those making
less than $50,000 per year, as favored by the president.

We expect headwinds to increase into 2014 as this top 1 percent actually
pays the higher tax rates. Remember that they are not 1 percent when it
comes to incomes, they are 18 percent of incomes, and likely about 15

Figure 1-20: Unemployment Rate by Education Level

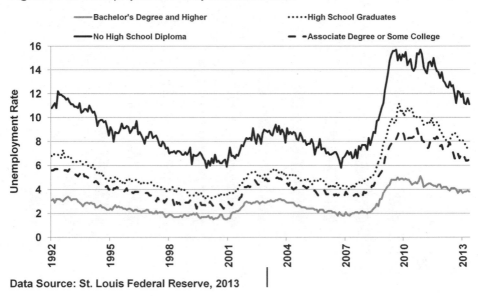

Data Source: St. Louis Federal Reserve, 2013

How's 3.5 percent unemployment sound? That's what college graduates are seeing even after the recession of 2008.

percent of spending! If they just cut back 3 to 5 percent in their spending, that would mean 0.3 percent to 0.5 percent lower GDP per year. That is significant when real GDP has been averaging roughly 2 percent since the great recession.

Given the extreme polarization in Congress, where Republicans feel bound to fight to the death to stop tax increases and Democrats fight similarly to stop spending cuts, we're unlikely to make much progress on our long-term deficit and debt problem. The United States is likely to be at least $26 trillion and possibly $30 trillion in debt ten years from now if they keep doing what they are doing, well before the United States reaches a better point in its demographic cycle and the economy turns upward longer-term. This projection is based on an annual deficit of $0.6 to $1.0 trillion in good years and $1.5 trillion plus in bad years. We can also expect two more U.S.

Figure 1-21: Top 10% of Households, Income by Age

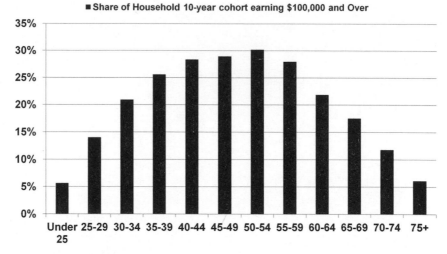

■ Share of Household 10-year cohort earning $100,000 and Over

Data Source: U.S. Census Bureau, 2012

The top 10 percent of households with well over $100K incomes tend to peak between ages fifty and fifty-four, versus forty-five to forty-nine for the average household. Given the skew of the trends on either side of the top, my estimate would be that this peak is about fifty-one. Note that Figure 1-2 showed a plateau in spending, first into age fifty and then into age fifty-three. In looking at Federal Reserve surveys of income by age, the top 20 percent peak around age fifty, the top 10 percent around age fifty-one, and the top 1 percent at ages fifty-three to fifty-four. That is what is driving this plateau after the average household clearly peaks around age forty-six. The drop-off would be more rapid without this more affluent segment, which is more dominant in the United States than in most other developed countries.

recessions before the next longer-term boom starts: the first likely starting in 2014, and the second in 2018.

If all of that is sobering, remember this: the global crash and financial crisis of 2008 was triggered by a subprime loan crisis that largely occurred in just four U.S. states: California, Florida, Arizona, and Nevada. Spain, Portugal, and Greece alone are similar in population and similarly could trigger

Figure 1-22: College Graduation Wave

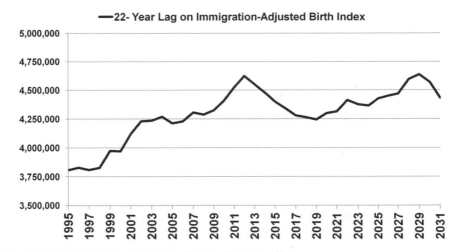

——22- Year Lag on Immigration-Adjusted Birth Index

Data Source: Dent Research, U.S. Census Bureau, Bloomberg, 2013

The first Echo Boom birth surge peaked in 1990. Roughly twenty-two years later, or around 2012, that group peaked in college graduations, as confirmed by the consumer expenditure survey, which shows college tuitions peaking at age fifty-one. This completion of college among the Echo Boomers removes a major financial burden from their Baby Boom parents, who tend to be in this top 20 percent of more affluent households. This represents another of the many cycles that are building toward the perfect storm between 2014 and late 2019. The stronger spending cycle from the top 1 percent to 20 percent will slow after 2013 or 2014, as their kids leave the nest and college-related spending slows from 2013 into 2019.

the next global crisis due to real estate busts and bank failures; not to mention any major breakdown in China or its real estate market, which would crucify high-saving upscale consumers who dominate 60 percent of its consumer spending, even more than in the United States.

Obviously, a concentrated subprime crisis in the United States should not account for a worldwide crisis, except that debt ratios are at unprecedented levels everywhere and demographic trends are slowing in almost all developed countries. Now, as governments stretch economies to keep the bubble going with increasing QE, it doesn't take much to trigger a crisis like 2008. Since the world has higher debt levels and worsening demographics ahead, the next crisis is very likely to be deeper, taking stocks and other financial assets like real estate to even lower lows. Just the suggestion that the Fed might taper off a bit in QE in mid-2013 caused a correction in stocks until the Fed capitulated a bit.

Europe embarked on a massive QE or stimulus program in late 2011 and early 2012 with $1.3 trillion in its LTRO (long-term refinancing operation) stimulus program (its form of QE or monetary stimulus)—as compared with QE3 in the U.S. of $1.0 trillion over a year. Yet Europe largely fell into a recession by mid-2012, just months later. There is a point where taking more of an artificial drug just doesn't work, as households and businesses are already stretched and overly in debt and natural demographic trends keep falling downward in spending.

I think that is what we're likely to see happen to the United States by early 2014. Then, from 2014 forward, Europe starts to fall off the cliff. So when other economists and analysts tell you we are finally in a sustainable recovery—don't believe them!

To keep up with our research and our views on current affairs, we have a free daily newsletter, *Survive & Prosper*, at www.harrydent.com.

If you need more persuading, the lessons of Japan may help.

CHAPTER 2

FOLLOWING JAPAN INTO A COMA ECONOMY

I just can't understand why more economists, government officials, investors, and businesses don't study Japan and look at what occurs when a supersized generation like the Baby Boom peaks, and is then followed by a smaller generation. The "new normal" that ensues is just not the same. Massive stimulus thereafter creates only modest growth, at best, and almost no inflation, which violates most monetary theories and models of the economy. Yet it is totally consistent with the winter season of my four-season model in Figure 1-10 in chapter 1.

In this chapter, I am going to look at how Japan's economy has evolved since its stock peak in late 1989, and its demographic peak, which had one final crescendo into late 1996, before Japan fell into a "coma economy." By that I mean an economy that has flatlined in the emergency room and takes endless life support (QE and stimulus) to keep it barely alive. It doesn't grow, it doesn't decline that much. Its population keeps aging and its debts keep growing, especially at the government level. Does that sound like a formula for success to you?

Countries that face a debt and demographic crisis and restructure such debt are the first to come out of it, even after a necessary period of austerity. Instead of doing that, however, governments are leaning instead toward bailing out and stimulating to avoid austerity. Such policies do not allow the economy to rebalance under its natural mechanisms, and that prompts the coma economy instead of regeneration and new growth, even when demographic trends become more favorable again.

Figure 2-1: Japan, Birth Index, 1900 – 2011

Data Source: Ministry of Health, Labour and Welfare, Japan, 2013

Note that not only is Japan's Echo Boom generation, born from 1956 to 1973, much smaller than that of the United States, but also births in its mini-boom on a forty-seven-year lag for growing spending again will last only from 2003 into 2020, largely an adverse time for the global economy.

Let's look more closely at the Japan story. That nation hit its first major demographic peak in births in 1942 (see Figure 2-1). It then hit a brief and sharply higher one in 1949 after the soldiers returned from World War II. If it hadn't been for their return, Japan's birth trends likely would have peaked well before 1949. I found that Japan seems to peak in spending around demographic age forty-seven, one year later in average age than in the United States. The reason for this would be very little immigration; immigrants tend to have lower education than average, which pulls down the average peak in spending a bit.

The first peak in Japan's economy on the forty-seven-year lag was in late 1989. The second was from the brief but strong surge after the soldiers returned, which, forty-seven years later, hit their economy from 1993 into late 1996. We saw the effect of that first peak when Japan's stock market tanked by 62 percent

Figure 2-2: Japan Spending Wave, Births Lagged Forward 47 Years

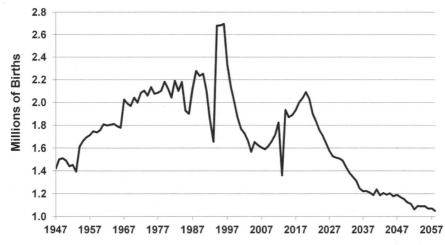

Data Source: Ministry of Health, Labour and Welfare, Japan, 2013

Japan hit its first demographic peak in late 1989, when its stock market first crashed, and then in late 1996 a second brief peak from the soldiers coming back from World War II. Since then, Japan's demographic trends were down into 2003 and should have bounced mildly into 2020. But its economy has not rebounded until recent extreme stimulus. This shows what happens when a larger generation is followed by a smaller one.

forty-seven years on, and its real estate market collapsed from 1991 forward (Japan's is a forty-two-year lag for peak real estate buying, one year later than in the United States). Its economy slipped into its first deep recession.

Note that while Japan has been doing QE or monetary injections and running massive fiscal deficits for seventeen years now, its economy has continued to fall back into recession and its stock market has continued to fall to new lows or near new lows after each stimulus-led rally. The last such low was in late 2012, before the big rally ignited by Japan's largest stimulus program ever. Again, though, it remains to be seen how long that will last if the world turns down again as I expect.

We need to pay heed to the lessons. *Every* country and *every* government should be studying Japan because it has already gone through most of what other developed countries in Europe and North America still face. Since its Demographic Cliff between late 1989 and late 1996, despite endless money printing and off-the-charts stimulus, the land of the rising sun has barely been able to lift its head off the pillow, let alone achieve a miraculous comeback—until 2013, when it basically tripled down on its QE stimulus. And I actually think there will be some follow-through to this only because Japan's demographic trends now point up a bit into 2020 and its economy needed a jolt to wake it up after two decades of flatlining.

When I published *Our Power to Predict* in 1989, I predicted that Japan would see a twelve-to-fourteen-year downturn while the United States and Europe would see their greatest booms ever into the 1990s. That was when most economists thought Japan was going to overtake the U.S. economy by 2010 and many everyday people worried they would buy all of our real estate and golf courses. But now we have the Fed stimulus and money printing, repeating the mistakes of the Japanese and creating a third bubble in the United States that looks likely to peak by very early 2014, as we hit new highs in stocks again. Just like Japan, each such effort has less and less effect, unless you increase the stimulus dramatically as Japan did from 2013 forward. But that's not the answer either, as it's like taking a massive dose of a drug to keep from coming down. Each desperate attempt at revival simply does more damage to an already very sick patient. And every crash to follow tends to take us to even lower levels.

After Japan's Nikkei nearly doubled (albeit from very low levels) from late 2012 into May 2013, it wasn't clear whether Japan will fall again to lower lows than its ultimate low in early 2009. This would only occur if the global economy crashes again as predicted, but perhaps less so in Japan, since its economy has been running contrary to those of most developed countries since 1990. Japan had falling demographic spending trends in the 1990s when Europe and North America had very strong trends. Now Japan has an upward trend from 2003 into 2020 while the rest of the Western world has downward trends into 2020 to 2023 or beyond. Will Japan see its stock market continue to edge up while the rest of the developed world falls? Note that our stock markets went up dramatically while Japan's fell in the 1990s.

Looking forward, it's hard to see Japan's market doing very well when the entire rest of the world is falling. Japan may or may not make new lows in the years ahead, but it is likely to see a major crash if the world sees one or two as I expect between 2014 and 2019, and most likely between early 2014 and mid-2015 or later. Ultimately, Japan will run headlong over a second Demographic Cliff after 2020.

This reality—that one major wealthy country after the next is sliding inexorably over the edge of the Demographic Cliff—explains the increasingly volatile world economy we live in. This is why it keeps taking more and more stimulus to keep economies growing at anemic rates at best, as in the United States and Japan, or in mild recessions at worst, as in much of Europe.

Japan has been in a coma economy for so long it has simply thrown in the towel and decided to up the ante on all developed nations and print money at 2.5 times the rate of the United States when adjusted for the size of its economy— and $1 trillion a year for the United States is already very aggressive at 6.5 percent of GDP. The thinking seems to be that if a policy hasn't turned your economy around after seventeen years, then just do it even harder. This is definitely not going to end well, but it has given Japan a welcome short-term jolt.

We'll look at Japan's economy over the last two decades and how little it has responded to seventeen years of QE and stimulus, but first let's look at how Japan was the miracle economy from the 1960s into the 1980s, just as the United States was from the 1920s into the 1960s.

Japan's Economic Miracle

I was speaking for Daishin Securities at a major financial conference in Seoul, South Korea, and stopped in Shanghai on the way. When I reached Seoul, I found it to be a great contrast to Shanghai.

The city is not as massive, though it's large by U.S. standards, and was more modern, livable, and upscale in its infrastructure than Shanghai. It is set within a majestic, mountainous environment with beautiful trees and landscapes, much like Japan. The broader population of Seoul is just over 10 million, smaller than the 23 million of Shanghai.

If I had to choose between the two to live in, it would be Seoul by a long stretch. Shanghai is too intense, too large, with endless high-rise urban sprawl and pollution, in contrast to Los Angeles, which has less pollution, but more low-rise sprawl. The GDP per capita in South Korea is more than three times that of China, even after adjusting for purchasing power. The infrastructures are better, the cars nicer, the stores and restaurants more upscale, the people more sophisticated and very gracious, although the culture is more formal, like that of the Japanese.

Unfortunately, what I observed in South Korea was simply a replay of the miracle of Japanese industrialization two decades earlier.

Japan was the first Asian country to industrialize and become a wealthy, developed nation. After the great leap to industrialization and urbanization in the West over many centuries, only a few island-like nations in East Asia have been able to accelerate beyond emerging-country status (GDP per capita of $2,000 to $15,000) to the living standards and higher-end industries, high-tech, and financial sectors that rival those in the West ($20,000 to $50,000). Japan was first, followed by Singapore, Taiwan, and South Korea. Only those nations have seen an S-curve progression in GDP per capita versus urbanization rates, as opposed to the more linear progression seen in most emerging countries in Asia, Latin America, and Africa (see chapter 6). What I mean by an S-curve progression is that new products or technologies, or GDP per capita in this case, grow exponentially until the trend starts to mature.

We don't yet see any major emerging countries, including China and India, doing the same in the coming decades, although that could happen in the future. But in China, that optimal S-curve progression is perhaps least likely due to its rapidly aging population stemming from its one-child policy dating from the early 1970s.

Again, Japan was the first non-Western country to accelerate into industrialization, as Great Britain did from the late 1700s forward with the Industrial Revolution (as I show in Figure 2-3). Is there something about island nations with limited resources or colder nations with greater challenges to survival that makes them great? Larger challenges seem to create greater innovation, just like downturns in any cycle (that's why we need downturns and not endless QE to prevent them!). Japan experienced the first emerging world S-curve acceleration in GDP per capita versus urbanization in far less

Figure 2-3: Japan, GDP per Capita vs. Urbanization

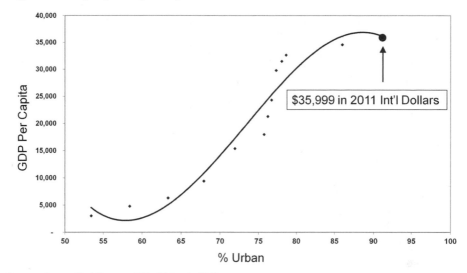

Source: Angus Maddison and World Bank, 2013

The Japanese progression accelerated from the 1960s to the mid-1990s, as the average Japanese went from about $6,000 in GDP per capita in world dollars adjusted for inflation and purchasing power to $32,000 in less than four decades. That's better than a five-times increase in the standard of living. South Korea did the same in just three decades since the early 1980s, as Figure 2-4 shows. It took Great Britain close to two centuries and the United States 130 years to achieve a similar acceleration in wealth and urbanization!

time than any major country after the English offshoots of the United States, Canada, Australia, and New Zealand. Only South Korea beat it from the 1980s into the 2000s, as Figure 2-4 shows.

Japan's peaks in stock and real estate bubbles came as a result of its Baby Boom generation maturing earlier. South Korea is slightly less wealthy in GDP per capita in international dollars (adjusted for purchasing power and fluctuations in the U.S. dollar), which is the best relative measure, according to the late University of Groningen economics scholar Angus Maddison's brilliant research. GDP per capita for Japan in U.S. dollars today is much

Figure 2-4: South Korea vs. Japan, GDP per Capita on 25-year Lag

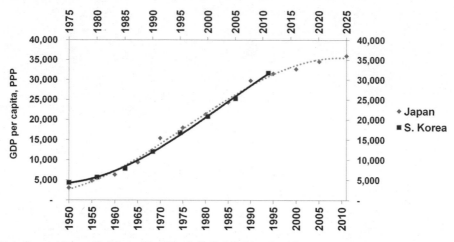

Data Source: Angus Maddison, World Bank, United Nations, Dent Research, 2013

South Korea saw its GDP per capita accelerate in a similar S-curve fashion on a twenty-five-year lag to Japan. The lag in the South Korean demographic peak actually is around twenty-two years due to a peak in its Baby Boom spending wave that comes around 2018, twenty-two years after Japan's in 1996. However, our best data from the United Nations comes in five-year age cohorts; hence, we use a twenty-five-year lag in the chart. But there are no two ways about it: there is a clear demographic influence with South Korea having a later Baby Boom, and an unbelievable correlation in economic progress.

higher, at $45,870, versus $22,424 for South Korea (for the United States it is $48,327). But Japan is a much more expensive place to live, especially Tokyo, and I can tell you from visiting Seoul that the Japanese do not have twice the living standard of South Korea. I would see it as more similar, consistent with Maddison's adjustment for purchasing power.

Such acceleration can come only from a leap into industrialization and from competing worldwide in value-added products like steel, autos, appliances, and computers, and not so many countries can rise to dominance in the highest value-added products and services, just as a given country can have only so many wealthy people on a relative basis. Again, only a few East Asian, urbanized, island-like nations have achieved an S-curve acceleration in GDP per capita versus urbanization rates, compared with the more linear correlation in almost all emerging countries.

To put it another way, not so many emerging countries will ever be as rich as the developed countries in North America, Europe, and East Asia, even though they are urbanizing and their incomes are growing and will for decades. The Western model of industrialization and urbanization that East Asia has followed has realized accelerating incomes like no other region of the emerging world, but at the same time, rising wealth and urbanization always lead to lower birth rates and falling demographic trends (on a lag of forty-six to forty-seven years for peak spending in wealthier and middle-class economies).

Lessons Learned in Japan

Japan's citizens have done what all increasingly urban and affluent societies do: They have fewer children because the cost of raising them goes up in an increasingly urban society. There's nothing immoral about this. It is simply a natural human impulse. Have fewer kids. Educate them better.

However, focusing on individual goals may not always be good for collective and long-term economic growth, and this is another reason why boom cycles always turn to bust naturally. Japan's government responded to its slowing economy by printing more and more money to stimulate it out of the coma. Such money printing counters the economy's natural inclinations to balance debt and asset bubbles and to bring the economy back to a more efficient and sustainable environment where it can grow again. Ironically, that's especially true for the young new families that should be driving the economy and workforce into the future.

These younger households cannot afford the sky-high housing costs, or the bubbles in education and health care costs. And how will they be able to invest profitably long-term in stocks and financial assets that are already bubbly and overvalued?

On top of that natural human tendency toward lower births in more urbanized settings, the Japanese have shunned immigration. This is also natural. Most cultures want to preserve what made them great, especially if they have cultivated and honed that culture over centuries or even thousands of years. But if you are not going to have enough kids to sustain or grow your population, then you should seriously consider the merits of at least selective immigration. Unfortunately, Japan has yet to open itself to this possibility. The fact that English is not commonly spoken there is another obstacle, unlike in Singapore.

This is one area that sets the United States, Australia, Canada, and New Zealand apart from Japan. These countries have been immigrant nations from the beginning. Hence, their Demographic Cliffs are not as dramatic as those of the East Asian countries or southern and central European countries.

Japan's situation gets darker. Japan has emasculated its smaller, younger generation in response to this Demographic Cliff and its slowing economy. The country's larger Baby Boom generation has locked in its very generous entitlements and lifetime employment programs, leaving the Echo Boom generation with much lower wages, more part-time work, higher unemployment, and fewer entitlements. Older Japanese are also staying in the workforce longer as they realize they can't afford to retire, crowding out the younger entrants.

A recent survey by the Ministry of Health in Japan showed that 35 percent of young males ages sixteen to nineteen have little or no interest in sex. That's because they see marriage and having kids as an obligation they simply can't expect to meet. They have given up on the Japanese dream. Even worse, 42 percent of marriages were classified as "sexless," meaning no sex for a month or more. These couples don't seem inclined to take the chance of having kids, either, in a bad economy.

To some degree, this problem extends to all major countries, with the exception of Australia (somewhat). Nations are locking in entitlements for older people, which the younger people increasingly have to pay for even though they have fewer job opportunities (because the older generation is staying in the workforce longer). The Baby Boomers see no better option: they can't afford to retire in a difficult economy, with much lower investment returns. Meanwhile, governments are running up massive debts to fight the great recession. Guess who will have to pay these debts off?

In the United States, immigration is falling. Our economy and the opportunities here aren't as appealing as they once were. We're becoming more anti-immigration, just when we need immigrants the most. In fact, we persistently turn away the highest-educated immigrants who graduate from our universities. How stupid is that? We will look in chapter 9 at how economists' projections for population growth in the United States are greatly overstated as they are not seeing the decline in immigration and births that we saw twenty years ago from this deep and lengthy downturn, which was predestined by demographic trends. Fewer immigrants and lower births ahead will increase the ratio of retirees to workers for many decades to come, even more than forecast.

If aging, wealthy countries do not restructure their massive private and government debt, and restructure their bloated, unwieldy entitlement programs to account for longer life expectancies and more realistic benefits, their youth will follow in the footsteps of their Japanese counterparts. Here in the United States, we will lose the American dream and commit economic suicide as each generation to follow chooses to have even fewer marriages and children.

Flatlining in Japan Since 1997

Let's look at the hard, cold, and clear facts on Japan's economy over the last two "lost decades." Japan's experience illustrates clearly what lies ahead for us if something earth-shattering doesn't shake us off the path we're on—and it's not likely the whole world can go into a coma without everything collapsing. Japan had the luxury of going through its worst crisis when the rest of the world was booming. We don't.

The key fact: real GDP has averaged just less than zero growth in Japan since 1997, as Figure 2-5 shows. That, in short, is a coma economy. More ominous for us, the United States is following roughly the same cycle as Japan: a bubble followed by dramatic weakening followed by stimulus trending into weakening again and again (which happens because stimulus only

Figure 2-5: Real GDP, U.S. vs. Japan on an 11-year Lag

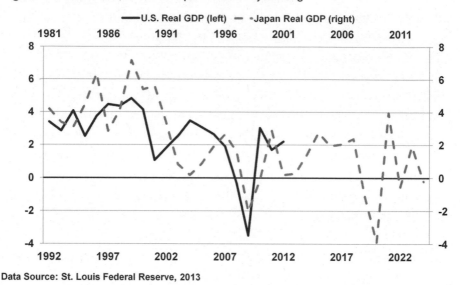

Data Source: St. Louis Federal Reserve, 2013

This chart looks at changes in real GDP growth for Japan versus the United States on an eleven-year lag, from 1981 to 2011 for Japan, from 1992 to 2011 for the United States. The eleven-year lag is the difference between the final Japanese birth peak in 1949 and that of the United States in 1961, with a one-year adjustment for the difference in spending peaks (one year later in Japan).

works short-term and works less and less over time). If the United States continues to follow this cycle, then growth will drop to zero (maybe even lower) in the next few years . . . rebound for three years or so . . . and then turn downward even more deeply into 2020, when our demographic cycle in spending bottoms out and then starts to turn up again with the next generation around 2023 or 2024.

This pattern fits with the predictions of our demographic cycles for the United States and many other developed economies. However, the pattern doesn't fit as well with the normal debt crisis cycle, wherein the worst economic and financial crisis of the economic winter season happens early in the season as a result of the deleveraging of debt and the banking system (following a fall bubble boom season). This misfit results from the unprecedented Keynesian stimulus programs we see all around us today. Governments simply are not going to allow recessions and debt deleveraging now that they have discovered the new drug QE.

In other words, the United States will very likely experience the same results as Japan if we continue to stimulate the economy for as long as Japan did. Unfortunately, this is exactly what it looks like we're going to do.

This continued high level of stimulation may have little or no effect by 2014. Those who could refinance their mortgages have already done so. And considering that mortgage rates are now rising, how will the rebound in housing prices in the United States continue for long, especially now that speculators are increasingly pulling out of the market as prices are rising and it is less profitable?

The 1990 to 1992 crash in Japan was similar to the crash in the United States from 2000 to 2002, as Figure 2-6 demonstrates. Likewise, the rally in Japan from late 1992 into late 1996 was somewhat similar to the American and European rally from early 2003 into late 2007. The difference was, thanks to continued advancing demographic trends, we had our next bubble in that time frame. The U.S. market reached new highs in stocks, while Japan's did not. Japan did not employ QE significantly to fight that crash. The rebound from late 1992 into late 1996 was fueled largely by the last surge in spending from the final sharp wave of births from 1946 into 1949 (four-year surge, four-year stock advance on a forty-seven-year lag).

The next crash in Japan after 1996 dovetailed largely with the 2008 to early 2009 crash in the United States and Europe. This crash was not as severe as the first one as it started from lower levels and valuations. It was the result of Japan's finally and fully falling off the Demographic Cliff. That's when Japan started panicking and using QE to fight the downturn. They have been doing it largely ever since.

Note that Japan's stock market has kept rallying on stimulus, then falling to new lows, as in 1998, 2003, 2009, and 2012. Also note that no rallies have lasted more than 4.5 years, as in early 2003 to late 2007, and from mid-1992 to mid-1996, on stimulus given continued falls in the demographic trends until 2002–03. The rally in the United States from early 2009 was

Figure 2-6: Japan Nikkei Stocks Index, 1988-2013

Data Source: Yahoo Finance, 2013

The bubble market in Japan first peaked at the end of 1989. Japan saw its first major crash as the first demographic dip from the steep drop in World War II births hit on a forty-seven-year lag. The real estate collapse on a lag after 1991 only made that downturn worse. The year 1991 was a forty-two-year lag on the birth peak where home buying peaks.

due to hit 4.5 years by September 2013 when this manuscript was in its final edit.

The first crash brought the Nikkei down 62 percent. The final low, at least thus far, in early 2009 saw the Nikkei down 82 percent from its top. And most of this downturn occurred when the rest of the world was booming! That's how strong demographics are and how dangerous the cliff is.

Should a more modest recession and stock crash occur over the next few years, they are likely to be fraught with growing banking problems apparently "fixed" by another round of massive stimulus and less-extreme debt deleveraging (as occurred in Japan). But I believe the United States and Europe are in for the next deeper economic and financial crisis starting by early 2014 and lasting into at least early 2015, and likely longer into mid-2015 to mid-2016.

We expect the lesser economic and debt crisis to strike between late 2017 and 2020, yet that could still take us to new lows after a less robust bounce into 2017 or so. But if we do have a more modest crisis in the next few years, the deeper crisis will very likely come between late 2017 and early 2020 or beyond.

This is because the world is a much more fragile place today, and debt ratios are now much higher in Europe and the United States than they were for Japan in the 1990s. Governments have so stretched economies and bubbles with their unprecedented stimulus that any financial crisis is likely to mushroom into something larger than what we experienced in 2008 and 2009. Very little private debt has deleveraged, and public debt just keeps growing. Banks and leveraged investment funds are speculating again as they did into the 2000 and 2007 bubbles, with even lower interest rates to fuel such leverage.

The most salient point concerning the Japanese Spending Wave is that the country should have had a stronger Echo Boom–driven economic expansion from around 2003 into 2020 as Figure 2-7 would suggest. However, the massive real estate bust and the lack of debt deleveraging from the endless stimulus programs to "ease the pain" ultimately weighed down the Japanese economy after its 1990s crisis. As the saying goes, "No pain, no gain!" Japan has done everything in its power (and continues to do so) to avoid the necessary pain. As a result, it has had no gains over the last two decades. With the U.S. and European efforts to avoid the pain at all costs, we will suffer the same fate unless a crisis ahead forces us into reality, and that is what I see as the likely scenario until something goes wrong as in 2008.

I predict a much longer decline for Japan after 2020 into the 2040s and likely beyond, as its Spending Wave dictates. Japan will never get back to "normal," given the high debt ratios and never-ending slowing of demographic trends. Unless, that is, it encourages debt deleveraging and a strong immigration policy, and builds a much stronger export machine (as has South Korea). Higher birth rates should be encouraged as well, but that would take

Figure 2-7: Spending Wave, Japan vs. U.S., 1947-2060

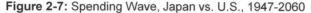

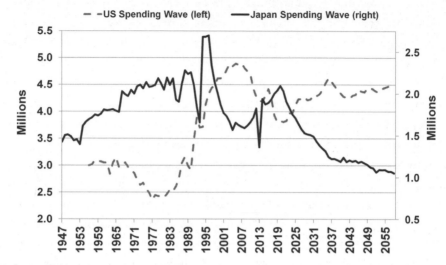

Data Source: Ministry of Health, Labour and Welfare, Japan, HS Dent Research, U.S. Census Bureau, Bloomberg, 2013

Note that for the Japanese Spending Wave the first stock peak in late 1989 correlates with the first peak in births in 1942, just into World War II. The reason overall spending and stocks topped earlier for Japan is that its real estate bubble was even larger than the one that inflated in the United States . . . and real estate peaks about five years ahead of overall spending. The decline in births in Japan during World War II (on a forty-seven-year lag) coincided with, and helped to trigger, the real estate bubble burst from 1991 forward. That bubble burst was strong enough to largely outweigh the brief surge in births and spending that followed from 1993 into 1996 (again on a forty-seven-year lag) so that stocks never made new highs, not even close. Japan and the United States have moved in different economic cycles as their demographic trends are very different and largely opposite. Japan's Spending Wave points up from 2003 into 2020, while that of the United States points down from 2008 into 2023.

much longer to make an impact, as at least twenty years is required for a new generation to enter the economy and contribute to its growth.

The debt deleveraging must occur at some point, likely more so in the next decade. Japan is also stimulating feverishly to push its yen down to help its export industries advance. But substantially higher immigration is unlikely in such an insular society. Likewise, higher births will be a challenge when the young generation feels so insecure financially because the older generation has sold it out.

Again, in early 2013, Japan trumped everyone else in massively printing money to push its currency down and increase its exports. Such measures only increase the prices of imports and hurt already struggling young and aging households. Also, such artificial means of supporting exports do not tend to create lasting effects as other countries will retaliate, just as rising tariffs were self-defeating in the Great Depression and only hurt world trade further.

If we look back to Figure 2-5 (which shows GDP in Japan in yen) and take out the external fluctuations in the U.S. dollar, we see a coma economy from 1997 forward. GDP peaked in the fourth quarter of 1997 at 131.1 trillion yen. At the most recent top in the second quarter of 2007, it was 128.8 trillion yen. That's a flat decade. In the fourth quarter of 2012, GDP was 117.7 trillion, down 10 percent from its peak sixteen years ago. Yes, in 2012 Japan's GDP is lower than in 1996, sixteen years prior.

This is much like the U.S. GDP from 1929 to 1940, where it peaked at $103 billion in 1929, dropped to as low as $56.4 billion in 1933, then climbed back to $101.3 billion in 1940. No net progress in economic growth for a decade! That's what happens in the winter season.

Government stimulus in Japan in recent years allowed the economy not to sink as low as it did in the United States in the 1930s. The private sector, called "total production" in Japan, actually declined by 4 percent between 1990 and 2011, following a 12 percent decline into 1993 and a 28 percent decline into 2009, all of which is evidence that Japan had a mini-depression in its private sector.

The fact that all of the growth in Japan since 1990 has come from government stimulus and rising government deficits is the ultimate definition of "denial"—and of an economy not only in a coma but on life support.

Mark my words: this cannot possibly end well. Japan will experience some shock if the global economy goes down between 2014 and 2019, but it will certainly experience a shock after 2020, when its demographic trends turn down sharply again and interest rates turn back up with global growth. How will it fund its massive debt if interest rates ultimately rise back to 6 percent in the range of historical norms versus 1 percent recently?

Another sign of a lifeless economy? Prices in Japan have remained largely flat, with minor bouts of deflation here and there (see Figure 2-8). So here's a question for those people who believe we're on a runaway train to

Figure 2-8: Consumer Price Index (CPI) Japan, 1960-2012

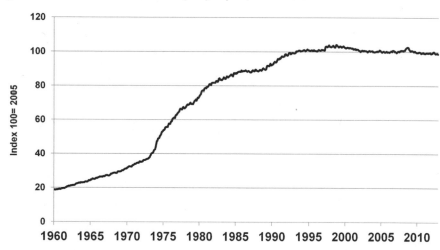

Data Source: OECD, 2013

The lack of deeper deflation is simply the result of massive and extended quantitative easing and endless government stimulus. Don't let anyone tell you that inflation is the trend in such a coma economy. Governments actively state that they are fighting deflation, hence that is the trend. And when such policies ultimately fail for a great variety of reasons, deflation will set in. Hyperinflation as preached by gold bugs is not even a possibility in this environment. Otherwise, we would have already seen very substantial inflation from the most massive monetary stimulus in history by far for over five years!

hyperinflation: how do you explain the massive and extended stimulus and money creation that created zero net inflation for two decades in Japan?

Here's the answer: asset bubbles bursting and debt deleveraging led to a deflationary environment, as they have after *every* debt and asset bubble in history. The difference this time around is that governments have chosen to actively fight deflation and prevent a major banking and debt-deleveraging crisis. This move is a very dangerous one. You don't want to mess with Mother Nature or the invisible hand of the free markets; both always come back with a vengeance.

Monetary policy can ease the crisis, but it cannot recreate substantial inflation when consumers and businesses can't or don't want to borrow any more than they already have in a debt bubble. And debt will continue to trend toward deleveraging to some degree even with massive stimulus.

RIP for Japanese Real Estate

The stimulus in Japan ultimately did not stop stocks from collapsing by over 80 percent. It did not prevent real estate from sinking by over 60 percent. And it's done nothing to assist these sectors in recovering longer-term— until the massive QE of 2013—and who knows the full implications of such a desperate move? Before this radical measure stocks up until late 2012 were near rock bottom after twenty-three years of falling, and they'll likely never recover longer-term, given Japan's "ease the pain and take more drugs" policy. The Nikkei would do well to get back to 23,000 at best by 2020 after peaking at 39,000, if it even gets there. Then it could fall again even in a global boom as Japan's demographics get even worse.

In comparison with hard news in the Japanese real estate market (see Figure 2-9), the U.S. residential sector in the recent book bubbled up 120 percent (2.2 times) from 2000 to 2006; then it fell by 34 percent into 2011. We project that ultimately home prices will crash by more than 55 percent in the United States. The real estate bust is not over here yet!

Such bubbles and bursts prove our general principles from studying all types of bubbles over hundreds of years: first, the greater the bubble, the

Figure 2-9: Japanese Real Estate Prices, by Sector, 1964-2012

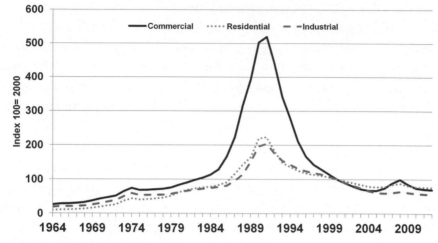

Data Source: Land Institute of Japan, 2013

This graphic represents the real estate crash in Japan, divided by its commercial, industrial, and residential sectors. As you can see, the commercial bubble was the most extreme, quadrupling from 1986 into 1991. This bubble then crashed by 87 percent! The industrial sector advanced by 150 percent (2.5 times) and then fell by 70 percent. The residential sector bubbled by 135 percent (2.35 times) and then crashed by 64 percent. It's also important to note that all three sectors of the Japanese real estate markets are still at or very near their initial 2004 lows and that these lows were even lower than prices at the start of the bubble in 1986.

greater the burst; and second, bubbles tend to deflate to where they started or to go a bit lower.

Scared by the numbers? People are always shocked by our forecasts and consider them extreme. But these types of stock and real estate declines are very typical of deflationary crashes that take place on and off in the economic winter season that follows the fall bubble boom season. Bubble boom, bubble burst . . . volatility on the way up, volatility on the way down. That has been the trend for decades now in Japan and in most developed countries.

Don't expect the soft landing that most economists expect in the United States, Europe, and especially not China today.

The extended and lengthy decline in Japanese real estate prices is one of the reasons we tell real estate investors to avoid property as a long-term, appreciating investment. That strategy is now dead. Instead, the best strategy for years to come is to buy real estate cheaply in foreclosure and then rent it out for positive cash flow, or to flip it quickly. There will be no quick return of the peak property prices achieved before the bust. In fact, I don't see real estate prices ever seeing their peaks in most developed countries again.

The United States (and other countries with strong demographics, like Canada, Australia, and the nations of northern Europe) may expect some minor appreciation in real estate, but substantial appreciation is unlikely before the early 2020s forward, and even then is likely to be limited to inflation rates at best, which means a zero real return. For what remains of this decade, any appreciation we do see will be most visible in low-end starter homes and the rental apartment markets.

That said, it is important to note that there is a new dimension of real estate I am just exploring. I call it "buyers versus dyers" and I'll talk about that in a U.S. context and in other countries in the next chapter. But it's an important factor in Japan, too.

This is the first time in modern history that the new generation is smaller than the preceding one. As we've seen, the peak in home buying is around ages forty-one to forty-two, several years before the overall peak in spending at around ages forty-six to forty-seven in developed countries. What is unique about real estate and housing is that it lasts nearly forever. When a larger generation like the Baby Boom starts to enter nursing homes or die, you don't need to build new homes for the younger generation. Existing homes simply come back onto the market from dyers and will outweigh the demand for new homes at some point.

If we look at peak buyers versus peak dyers in Japan specifically, then real estate should continue to rise in supply after 2015 forward as more people die and their homes become available on the market again. With more of these homes available, the need to build new homes or infrastructure is stunted for decades. Home builders beware! Commercial real estate developers as well need to be wary, as the workforce peaks and slows in one country after the next.

Excess supply for decades ahead means home prices in Japan may never appreciate substantially again. In fact, they could actually fall even lower in the years and decades to come. To reiterate this very important point: real estate will never be the same in most developed countries. Hence, you need to buy real estate only if you need it long-term, or to buy foreclosures in this global real estate bust with the intention of renting them out for positive cash flow. The old-fashioned way of making money on real estate (i.e., the Monopoly game) is back. You don't buy it for appreciation—you buy it for the rents.

But not only have Japanese investors seen real estate slide for two decades with no real bounce, they've also seen very volatile stock markets that were still down by close to 80 percent as late as 2012 and will likely see lower prices yet again in the years ahead, and possibly for decades.

Now consider another warning sign. Japanese investors can purchase a "safe" ten-year government bond for their retirement—for which the interest paid is 1 percent or lower! That level of return and the status of the equities market explain why the Japanese have almost negligible holdings of stocks and bonds compared with investors in the United States and Europe. In fact, Japanese hold only 2.4 percent of their financial assets (outside of real estate) in bonds, 2.6 percent in investment trusts, and 5.8 percent in stocks. That's a total of 10.8 percent in traditional financial securities. Approximately 56.3 percent of the money in Japan is in deposits and savings accounts. Why not, when long-term bonds yield 1 percent and stocks have gone sideways to down for two decades?

The other big chunk is in pensions and insurance at 28.3 percent. U.S. investors have only 14.4 percent in deposits and savings accounts and 52.8 percent in bonds, trusts, and stocks. Yet we're about to get our retirement asses kicked, just like the Japanese.

The Retirement Disaster Unfolding

Japanese savings rates peaked at nearly 15 percent of disposable income in 1992 and dropped to 2 percent recently. There are two reasons: there is no

way to get a decent return in a deflationary environment drowning in governmental QE policies, and after age sixty-four, people live off and spend
down their savings, becoming negative savers.

Given that Japan has the largest and fastest-growing segment of people
age sixty-five and older of any major country, how have Japanese standards
of living and civil stability remained as good as they have, given an aging
society, a long-term demographic and economic slowdown, and near-zero
returns for investors and retirees for two decades?

The answers are to be found in government-driven near-zero short-term
and long-term interest rates. We're back to quantitative easing again, on a
huge scale in which money is injected into the banks, which keeps them from
failing or being forced to deleverage. That money is then reinvested in Japanese government bonds to keep yields low and deficit spending more tol-
erable. Add to that massive government deficits, which fund increases in
entitlements and social welfare, but only for the older generation, not sustainably for the new younger one.

Let's go to the numbers. The discount rate, or short-term government-
dictated interest rate, in Japan dropped from 6 percent in 1990 to 0.5 percent
in 1995. It dropped to near 0 percent from 2001 forward. The discount rate
presently is 0.25 percent, or near zero, just like here and in Europe.

At first, rate decreases encouraged a little refinancing and minor borrowing among consumers, but not among companies. Japan's real estate bubble began to burst when rates were raised to 6 percent into 1990, but
without this increase, consumer home buying would have peaked anyway,
as it did around 1991 on about a forty-two-year lag on births (1949 + 42 =
1991).

As a percentage of GDP, securities purchases in the United States
still have not come close to the levels of easing in Japan, even though
they are projected to go toward 30 percent of GDP by the end of 2014,
and then more likely beyond that if the economy weakens again as expected
(see Figure 2-10). Southern Europe has already seen QE policies 50 percent or so higher than in the United States due to that region's weaker
demographic trends and less competitive economies. So, are you wonder-
ing why the U.S. dollar hasn't collapsed against other major currencies?

Figure 2-10: Central Bank Balance Sheet, Japan vs. U.S., 2009-2033

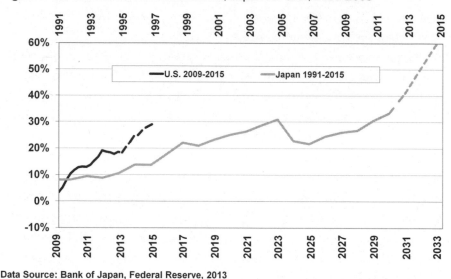

Data Source: Bank of Japan, Federal Reserve, 2013

Under Japan's QE policies, government securities were purchased to inject money into the banking system and economy. Such purchases advanced from $300 billion in 1991 to $1.2 trillion in 2004. That's an increase of $900 billion—massive, given the size of the country's economy (which is about 38 percent of the U.S. economy). That's the equivalent of $2.4 trillion in the United States. Although Japan backed off QE in the good years of 2006 and 2007, presently, purchases are approaching the $1.2 trillion level and are hence set to increase greatly over the next few years. Japan's purchases of bonds are targeted to double during 2013 and 2014, rising to a whopping cumulative 60 percent of GDP—twice the projections for the United States.

Other major countries are out-stimulating us and we are being very aggressive!

But guess what? Europe's economy sank into a recession in mid-2012, and it's getting worse. There comes a point where stimulus can't stretch an already stretched economy much further. Ultimately it fails to prevent the natural forces of demographics and debt deleveraging, which want to correct the massive imbalances for the good of the longer-term picture.

Going Off the Deep End

Japan's January 2013 stimulus plan is far beyond what the United States and Europe have done when compared by the relative size of the economies. Japan's $116 billion in fiscal stimulus for 2013 and roughly $1.1 trillion in QE is like $3 trillion in QE for the United States. And Japan proposes even more for 2014, to the tune of $1.7 trillion a year for as long as it takes.

There is an important distinction to note here. Japan's financial structure differs from ours and from most of Europe's. The basic reason it can go further in such stimulus is that Japanese financial institutions hold 81 percent of Japanese government bonds (39 percent by banks, 23 percent in pension funds, 10 percent in national pensions, and 9 percent by the Bank of Japan). Foreigners hold only 7 percent of these bonds, and Japanese households hold only 4 percent. Almost all of the savings/investment in Japan now comes from its own government and financial institutions. Also, Japan is buying much shorter-term bonds than the United States, which means its QE does not accumulate as much over time as these bonds mature and disappear.

Furthermore, an under-the-table understanding exists that while governments will bail out the banks with monetary injections, the banks must buy enough government bonds to keep yields down so the government can afford to finance its growing debt and deficits. In this way, the government and the banks keep the bubble from bursting and debt from deleveraging excessively. Unfortunately, they do it at the expense of ever-rising government debt and, ultimately, at the expense of consumers and businesses, who never find the longer-term relief that comes with the deleveraging of private debt. With aggressive easing to push down the yen, Japanese consumers pay more for imports, including energy and gasoline, which they produce little of.

In contrast, the United States typically relies on foreigners for over 50 percent of its bond purchases until the recent Fed acceleration in bond buying. In Spain, financial institutions own 67 percent of Spanish bonds, and this percentage is rising in a depression-like economy with over 27 percent (and rising) unemployment. However, that remaining 33 percent can still tank the market if investors think they'll face a default or repayment in a weaker currency. This is already happening in the United States in 2013.

Do bondholders allow the United States and Europe to continue to implement QE policies as has Japan? Or do the higher (although declining) levels of foreign holdings eventually force rates to rise, given increases in debt and stimulus plans that continue to have less of an effect? In other words, can central banks keep recycling QE into purchases of their own bonds so they can continue to raise debt levels and fund never-ending fiscal deficits at unprecedented low interest rates? Or will citizens in weak countries like Japan and southern Europe revolt against policies that save the banks and financial institutions, and the euro, against the interests of everyday citizens whose wages decline and whose retirement investment returns tank?

I think this desperate money-printing approach began to fail in Europe in mid-2012, when $1.3 trillion in QE was followed soon after by a recession. We anticipate the same thing happening in the United States by early 2014 forward . . . and then in Japan on a lag as well. Eventually the global slowdown will hit the biggest bubble economy of all: China.

All of which brings us to the final issue: how high can public and private debt ratios go before the system simply collapses from a short-term shock and/or bond rates spike (as in southern Europe)? We have already seen total debt ratios in major countries at two to three times the levels reached before the 1930s Great Depression in the United States.

As a result of massive QE over time, Japan's fiscal deficits, and rising debt (Figure 2-11), the country's private sector has barely deleveraged. This lack of deleveraging is the opposite of the massive "cold turkey" deleveraging of the 1930s, especially in the United States, wherein total debt fell from around 190 percent of GDP to 50 percent.

Looked at realistically, then, Japan is already bankrupt; or, as our respected colleague John Mauldin says, "Japan is a bug looking for a windshield."

The Japanese financial sector is at 160 percent of GDP (much higher than in the United States) and has not deleveraged at all. The consumer sector is lower than that of the United States, at 64 percent, but these are nearly the same levels as 1991, so this sector has not deleveraged either. Only the corporate sector has deleveraged modestly, falling from 150 percent in 1990 to its present level of 103 percent. The government debt has risen sharply to

Figure 2-11: Japan, Debt to GDP Ratios by Sector, 1980-2011

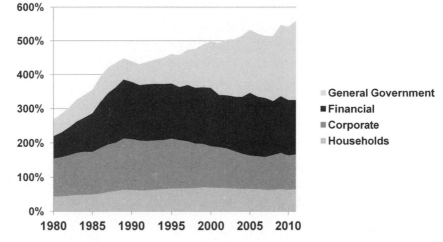

Data Source: Cabinet Office, Annual Report on National Accounts, 2013

As you can see, the country's government debt rose from 60 percent of GDP in 1990 to 217 percent in 2010. It is now at 250 percent and rising, the highest in the developed world by a long shot. Japan used this debt to plug the economic gap from the flat-to-declining private sector, a classic example of Keynesian economics: again, keep taking more of the debt drug to keep from coming down off the bubble high! The only reason Japan has been able to do this is that long-term bond rates are at 0.5 percent to 1.0 percent and short-term rates are near zero.

offset the slowing private sector—from 60 percent in 1990 to near 250 percent in 2013! Total debt for Japan, private and public, rose from an already colossal 437 percent of GDP in 1990 to 543 percent in mid-2013.

Japan increased debt during the economic winter season instead of deleveraging and thus, ultimately, will face a much larger debt crisis and deleveraging down the road. I expect this to start happening in the next several years. In an economy that is stretched so far, by such a high level of debt, it is inevitable that any shock to the system will cause a crisis the government can't control.

Why Can't Other Countries Keep Printing Money and Stimulating Like Japan?

That's a question I'm frequently asked during media interviews and speaking engagements: Japan has stimulated endlessly, why can't we? The most obvious answer is that the Japanese demographic and debt crisis occurred at a different time, when the Japanese were in a different financial position.

The financial crisis hit Japan in the early 1990s, a time when the rest of the world was experiencing the greatest boom in history. As a result of a bubble boom in the 1980s, Japan was a net creditor when its Demographic Cliff opened up beneath it. The country had trade and budget surpluses, unlike the United States in 2008. That's one factor.

The more important answer to that question is: Although a governmental policy of extended stimulus and quantitative easing relieved some of the pain of the debt and demographic crisis in Japan, the price of the easing was that Japan never dealt with its massive private debt. It never rose from the ashes of the crisis. It never woke up from the coma. The money printing and stimulus only accomplished an increase in the burden of debt on the government. That alone is now 250 percent of GDP and rising, way higher than Greece, and 2.3 times that of the United States.

The result is that Japan is still carrying an impossibly heavy weight on its back, one that is growing heavier every year. How far and fast can *you* run with such a weight strapped to your shoulders, especially while aging rapidly?

In the twenty-three years since its peak, Japan accumulated the highest total private and public debt of any major nation. It has the fastest-aging population. This is not a model of success, but a formula for disaster, especially after 2020 when Japan goes off a second steep Demographic Cliff, when interest rates rise around the world again, causing its debt burden to skyrocket in interest costs.

Europe and the United States are headed in the same direction if a financial crisis or bond market reaction doesn't prevent endless fiscal deficits and money printing. Built over decades, these two powers came into this crisis with major budget deficits and in many cases major trade deficits. Also, at this point the whole world is melting down, which makes it much harder to stimulate effectively or avoid crises that trigger panics and collapses. If southern Europe blows up, that will trigger a recession in the United States, just as our subprime crisis did for Europe and the world from 2008 forward. The only way we will not follow in Japan's footsteps is if the Federal Reserve stops printing new money.

Killing the Golden Goose

Let's look at the real consequences of endless stimulus. Economists are constantly debating how far QE and money printing, and rising budget deficits and debt, should be allowed to go. But the main issue seems to be: as long as it doesn't cause significant inflation then there are few or no consequences.

Since I have been predicting that we won't see inflation as a consequence given that we are in a deflationary environment, I'm not worried about inflation either. But astute economists like Ken Rogoff worry that government debt levels will get so high that they will weigh on the economy and, when interest rates ultimately return to more typical levels in a more inflationary environment, many governments will see much or all of their revenues go to paying interest on the debt. Especially Japan. I do worry a lot about that, as I think it's inevitable.

My greater concern, however, coming from a real-life business background of starting businesses, consulting to businesses, and running businesses, is, again, the death of the "invisible hand." Government's interventions to prevent recessions, debt deleveraging, bank failures, and business failures through endless stimulus all help undermine the very dynamics that drive free-market capitalism.

If you want to really understand how persistent and pernicious the corruption of capitalism has been, read an excellent and thorough book that chronicles the endless stimulus and bailouts since 1914 when the Fed was created: *The Great Deformation* by David Stockman.

It's a monumental mistake—and a misunderstanding shared by the great majority of economists—to think the economy can become a "machine" with constant 3 percent to 4 percent growth, 1 percent to 2 percent inflation, and no recessions. This involves such a misconception and disconnect from the real world that it is unforgivable. As Jim Cramer would say, "They know nothing!"

Central banks and governments around the world are targeting growth and inflation rates, using monetary and fiscal policy to achieve a constant economy. How many economists do you know who have actually run a business? Despite very high intelligence, these people simply don't live in the real world. You can know a lot about something and not understand it at its most basic level. As Einstein used to say, if you can't explain something to a ten-year-old, then you don't really understand it yourself. Listen to most of these economists sometime.

My point is actually pretty easy to make: The economy is not a machine. It is not an inorganic or a man-made process that can be run at a certain rpm with a constant output and fixed energy input. Economists have lost the great insight of the eighteenth-century Adam Smith about the invisible hand— despite the fact that today authors like George Gilder have shown how this invisible hand is operating at new and higher levels than Adam Smith could ever conceive! The economy is an organic process, like life itself and our own bodies, one that evolves through a constant interplay between opposite dynamics: growth and slowing, inflation and deflation, innovation and creative destruction, success and failure.

Does the invisible hand drive machines? No: human engineering and energy do. Do machines innovate and create entrepreneurial breakthroughs? No, a tiny percentage of human, contrary-thinking monomaniacs do.

Can your body stay awake and work constantly and never sleep? An economist would look at sleep as if it were a waste of time and productivity, and then give us speed pills and steroids or whatever to keep us awake and productive (sound like QE?). How would that work out? It would last for a time, then you'd die, go insane, or fall asleep regardless of the pills. Organic processes see sleep as restoration, rebalancing and purification, innovation and creative resolutions (working out things in dreams).

Ultimately, which businesses and people succeed? From my experience, especially with entrepreneurs, it is those who take the most risks and, ironically, both succeed and fail the most. You can't learn through success and growth alone. Such people and businesses only get more complacent and overconfident, and then make huge mistakes or become blind to threats and opportunities. Without disruptive entrepreneurs and economic challenges, businesses, countries, people, and species don't grow and evolve effectively. Why do you think the universe keeps throwing earthquakes, lightning, ice ages, and so on at us? Challenges create innovation and growth.

That's why life has at its very core the play of opposites: male and female, dark and light, pain and pleasure, nurturing and challenge, growth and failure, good and evil. Who would watch a movie that doesn't have the drama of good and evil, love and betrayal? Life would not be interesting, and certainly not dynamic, without this natural play that occurs in all organic systems, unlike inorganic machines, or rocks. Rocks can be beautiful, but try having a relationship with one—or with a machine!

The point here is that Japan remains in a coma economy precisely because it never let its debt bubble deleverage; it never let banks and major companies fail. It killed the golden goose that drives the invisible hand of the free-market system. What major innovation has come out of Japan since 1990? Innovation and evolution come to a near halt when governments protect the old system with endless stimulus and don't let the economy rebalance itself and innovate to generate a new, better system out of the ashes.

The economic truth is that you can't have success without failure, you can't have accountability without consequences. Governments are eliminating these crucial factors to give short-term relief, at the expense of killing long-term growth and innovation. Without innovation there is no long-term growth and evolution—especially in an era when all developed countries will see demographic growth flatten or even contract substantially in the decades ahead. And even the higher-growth emerging countries will hit such a Demographic Cliff in the decades farther ahead.

Whom are governments giving relief to? Not the average citizens who are often underwater on their mortgages, with falling real wages and ruined credit, underemployed and fearful of losing their jobs. Governments are saving the banks from their bad loans, and major companies and investment firms from overexpansion and leverage. Remember that the stock gains from monetary injections are going mostly to the top 1 percent to 10 percent income brackets, especially in the United States. And the top 20 percent with college degrees are only experiencing 3.5 percent unemployment.

Governments are protecting the old order in business, and the democratic system should call for a halt to this. But we're not, as there is no leader explaining this to us. The U.S. government just brings out Warren Buffett to say everything is okay while he is getting preferential investment deals.

So let's look back to Adam Smith's day. The ultimate play of opposites that emerged in the late 1700s was democracy and free-market capitalism. These two principles have worked so well together that most people see them as one and the same—but they are as opposite as men and women.

Free-market capitalism rewards those who produce and innovate the most, as does nature with its survival-of-the-fittest drive. Democracy is a truly human innovation that gives everyone the same vote. Democracy says the system must work and have sustainability for the good of the whole, not merely the profits of a few. It doesn't say that some people can't make more than others. It's just that the system has to spread the wealth a little more fairly. Otherwise, the ill-treated at the fat bottom of the pyramid ultimately revolt. In fact, the American and French revolutions in the late 1700s were all about revolting against a system in which kings, queens, royalty, aristocrats, and landholders (or, in the case of the United States, foreign royalties) garnered almost all of the gains in societies in which most of the people could barely feed themselves and did all of the work (like North Korea today).

Such systems are not sustainable, as people eventually revolt or flee. The pilgrims and early Americans fled the Catholic Church that was the dominant power in Europe at the time and look what they started! By the way, the first settlers at Jamestown saw 88 percent perish within the first two winters, about the same failure rate of start-ups funded by venture capitalists. How could anyone be expected to be prepared for a totally unknown environment, as radical new entrepreneurs face in any such new endeavor? That was akin to free-market capitalism at its best, but of course with unexpected risks.

In a sense, then, democracy is in effect "socialism." It only works in balance with a healthy and dynamic free-market business environment.

Socialism on its own would end up with everyone voting not to work and to be supported by the government—does this sound like southern Europe today? Free-market capitalism on its own almost always ends up with the eight-hundred-pound gorilla getting all of the females and most of the food. That's what happens in nature, according to the principle of the survival of the fittest. That's what happens sooner or later in an inheritance-based political system, or with the mafia, dictators, or tribal leaders who simply strong-arm their way to power. The strong take over and rig the system to their advantage, then exploit everyone else out of fear and coercion.

The marriage of two opposite principles—free-market capitalism and democracy—is likely the single greatest cause of the unprecedented expansion in the standard of living in all of human history. Are we going to let governments kill the free-market side of this equation in the name of preventing an economic slowdown at all costs? Japan is already proof of what happens when you take the easy way out and prevent most of the pain or failure.

Japan has already seen a new, albeit smaller generation come along since around 2003, and its economy has not turned around, nor have home prices. Its government has now gone off the reservation in taking monetary stimulus or QE to a new and even more dangerous level since early 2013. This is desperation, not intelligence. After seeing *The Iron Lady* starring Meryl Streep, I wished we had major politicians with "balls" like Margaret Thatcher. She persuaded Great Britain that it had to go through austerity in the early 1980s recession (as did Ronald Reagan in the United States) in order to balance out the worst recession since the Great Depression, and the country came soaring out of that downturn.

We have no such leadership today, so we either have a crisis forced on us by the next trigger that bursts the bubble that governments keep stretching to new extremes to keep the high going, or we go into a coma economy for decades like Japan.

The moral of the story is that you don't get something for nothing. You can't cure a debt addiction with more and more debt. Japan has proved this already and is likely to keep proving it in the coming decades. The top-down, state-driven model of capitalism, China, is going to be proven unable to trump free-market capitalism as its massive overexpansion and bubble bursts in the next several years.

I believe the great reckoning is coming over the next decade, likely most dramatically in the next two years. I think by early 2014 the economy will begin to demonstrate the limits of endless stimulus in a world bubble that is like an overinflated balloon—heading directly for a nest of sharp-tipped pins.

But let's shift our lenses to home prices, and not only in Japan, which has seen a twenty-two-year fall in home prices that no one would have thought possible. I'm afraid our love affair with real estate, here and there, has come to an end.

CHAPTER 3

WHY REAL ESTATE WILL NEVER BE THE SAME

When I give speeches anywhere in the world, I get the most questions about real estate. People love real estate, and globally we've seen the greatest bull market in modern history. But real estate is also very regional and local, unlike stocks, which tend to move together more globally. Hence, people don't necessarily assume that just because real estate bubbles are bursting in some areas of the world they will in others. Most people want me to tell them that although real estate is crashing in many areas, their real estate is special and won't.

Unfortunately, I generally can't tell people what they want to hear, given my demographic analysis and study of bubbles.

We have seen the greatest real estate bubble in modern history, one fueled by very low interest rates, unprecedented liberal lending, and the demand of the largest generation in history. Both of these trends are over, or nearly over. Try thinking of real estate as a popcorn popper with different segments popping and bursting at different times. The bubbles that have not peaked or burst yet will in the next few to several years.

Real estate, along with infrastructures, will be the sector most affected by this new trend of a smaller generation following a larger one and with declining birth rates around the world. Aging in virtually all developed countries is the trend for decades to come. Real estate is most affected simply because it lasts nearly forever, meaning it does not need to be replaced, like cars, furniture, and food. Mostly just remodeling is required, now and then. This means that when population slows or declines, and when there are more dyers than young buyers, developers and investors are in a whole new ball game.

Let's first review the demographics of real estate. It is one of the most demographic-driven of any sector and very concentrated. Did you know that the great majority of homes are bought by buyers between ages twenty-seven and forty-one? That does not bode well for developers or rising home prices in aging societies around the developed world.

The first real estate surge is in apartment rentals at around ages twenty-six to twenty-seven (see Figure 3-1), when the average person gets married. For the Baby Boomers it was age twenty-six, but this has risen to around age twenty-seven-plus for the Echo Boomers and is likely to continue to rise (it

Figure 3-1: Consumer Real Estate Life Cycle

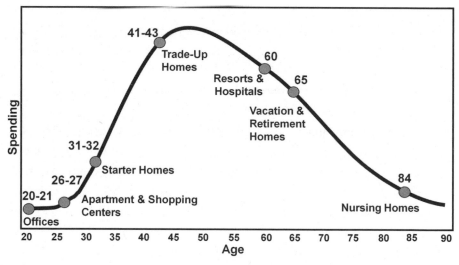

Data Source: U.S. Census Bureau, Bureau of Labor Statistics

The life cycle of consumer real estate buying, based on our demographic research, which combines the Consumer Expenditure Survey (CE) and statistics from real estate associations.

was age twenty-two for the Bob Hope generation). Marriage also produces a strong surge in spending on everything to build a household—cars, furniture, appliances—including when shopping centers are built for these new rising consumers. As a result, ages twenty-six to twenty-seven are also the peak for shopping centers.

The average child is born to parents age twenty-eight to twenty-nine (again, twenty-eight for the Boomers and more like twenty-nine-plus for the Echo Boomers). Marriage and kids create the impetus to buy a starter home, which peaks around age thirty-one. But as the kids become teenagers with all of their hormones, you want a bigger house. The greatest surge in home buying comes at age thirty-seven, but it plateaus into age forty-one. That means age forty-one is the best number for peak trade-up home buying, and that is likely to rise a bit in the future as well.

Thus, spending on housing peaks five years before the overall peak in spending around age forty-six. In the Roaring Twenties, home prices and housing starts peaked in 1925 and the stock market and overall economy peaked in 1929–30. In Japan, more recently, real estate prices peaked in 1991 and the overall economy in 1996. The subprime bubble in the United States kept home prices going up longer than they would have otherwise, into late 2005 to early 2006.

When the kids start going off to college or leaving the nest between parental ages forty-six and fifty-four, the first surge of vacation home buying hits. Note that only about 10 percent of households buy a second home, although that was certainly much higher in the bubble from 2000 to 2006. This first surge in vacation homes peaks around age forty-eight. One of the motives here is to lure your kids to come back and see you. Then empty nesters focus on travel here and overseas. Hotel and resort demand surges into age fifty-four and plateaus into age sixty. So age sixty is the best number for peak demand for hotels.

Then more people decide that travel is too stressful and focus on easier cruise ships into age seventy. But there is also a second round of vacation/retirement home buying, and one of the motives here is to be near the grandkids. This peaks between ages sixty-three and sixty-five, the typical retirement years. Some people move to a retirement community or area altogether.

Others keep their main home (or downsize) and then get a second home in a vacation area. The best of all worlds is to have a home near your grandkids and a vacation home in a very desirable area. The last destination is nursing homes, which peak around eighty-four, dominated by longer-living women.

Baldly stated, the progress of the aging Baby Boom is from a 4,000-square-foot McMansion to a 2,500-square-foot townhome to a 300-square-foot nursing-home room to a 20-square-foot grave plot. That's not a happy picture for real estate in an aging market, especially those looking to build or sell larger trade-up homes.

Now, we can use the same simple technique we use with the Spending Wave for overall spending to project the general trends in spending on real estate in these various sectors starting with the commercial or office sector (see Figure 3-2). Instead of a simple twenty-to-twenty-one-year lag (twenty for past, twenty-one for future) in this sector we can get more specific. We can project the number of people who will enter the workforce at ages twenty to twenty-one, then subtract the number who will exit at age sixty-three and higher in the future. After all, the need for offices follows workforce growth.

When looking at individual consumer sectors, keep in mind that overall economic trends will obviously affect sector trends. In apartments, the housing crash has caused young households to stay with parents longer or to rent longer rather than buy. This has caused the demand for rentals to be even higher than demographic trends would suggest, and conversely the demand for starter homes has been lower. Shopping centers (Figure 3-3) have not been built as aggressively with overall consumer spending slowed by the crash and great recession of 2008. This economic recovery has been the slowest in the last century.

Also note that the Echo Boom had two major surges in births, one from 1976 into 1990 and the second from 1998 into 2007, with a seven-year decline in births from 1991 into 1997. Hence, there are two distinct surges in this generation, whereas the Baby Boom was mostly steadily up. The overall spending peak on a likely forty-eight-year lag in the future hits around 2055, but overall home buying will peak more around 2050 for trade-up homes.

Figure 3-2: Offices, Workforce Growth, 20 – 21-year-olds minus 63 – 65-year-olds

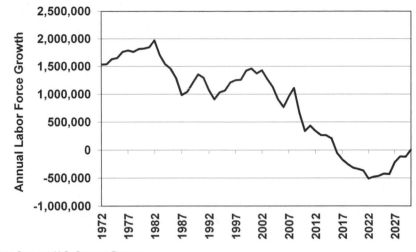

Data Source: U.S. Census Bureau

Offices already peaked in 2010 (and earlier due to the Great Recession of 2008), and this sector is the most sensitive to upward and downward moves in the economy, especially job creation or losses. Given the weak recovery and further downturns in the economy ahead, this is the very worst sector to be in. This sector does not turn upward until around 2023, so I would advise generally waiting until then to build office buildings or invest in them. It is better to lease than to own here for the next decade.

However, since the second surge in Echo Boom births is only about as high as the first, we will not see much progress after 2032.

These charts in Figures 3-4 to 3-7 are a lot to absorb. But investors and real estate developers who are savvy enough to see the slowing and even declining demand for most sectors of real estate ahead can start to focus on health care facilities, nursing homes, and assisted living facilities for decades to come, along with a final round of vacation and retirement home buying into 2026 or so. After apartments peak around 2017 or 2018, starter homes will be the next best sector, then trade-up homes after 2023.

Figure 3-3: Apartments and Shopping Centers, 26 – 27-year Lag

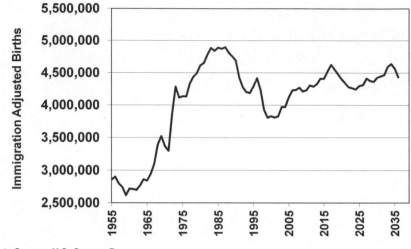

Data Source: U.S. Census Bureau

This reveals a twenty-six- to twenty-seven-year lag on the immigration birth index for apartments and shopping centers. We use twenty-six for the past and twenty-seven moving into the future. The demand for apartments and shopping centers should rise into 2018 and then fall for seven years into 2025, then rise again into 2034–35 (allowing for a continued rise in peak spending down the road).

The New Insight: Dyers Outweigh Buyers

The reality is stark: when dyers start to outweigh buyers, the market changes. What I call the most important and unique economic shift in modern history, the Demographic Cliff, means much more than that, as a generation peaks in its spending, and the economy slows until the next generation comes along, as we saw in the 1930s and 1970s.

We're also talking about a smaller generation following a larger one for the first time since the Black Death in Europe. Fewer spenders, borrowers, and investors will be around to participate in the next boom. As I mentioned in chapter 1, economic growth will be slower (and even declining in many

Figure 3-4: Starter Homes, 31 – 32-year Lag

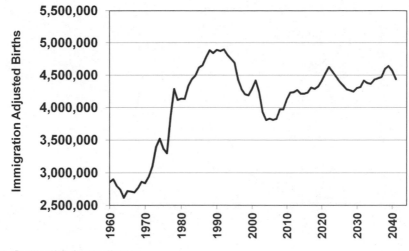

Data Source: U.S. Census Bureau

Here's the projection for starter home buying. This is already in a mild up-trend, though it has a weak recovery as a headwind. Still, this sector should accelerate from around 2015 forward and then have a first peak around 2022 and a second similar peak around 2039–40. This will be the best sector to invest in or to buy after the next real estate downturn, which is likely to occur in the next two to three years.

countries and regions), barring a medical or technological breakthrough that allows for greater productivity among the aging (which is likely in the decades ahead, but not yet). However, the implications for housing and real estate, as a result of this smaller generation, are even greater.

Again, the difference between real estate (housing, commercial, and many infrastructures) and other consumables is that real estate lasts "forever" (many homes in Europe, for example, are hundreds of years old, some even thousands). The longevity of housing stock means that, at some point, the *dying* of the larger, older generation will start to offset the real estate *buying* of the younger one. That means increasing supply versus demand, as net housing demand slows and ultimately even declines when the homes of

Figure 3-5: Trade-up Homes, 41 – 43-year Lag

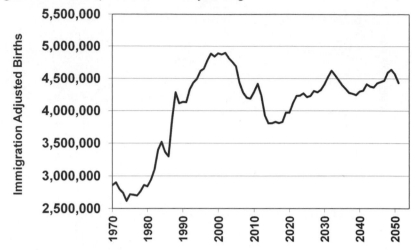

Data Source: U.S. Census Bureau

Look at the projections for the largest homes and McMansions on a forty-one-(past) to forty-three-year lag (future projections). The trend here does not begin to turn up until around 2018 and will see a first peak around 2032 and a second peak around 2050. This will be the worst sector for price declines if we are right about real estate falling to substantial new lows in the years ahead. This will be the best sector from 2024 to 2032 or so in the next boom.

older (dying) people go back on the market and counter the need for new construction.

One impact is that home prices fail to advance beyond modest inflationary trends and replacement costs even in the next, longer-term boom, and may even decline further among countries with the weakest demographics. In emerging countries we will still see growing demographic trends and larger generations to come. That will be where real estate will fare best in the next global boom from 2023 or so forward.

Most people do not realize that the peak in demographics in Germany was earlier than in most southern European countries—and the falloff dramatic. Germany had no significant Echo Boom generation. It already has in

Figure 3-6: Vacation Homes, 65-year Lag

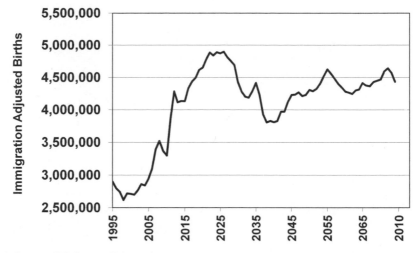

Data Source: U.S. Census Bureau

The vacation home market is generally about 10 percent of the overall home market, so not nearly as important. It is dominated by the top 10 percent of households that can afford a second home. There are two surges in vacation home buying: the first when the kids leave the nest during the midlife crisis; the second around retirement when most people have the most time to enjoy a second home. Note that in the second surge into around age sixty-five, people tend to pay more for their vacation homes. Hence, I put the overall peak at age sixty-five, with a sixty-five-year lag for vacation home buying. Given that the first surge peaks around age forty-eight in Figure 3-6, this market would have first peaked in 2011. The great recession brought a downturn earlier. The final peak should be around 2026, and the next bull market in prices could start around 2016 after another crash in prices. Since vacation homes are bought more by the affluent and are discretionary in nature, they are the most sensitive of home purchases to economic and home price swings. I expect vacation homes to tank the most if there is a second home price slide in the next two years or so, then they should be the best place to buy, invest, or build. So sell now if you can and look to buy a vacation home in 2016 or later. The next Baby Boom round of vacation home buying will peak around 2024–26, and it will be a long time before the Echo Boom is interested in vacation homes in large numbers. So sell your vacation home by then unless you really love it!

Figure 3-7: Nursing Homes, 84-year Lag

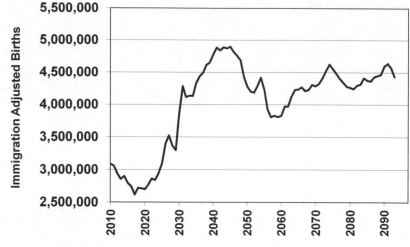

Data Source: U.S. Census Bureau

The opportunity of our lifetimes in real estate development and investment is likely to be nursing homes and assisted living facilities with projections on an eighty-four-year lag. There are already shortages of nursing homes in many areas, and the massive Baby Boom has not begun to enter this sector yet. The first real growth demographically starts around 2018 and then will rise until at least 2045—talk about a long-term growth market! This market is the least sensitive to the broader economic cycle and is something to invest in and put in a trust for your kids.

place public policies for tearing down residential and commercial developments and converting them into public parks to hide the demographic decline. We're going to be seeing that a lot in East Asia, southern and central Europe, and in the middle and northeastern parts of North America—think Detroit!

To get an idea of what can happen to home (and commercial real estate) prices, let's look again at Japan, the first wealthy country to go off the Demographic Cliff. We saw in chapter 2 how Japan's real estate bubble peaked two years after its stock bubble in 1991, an exact forty-two-year lag on the final peak in births in Japan in 1949. But note that home prices in Japan should have turned back upward from around 1998 forward, as the Japanese Echo Boom generation entered its housing cycle and, especially, as the global economy boomed from 2003 into 2007. But home prices didn't rebound. In fact they're still flat or falling, twenty-two years after the peak in late 2013!

The explanation for those prices is the selling out of the young by the older generation in Japan. Those in the younger generation will not have the wages, lifetime employment, and benefits promised to their parents. Hence, Japanese males have much lower interest in sex and marriage. They simply can't afford to support a wife and kids. And if you don't get married, you're much less likely to buy a house and expand your housing ownership over time. That has an impact on the real estate market.

This phenomenon is growing. All wealthy countries are requiring the younger generations to underwrite their parents, assume massive debts, face scaled-back entitlements over time, and find less attractive jobs and wages on average. Youth unemployment is much higher almost everywhere, and especially in southern Europe. So what is happening in Japan will happen broadly in wealthy, aging countries during the next decade and possibly longer.

Another factor may be even more sobering.

What if we adjust for the average age of death (at birth) in Japan and subtract the people who will die and free up new housing structures for the younger buyers (Figure 3-8)? We make this adjustment in a manner similar to how we projected workforce growth and inflation trends back in chapter 1 in Figure 1-8: that is, where we added the young entrants at age twenty on average and subtracted the retirees at age sixty-three. Think of this indicator of adding peak buyers versus dyers as the required "housing stock" similar to the stock of workers.

Here we add the younger people who are buying the housing and subtract the older people who are dying and thus leaving the real estate market, on average at age eighty-four. We know that fewer young people will buy homes in the future due to lower numbers of peak buyers, especially if housing does not seem to be the great investment bonanza it was for so many

Figure 3-8: Japan, Net Housing Demand, 42-year olds-minus 84-year-olds

Data Source: Ministry of Health, Labour and Welfare, Japan, 2013

Note that Japan's life expectancy at eighty-four is five years longer than life expectancy in the United States. It's actually the highest of any major country. I don't know if it's the sushi or the seaweed or the sake, but they are doing something right there.

years after World War II, and also if marriage and birth rates are even lower in Japan, which appears to be the case as far into the future as the eye can see. But when more people die than buy, then the supply of homes on the market rises faster than demand, which just can't be good for home prices. It certainly is not good for home building!

There's a clear correlation in Japan between the net demand projection and the trend in house prices, which certainly makes sense. It explains why home prices did not bounce significantly even when the next generation of young new buyers came along.

Why would developers in this economic situation ever build new real estate, except in areas that are growing due to better climate or new industries? Rather, the key will be renovating existing structures for the downsizing, aging Baby Boomers and the younger, rising Echo Boomers, both of whom will need smaller homes. Expect a general trend away from larger homes in the next decade. Forget the fact that in 2013 large mansions were in short supply. That trend will reverse when the next bubble bursts and most affects the top 0.1 to 1 percent. Compare Figure 3-9 with Figure 3-10 for the United States when we first look at peak buyers and then adjust for dyers.

Figure 3-9: U.S., 41-year Lag for Peak Home Buying vs. Home Prices

Data Source: US Census Bureau, Dallas Federal Reserve, 2013

There's a strong correlation between the housing peak and a simple forty-one-year lag in the birth index in the United States. Our housing bubble extended a few years longer than analogous bubbles for Japan and many other countries because of subprime lending. According to this graph, the U.S. housing market should bottom out a few years from now at levels not much lower than the lows in early 2012 and should start to rebound modestly over many years (until roughly 2032), starting with the first wave of the Echo Boom generation. However, that turnaround is not likely to start until at least 2015, as we have been warning. That's good news, but not great news. But what if the trend in the United States instead follows the net demand shown in Figure 3-8 for Japan, which adjusts for people who die? Japan is ahead of us in the aging and bubble-burst cycle by eleven years plus, so the impact of dyers would naturally show up earlier in Japan. The next great deflation is ahead: 2014–2019.

Figure 3-10: U.S., Net Housing Demand, 41-year-olds minus 79-year-olds

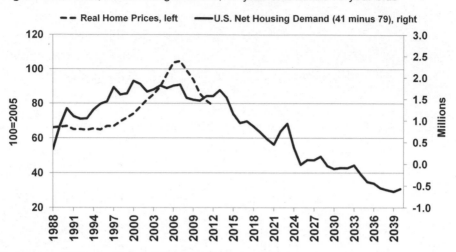

Data Source: US Census Bureau, Dallas Federal Reserve, 2013

After subtracting the number of people who will die at age seventy-nine on average in the United States, a different trend appears. Under this scenario, a continued minor bounce in the market in 2013 is followed by a continued trend downward from 2014 into 2021 or so. Ouch! Prices could go down even more into 2039 or beyond.

Increasing numbers of older people downsize their homes as they become empty nesters, and often move back closer to urban areas for convenience of services and entertainment. They also rent more, especially as they get very old. The new young generation also tends to buy smaller homes at first and tends to prefer more urban over suburban areas until they have kids.

So who's going to buy the larger McMansions from aging Baby Boomers in suburban areas? There will be a trend back toward smaller homes and more urban than suburban, especially in the coming decade. Many Baby Boomers will get stuck in larger homes that they can't sell, which will be the worst part of the real estate market until around 2024 forward.

Canada has the strangest chart and least correlation under either

Figure 3-11: Canada, Net Housing Demand, 40–44-year-olds minus 80–84-year-olds

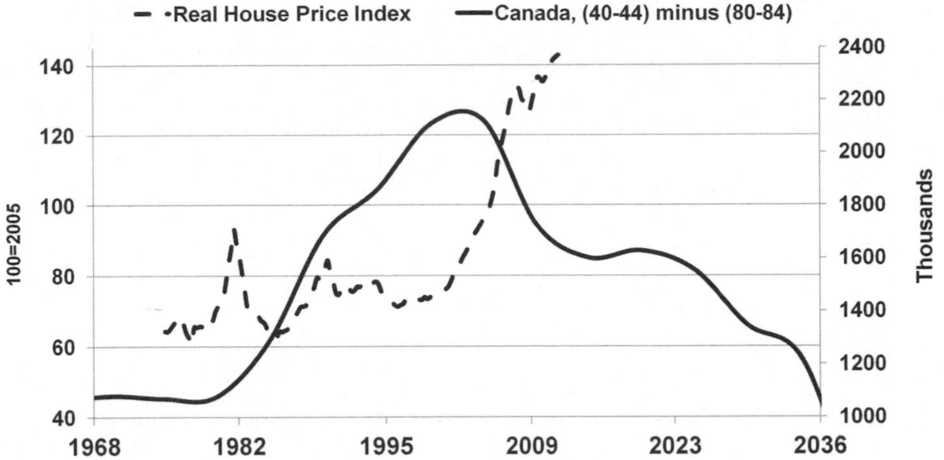

Data Source: United Nations Population Division, Dallas Federal Reserve, 2013

Did the Canadians learn nothing from our bubble burst? Their personal debt/disposable income is 57 percent higher and home prices 47 percent higher than in the United States. Hence, their consumers and real estate are more vulnerable in the years ahead, especially in the face of another crash and/or slowdown between 2014 and 2015 and between 2018 and 2019. Like Australia, Canada is likely to get hit more this time due to continued falling commodities prices since the nation is a major resource exporter.

assumption (see Figure 3-11). One thing is for sure, the Canadian housing bubble has extended much longer than in the United States, and has lasted well beyond due to faster growth in households, which is due to turn down again in the years ahead. The peak spending model at age forty-one suggests that only a 20 percent or so correction is coming in the years ahead. Canadian households are now 55 percent more in debt and real estate is priced 65 percent higher than in the United States on average. But the net demand model suggests much lower home prices ahead in Canada and a fall greater than that of U.S. prices given that Canada is only finally peaking in 2013.

Next, let's look at Spain, as it has the largest real estate bubble in Europe. This bubble could be a major factor in the next debt and banking crisis in Spain if its economy keeps weakening and real estate prices keep falling, as they did into late 2013.

Note that Spain's overall spending wave in housing does not peak until around 2020 (see Figure 3-12), and its broader Spending Wave doesn't peak until near 2025. Spain is the last wealthy country to go over the Demographic Cliff, after South Korea and Italy. The fact that Spain had such a large bubble that has burst to this degree suggests that much of the bubble

Figure 3-12: Spain, Net Housing Demand, 40–44-year-olds minus 80–84-year-olds

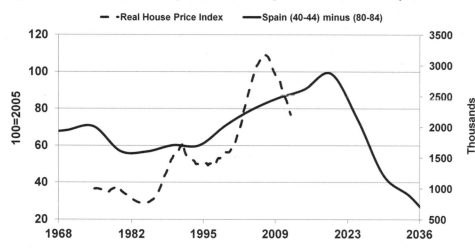

Data Source: United Nations Population Division, Dallas Federal Reserve, 2013

Given that Spain's net housing demand points up into around 2020, it is possible that Spain will have a final boom in housing after a few more years of bust. But the overall trends in Europe's demographics would suggest that its economy will not rebound much if at all, and, after such a major bubble, any such boom is likely to be muted, if it occurs. Spain is rumored to have 2 million unsold homes, which makes the U.S. shadow inventory look like nothing when adjusted for population. Spain looks to be facing a 65 percent or greater decline in real home prices over the coming decade.

in prices came from the highest home ownership in the developed world (92 percent and foreign buyers and speculators with such homes often built with immigrant labor. Those immigrants are rapidly leaving Spain with 27 percent unemployment and the depression in real estate, hence Spain's demographic trends will not be as strong as statistics suggest.

Finally, let's take a look at Germany, the stalwart of Europe and the first major country there to go off the Demographic Cliff. In Figure 3-13 you can see how dire Germany's housing picture is as we continue into the future, and why the nation has already been covering over commercial and housing developments and turning them into parks.

Perhaps the most important point about real estate comes from Robert Shiller, a prominent Yale economist (and one of the very few economists I really like). He charted home prices adjusted for inflation and for the size of

Figure 3-13: Germany, Net Housing Demand, 40–44-year-olds minus 80–84-year-olds

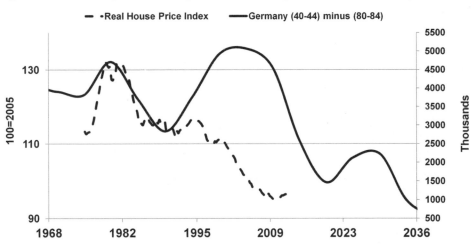

Data Source: United Nations Population Division, Dallas Federal Reserve, 2013

The rest of Europe will follow Germany's dire cliff in net housing demand. Europe's future overall and in this arena is second only to Japan and East Asia in the decline in the coming decades. Developers are going to have to get into health care and nursing facilities to survive.

Figure 3-14: Long-Term Home Prices in U.S., Adjusted for Inflation

—Real Home Price Index

Data Source: Figure 2.1 in Robert J. Shiller, Irrational Exuberance, 2nd. Edition, Princeton University Press,2005, 2009, Broadway Books 2006, also Subprime Solution, 2008, as updated by author, accessed on 8/1/2013

We have lived in a time period where we have mistakenly accepted the illusion that home prices always go up and rise at high rates. Home prices follow inflation and hence deliver a net zero return when adjusted for inflation. The days of home prices growing faster than the economy are over, likely forever, in the developed world, especially given the dying-versus-buying trends.

homes and features (homes are much larger and nicer than they were decades ago). Shiller's analysis (see Figure 3-14) was a breakthrough for understanding that home prices basically follow inflation or replacement cost, unlike stocks that tend to grow with earnings and the economy.

It will take time to see which forecasting approach is the more accurate, but the long-term results from Japan already suggest the net demand model is best. This model makes more demographic sense, given that housing's uniqueness is that it lasts forever.

The most important insight is this: we need to give up our long love affair with home buying and real estate as a means to wealth. A longer view of history does not support this.

The United States (and almost all developed countries) experienced the greatest real estate boom in modern history, initially as a result of being home to the first middle-class generation that could broadly afford homes after World War II, and then as a result of the massive Baby Boom generation, which now clearly has peaked and is being followed by a smaller generation. The result was to create a temporary illusion that real estate only goes up and it outperforms economic growth. The great real estate boom from 1933 to 2005 will not be seen again anytime soon—and perhaps never—in the developed countries.

Instead, we go back to the old model: Own real estate because you love it and want to live in it and improve it long-term, or because it is strategic to your business. Or invest in it if you can rent it out for positive cash flow. But don't buy real estate because you think you are going to get rich sitting on it.

Real estate developers should consider future building projects carefully, especially given the huge shadow inventory (from foreclosures) that has not fully hit the markets, as banks are hoping the Fed will turn around the economy and home prices will come back to their highs and they won't have to write off their losses—this will not happen! Build only in areas growing as a result of in-migration. If you build to rent, be aware that many hedge funds are buying rental properties and that the rental market has gotten to be very competitive.

The Worst of the Crash Is Yet to Come

I've written before about how the most unique aspect of the greatest debt bubble in history was its real estate component. After the tech stock bubble burst in 2000 and speculation shifted, everyday households in developed countries could borrow massive amounts of money for mortgages for the first time in history. Interest rates were falling, making housing more and more affordable. In countries like the United States, this situation was even more extreme. Government agencies like Fannie Mae, Freddie Mac, and the FHA were involved. Even though the United States had lower standards for lending encouraged by the government, all countries saw massive expansions in

Figure 3-15: Mortgage Lending vs. Pre-Tax Income

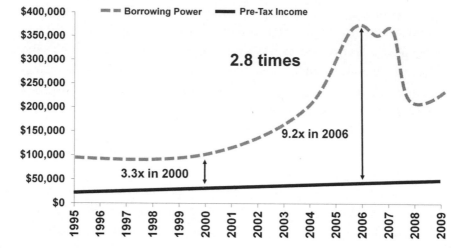

Source: Amherst Securities

A summary of the bubble in the United States: At the beginning of the bubble in January 2000 the average household could borrow 3.3 times their pretax income for a mortgage. By the top of the bubble in January 2006, they could borrow 9.2 times—that's 2.8 times as much, in a time period when incomes rose only modestly and other consumer debt was rising.

loan-to-income ratios due to huge Baby Boom demand, falling mortgage rates, and limited supply, especially in coastal cities in the United States as Figure 3-15 shows. Real estate bubbled everywhere in the world.

A plethora of low- or no-down payments and no-doc loans caused the subprime crisis in the United States in 2008, but the real estate bubbles in most developed countries were as great as the one in the United States and even greater for many countries, including Ireland, Sweden, Spain, the United Kingdom, Canada, and Australia. But it has been a whole other story in the major cities of most high-growth, emerging countries, in which the surge of new, middle-class households is the greatest and the concentration of wealth in the top 10 percent even more extreme. The greatest real estate bubbles have come in cities like Beijing, Shanghai, and all of China, and in Dubai, Bangkok, and Mumbai.

I have always stressed that this is a global real estate bubble. Again, it is like a popcorn popper: bubbles crescendo and crash at different times. However, deflation and a worldwide crash down to sustainable levels will happen over the next decade, most likely over the next two to three years. Hence I don't think that you are okay holding real estate in places that have not yet crashed or that have barely crashed thus far; you are only safer in areas where there was no major bubble in the first place, like Dallas or Frankfurt! The cities that have continued to bubble are now the most vulnerable: Beijing, Shanghai, Shenzhen, Hong Kong, Singapore, Sydney, Melbourne, London, Paris, Vancouver, New York, and many others.

In Figure 3-16 we can see average home valuations in major cities in the developed world, with Paris at 17 times income and London at 13.3 times. New

Figure 3-16: Price-to-Income Ratio In Developed Countries, 2012

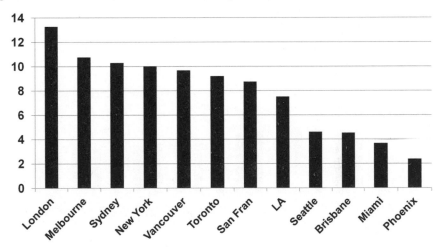

Data Source: Numbeo.com, 2013

These are key cities in developed countries with high average home valuations. London is very high at 13.3 times income. For reference in Europe, Paris is 17 times, Madrid is 11, and Frankfurt is a mere 5.5. Then there is Melbourne, Australia, at 10.6 times and Sydney at 10.2 times. Note that that is slightly higher than San Francisco and key California cities hit before the bubble burst in the United States.

York is at 10 times, now the highest in the United States. In Canada we have Vancouver, the most expensive at 9.7 times, and Toronto at 9.2. Due to a lack of subprime lending, Canada did not see the real estate fall that the United States did and has trended higher and is now substantially more overvalued than the United States in general. San Francisco and Los Angeles are next in the United States at 8.8 and 7.5 respectively—and this is after the big crash. These cities are quickly getting expensive again. The more reasonably priced major cities that bubbled before and have been set back somewhat include Seattle at 4.5; Brisbane, Australia, at 4.4; Miami at 3.7; and Phoenix at 2.3. These areas are seeing bounces into 2013 due to such attractive prices again.

Note the absolutely astounding price increases among cities in some of the fastest-growing emerging countries in Figure 3-17: Shanghai, at 530

Figure 3-17: Cities Around the World, Percentage Increases from 2000 to Peak

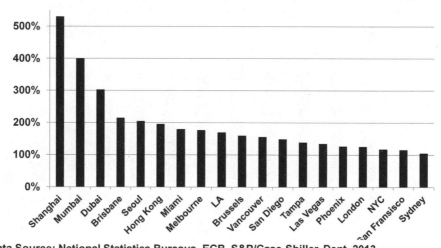

Data Source: National Statistics Bureaus, ECB, S&P/Case-Shiller, Dent, 2013

Here's a different angle on the bubble since 2000, with an overview of key cities in countries around the world. Price increases are graphed here in percentage terms, since the beginning of 2000. This chart understates the bubbles in the many places for which prices had already started to bubble in the mid-1990s or for which prices were already high, such as Australia, California, Hong Kong, and London.

Figure 3-18: Shanghai Real Estate Prices, 1999-2013

Data Source: Global Property Guide, 2013

percent, or 6.3 times (see Figure 3-18 for actual price history); Mumbai, at 400 percent or 5 times; and Dubai, at 403 percent or 3.03 times. Hong Kong was up 196 percent or 2.96 times, and Seoul was up 205 percent or 3.05 times. To erase the bubble that has been growing since early 2000, prices in Shanghai would have to drop by 85 percent; in Mumbai, by 83 percent; in Dubai, by 75 percent; in Hong Kong, by 70 percent; and in Seoul, by 66 percent!

The price-to-income ratios in Hong Kong are 45 times, in Shanghai 30 times, in Bangkok 27 times, and in Mumbai 17 times. In these developing-world cities, the top 1 percent to 10 percent dominate real estate buying along with foreign buyers; thus, the price-to-income ratios are distorted. But the real question is who in those cities is going to buy real estate in the future with such unaffordability, and the answer is: *no one*. Foreign buyers can suddenly flee when the economy goes sour and prices begin to crash.

Mumbai looks affordable compared with cities in China. Yet in my three trips there over the last seven years, I found that many workers in hotels were commuting in from two hours away because rents were not affordable. Such people would never be able to afford the much higher down payments on housing nearer to the city. Only the rich can afford to own a condo in Mumbai, and that is obviously even more the case in cities like Shanghai or Hong Kong. The suburbs in emerging countries are not as nice or as wired and the traffic is much worse, so the city is the place to be. Foreigners doing business in such high-growth cities drive up the prices to extremes, and then prices fall off once global growth and trade decline.

The issue in emerging-country cities is this: How do prices keep going up when even the small minority of upper-class households cannot remotely afford to buy in the best areas? What will happen as the unprecedented growth in China continues to slow down, as emerging-country exports to China and the developed countries drop more substantially, and as commodities prices continue to fall?

Now let's go back to the cities and countries in the developed world with the greatest bubbles. The peak values for the greatest bubbles from the beginning of 2000 forward are: Brisbane, Australia, 3.15 times, or 215 percent; Brussels, Belgium, 2.59 times, or 159 percent; London, UK, 2.26 times, or 126 percent; Miami, Florida, 2.86 times, or 186 percent (Figure 3-19); Los Angeles, California, 2.7 times, or 170 percent (Figure 3-20); Melbourne,

Figure 3-19: Real Estate Prices, Miami, Florida, U.S.1989-2012

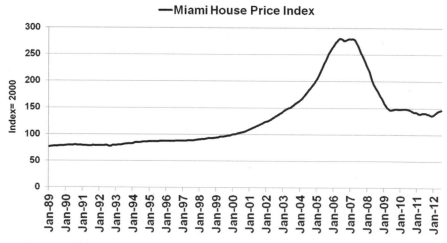

Data Source: Case-Shiller, 2012

Figure 3-20: Real Estate Prices, Los Angeles, U.S.1989-2012

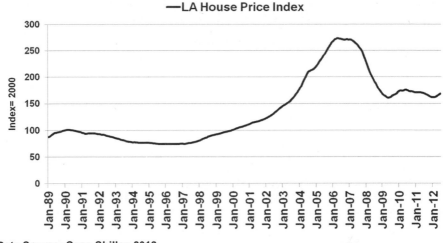

—LA House Price Index

Data Source: Case-Shiller, 2012

Australia, 2.77 times, or 177 percent; Sydney, Australia, 2.05 times, or 105 percent; Vancouver, Canada, 2.56 times, or 156 percent (Figure 3-21); and New York, New York, 2.15 times, or 115 percent (Figure 3-22). Cities like New York, London, Sydney, Melbourne, Vancouver, and Los Angeles were already expensive, so they are even more expensive than the price appreciation from 2000 forward alone would suggest.

There were bubbles that were a bit more moderate, in cities such as Paris, where prices were up 2.06 times, or 106 percent; Toronto, 2.01 times, or 101 percent; and Athens, 1.95 times, or 95 percent. We have some good charts with which to compare countries overall, including some for which we didn't have good data on major cities. Germany had the smallest bubble, at 1.12 times, or up 12 percent; prices for Italy and Finland rose 1.66 times, or plus 66 percent. For the Netherlands, prices rose 1.59 times, or 59 percent; for Norway, 2.14 times, or 114 percent; for Canada, 2.3 times, or 130 percent (see Figure 3-23); and for Sweden, 2.50 times, or 150 percent. The largest and most pervasive bubble was in Spain; prices rose 2.5 times, or 150 percent (Figure 3-24), versus 2.05 times, or 105 percent for the largest twenty cities in the United States; and 1.60 times, or plus 60 percent, for the euro zone overall.

Figure 3-21: Real Estate Prices, Vancouver, Canada,1990-2013

Data Source: Teranet, National Bank of Canada; 2013

Figure 3-22: Real Estate Prices, New York City, NY, U.S.,1989-2013

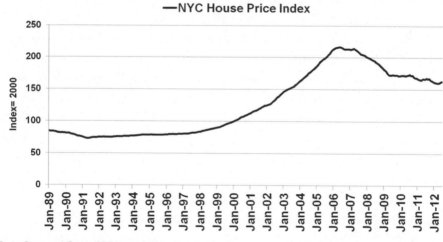

Data Source: Case-Shiller, 2013

Figure 3-23: Real Estate Prices, Canada, 1990-2013

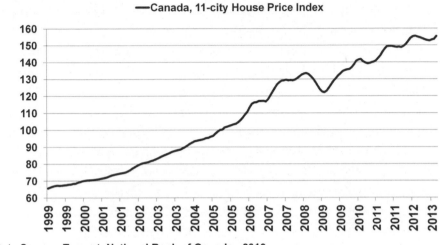

Data Source: Teranet, National Bank of Canada; 2013

Figure 3-24: Real Estate Prices, Spain, 1995-2013

Data Source: National Statistics Institute, Spain, 2013

Note that a decrease in prices to the levels from the beginning of 2000, when most bubbles were first accelerating, would still require a fall from recent levels of at least 59 percent for Australia, 48 percent for Spain, 35 percent for the euro zone, 29 percent for the United States, and only 11 percent for Germany (2003).

I have met investment groups in Australia and Canada that were looking to buy foreclosed homes in cities like Phoenix in order to rent them out for strong positive cash flow. Phoenix is perhaps the most undervalued major city that bubbled, and the Australian and Canadian dollars clearly are overvalued. Hence, Australian and Canadian buyers will win on cash flow, currency appreciation in U.S. dollars, and capital appreciation down the road.

Such strategies would be good in certain other countries as well, especially those with high real estate values, like Ireland, the United Kingdom, Spain, countries of the Middle East, and China. But as prices accelerated short-term into 2013, the game got more challenging, and, again, even large hedge funds have been backing off of buying foreclosures and renting them out or flipping them.

Bubbles Tend to Go Back to Where They Started or a Bit Lower

Going back hundreds of years, bubbles always burst—and they almost always go back to where they started or a bit lower. The crashes don't tend to erase the honest gains over time that correlate with inflation and replacement costs, just the irrational bubble phase. Japan's real estate bust was the perfect example.

The United States would have to fall 55 percent to erase the bubble from early 2000 to early 2006. The first crash took it down only 34 percent, and there has been a modest bounce from there into 2013. There is still a long way to go in the United States and much farther in countries where we have yet to see their bubbles burst or have witnessed only minor downtrends so far. Indeed, as I've been warning, the worst of the global real estate crash is still ahead of us, likely starting in 2014.

In summary, then, the United States led the first round of real estate collapses, due to its subprime crisis. But despite less reckless policies on down payments and credit quality in many other countries, real estate valuations still went as high as or higher than in the United States, and real estate valuations for these countries typically have not crashed as hard since 2006; some have even continued to rise. These high prices and valuations indicate that banks still lent at very high loan-to-income ratios. With higher down payments and credit standards, it simply takes longer for these loans to go bad when real estate continues to burst around the world.

That means that countries like Australia, Canada, Britain, and Spain have more potential downside in the next global crash and real estate crisis. Australia and Canada will be hit by the next downturn, with real estate bursting more strongly due to high-resource exports and a forecast collapse in commodity prices. Real estate and financial lending will be hit hard in countries like Britain, Ireland, and Spain.

However, the greatest recent extremes in growth and wealth concentration came in major emerging countries like India, and especially China. That means the biggest bursts almost certainly will be in these emerging countries, despite stronger demographic potentials, as these economies typically are based on high export-to-GDP ratios and/or are heavily dependent on high commodity prices, which will fall further (see chapter 6).

The big picture is that the largest generation in world history created huge increases in demand in the face of limited supply in the largest cities, which tend to be on the coasts. Extremely liberal lending standards allowed the new middle class that first emerged after World War II to broadly afford homes and to borrow at 9.2 times income in the United States and higher in some places. The greatest real estate bubble in history will continue to collide with the Demographic Cliff that will progress around the world.

Its encounter with the Demographic Cliff means that real estate will never be the same, and very likely we have not seen the worst of the financial crisis that started in 2008. But let's look at the why and the how of the greatest debt and real estate bubble in history.

CHAPTER 4

A LOOK AT PUBLIC AND PRIVATE DEBT

We have seen the greatest global debt bubble in modern history, one that reached around the world, spanning developed countries and emerging countries like China. Economists and politicians have acted like we can just wave a magic wand of endless monetary injections and bailouts and get over what they see as a short-term crisis. But the greatest and most unprecedented peacetime stimulus in history has only generated modest growth in the United States. Europe has fallen into a recession that it can't seem to get out of, and China is starting to see the cracks in its unprecedented government-driven investment and real estate bubble.

The moral of the story: You can't use short-term stimulus methods to deal with a long-term structural crisis in the face of adverse demographic and debt trends. Most countries have not dealt with the massive debt ratios that are twice that of the last bubble in the Roaring Twenties, or even much greater if you take into account the new entitlement bubble of unfunded promises. There will be a debt crisis ahead that is greater than the one that started in 2008. It will simply take a global trigger (like the subprime crisis in the United States) to show the fallacies of artificial monetary stimulus. All bubbles burst and governments have not let this one deleverage.

But let's start by looking at the development of the debt bubble in the United States from 1983 forward into the fall bubble boom. We always see debt and financial bubbles in this season, as we did in the Roaring Twenties. The bad news is that there are other negative factors, such as U.S. trade deficits since the early 1970s (we consume more than we sell) and government budget deficits during the same period (except for 1998–2001). But, again, the main story line is that private debt is much larger and has grown even faster than government debt.

Private debt more than doubled from $20 trillion to $42 trillion in the first years of the new century, as Figure 4-1 shows. At the same time, the federal government debt doubled from $5 trillion to $10 trillion under a Republican administration and Congress who billed themselves as more fiscally responsible. But I find that bubbles tend to go back to where they start. How could any economist not see a problem with debt growing at 2.5 times GDP for twenty-five years? Yet almost none warned of a problem in 2007.

Figure 4-1: Total U.S. Debt Growth vs. GDP

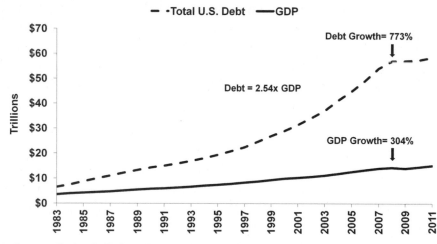

Data Source: St. Louis Federal Reserve, Treasury Direct, 2013

Here's the evolution of the debt bubble at the most summary level. Starting in 1983 total debt—private and governmental—started to grow much faster than the economy. At the peak in 2008, debt had grown 773 percent versus GDP growth of 304 percent. That is 2.54 times! But worse, private debt grew at 2.7 times GDP, even higher than government debt. So who's the "drunken sailor" here?

I showed in chapter 3 how banks shifted from lending at 3.3 times pre-tax income in early 2000 to 9.2 times in early 2006. Banks got greedy and so did we as consumers. Fannie Mae and Freddie Mac and FHA made available smaller down payment and lower interest rate loans with the implicit backing of the U.S. government. Why not buy a larger home than you can afford if the bank or mortgage broker tells you to? Why not speculate at low interest rates created by the government and buy a second home or more?

Note that total debt tends to peak a little earlier. As a percentage of GDP it peaks a few years into the crisis, as GDP falls dramatically in a depression or debt-deleveraging period as Figure 4-2 shows. The first peak in 1875 was

Figure 4-2: Total U.S. Debt as % of GDP, 1870-2012

Source: Courtesy of Hoisington Investment Management

Here's a longer view that reveals another important trend. This comes from Lacy Hunt at Hoisington, another of my favorite U.S. economists. Debt bubbles keep getting larger as a percentage of GDP over history, as our incomes and creditworthiness grows. Consumers and governments in wealthier countries simply can borrow more than those in emerging countries. And since we are greedy and always want more today at the expense of tomorrow, we use that leverage to extremes as bubbles develop and interest rates steadily fall.

at 156.4 percent of GDP (stock peak early 1873); the second in 1932 was 299.8 percent (stock peak late 1929); and the recent bubble peaked at 382.8 percent in 2009 (stock peak late 2007). And I see higher debt-to-GDP levels ahead in the next major downturn between 2014 and 2019.

Then debt deleveraging and deflation set in as Figure 4-3 demonstrates. I see deflation setting in again between 2014 and 2020, possibly lasting into 2023 off and on. That changes everything for investments and business strategies. We are used to dealing with inflation over our entire lifetimes.

Figure 4-3: Cycles of Inflation and Deflation, 1810-2013

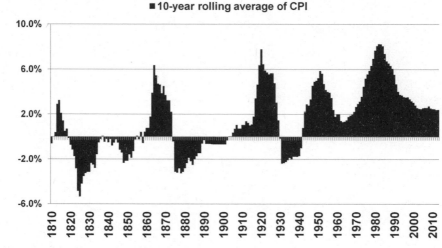

Source: Minneapolis Federal Reserve, 2013

Perhaps the most important conclusion and impact to draw from this: Deflation always follows debt bubbles when they finally deleverage. There are no exceptions to this pattern in major developed countries. Such periods of deflation and depression were 1837–43, 1873–77, 1929–38, and recently 2008–09. The difference in the most recent case is that central banks around the world are insisting that we can't deleverage—no depression will be permitted this time. We just won't take or deal with the consequences of our drunken orgy. This is very dangerous and will either fail dramatically or throw us into an endless coma economy, as in Japan.

Another useful way to think about economic activity is the so-called velocity of money, which Lacy Hunt explains better than anyone. Money velocity is simply the turnover of money (see Figure 4-4). The velocity is higher if money is being lent, invested, and spent; higher is better for the economy, because spending and investment drives the economy and productive capacity. The velocity is slower if money is increasingly being

Figure 4-4: Velocity of Money, 1890-2012

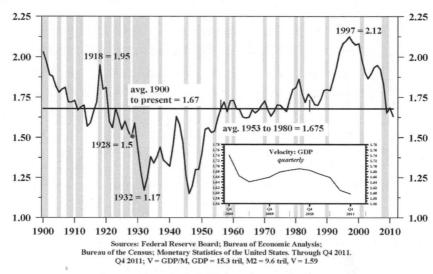

Sources: Federal Reserve Board; Bureau of Economic Analysis;
Bureau of the Census; Monetary Statistics of the United States. Through Q4 2011.
Q4 2011; V = GDP/M, GDP = 15.3 tril, M2 = 9.6 tril, V = 1.59

Source: Courtesy of Hoisington Investment Management

Money velocity peaked in 1918 just after World War I, and then fell into 1932. That fall showed that money was going increasingly into speculation. Did you know that in 1929, 40 percent of bank loans were lent to speculate in stocks? How's that supposed to work out? The speculation and rapid debt growth in the 1920s led to the depression, deflation, and debt deleveraging of the 1930s when money velocity actually fell. Similarly, velocity peaked in 1997 just as the speculative tech bubble was raging and has fallen since. We just crossed the line into negative territory in 2009 before governments started massive QE. This chart would strongly suggest that we have a period of deflation and further falling money velocity for many years ahead.

used for speculation that does not lead to longer-term productive capacity, but produces bubbles that burst. It goes negative when debt is actually de-leveraging, and money is not being spent and lent after a debt bubble finally bursts.

Falling monetary velocity is the reason that massive money printing is not creating significant inflation. Money is not being lent and spent, it is simply going into speculation and creating financial bubbles that look ready to burst again by early 2014 or so. That will lead to more debt deleveraging and deflation ahead. Your concern should be deflation, not inflation that the goldbugs are warning of.

The relationship of GDP to debt demonstrates the truth of my favorite statement: "Debt is like a drug!" (see Figure 4-5). I know that this analogy is being overused today, but I was one of the first to introduce it in 2008. The fact is that debt leverages growth today at the expense of tomorrow. It

Figure 4-5: GDP per Dollar of Debt

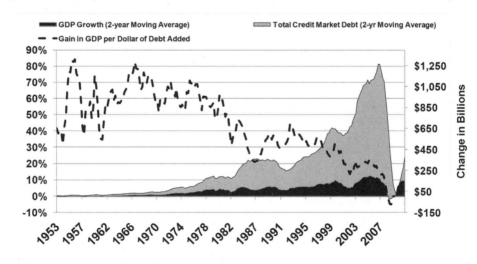

Data Source: St. Louis Federal Reserve, 2012

Since 1966, the growth in GDP for every dollar of debt added has fallen. It finally hit below zero in 2008 before the massive stimulus programs.

takes more and more debt to create less and less effect, just like any drug. At some point you collapse or die from the side effects and toxicity of the drug.

Central banks have to keep upping the ante for QE, but with fewer results. Europe saw almost no effect from its massive QE in early 2012, with a recession to follow by mid-2012. I see that happening in the United States and other countries in 2014 forward. One reason is the unprecedented debt ratios as I show for the United States in Figure 4-6.

Figure 4-6: U.S., Debt as % of GDP by Sector

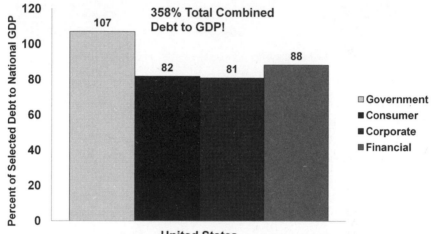

Data Source: Federal Reserve Flow of Funds, Treasurydirect.gov, 2013

Note that government debt is the highest, at 107 percent. It is rising as deficits continue to mount, and that will continue with entitlements kicking in during the years and decades to follow. Our consumer debt was closer to 100 percent in 2008 before declining with some debt deleveraging in mortgage and credit card debt, but now stands at 82 percent. Corporate debt at 81 percent has not deleveraged much. The largest debt deleveraging came in the financial sector, which was 114 percent at its peak and is now down to 88 percent. This sector will deleverage the most and the fastest in the next debt crisis ahead.

Figure 4-7: Unfunded Entitlements

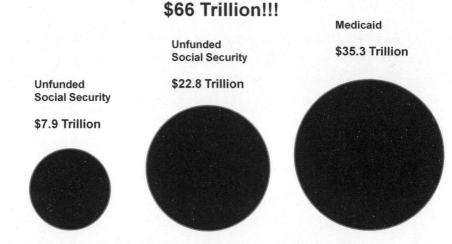

$66 Trillion!!!

Unfunded
Social Security

$22.8 Trillion

Medicaid

$35.3 Trillion

Unfunded
Social Security

$7.9 Trillion

Source: Kleiner, Perkins, Caufield & Byers - www.kpcb.com, USA Inc. February 2011

The U.S. Treasury estimates it has about $50 trillion in unfunded commitments for entitlements. Private estimates from Mary Meeker at Kleiner, Perkins, Caufield & Byers put that estimate at more like $66 trillion and growing every year, and there are other estimates as high as $84 trillion to $100 trillion. Meeker's estimates are $7.9 trillion for Social Security and a whopping $22.8 for Medicare and $35.3 for Medicaid. Such health care entitlements have no chance of being paid in a world where the ratio of retired to working-age people will only rise. And that ratio will be higher than projected as births and immigration fall, and tax receipts to fund these programs slow in the difficult decade ahead.

Entitlements represent the greatest long-term crisis (see Figure 4-7), while the private debt that peaked at $42 trillion in 2008 represents the greatest short-term concern. Workers everywhere in developed countries are going to have to get real about our rising life expectancies, and we are going to have to retire later, at ages approaching seventy-five instead of sixty-three. But high private debt has only one real solution: write it down

Figure 4-8: Total U.S. Debt

- **Total Government Debt**   **$19.8T**
- **Total Private Debt**   **$39.4T**
- **Foreign Debt**   **$ 2.3T**
- **Unfunded Entitlements**   **+ $66.0T**
- **Total**   **$127.5T**

8.2x GDP

Source: Dent Research

If we add up all of the debt in the United States it comes to a whopping $127.5 trillion or 8.2 times GDP. In comparison, at the peak of the last great bubble in 1929, total debt was just 190 percent or nearly 2 times GDP. Entitlements did not exist back then.

and restructure it, to take a huge and unrealistic burden off consumers and businesses.

With our debt at 8.2 times GDP in Figure 4-8, does anyone really think that adding more debt is the solution? Does anyone think we can grow at normal rates again with such a massive weight on our backs and slowing demographic trends?

The biggest problem when we go into such debt is that no one wants to see the end of the easy gains at little effort; people go into denial and feel safe exactly when they shouldn't. In 2013, people finally felt that the crisis was over and there was little chance of a recession. Hey, the economy was getting a little better, home prices were going back up again, stock prices were rising, and interest rates were still low. What is there not to like?

That's exactly when the next set of bubbles start bursting and you are back in a financial crisis again, given that the government never addressed this unprecedented debt, it just kicked the can down the road. Now, we're down the road and the odds of a major crisis are growing fast.

The Debt Crisis in Europe

After the U.S. subprime crisis, the financial woes spread to Greece, then on to Spain, Portugal, and Ireland. Then the too-big-to-fail Italy and maybe even France seemed at risk. None of these countries (outside of Ireland) are competitive in world markets; they have died and gone to heaven, with early and generous retirement plans and high government debt and deficits (just like a lot of public workers in the United States have). Germany, which is aging the fastest, has had to backstop the whole debt debacle in Europe.

The short story of Europe is: *"I've fallen and can't get up."* This is a problem that they keep putting Band-Aids on, but one that will not go away precisely because Europe never solved the root problems or restructured much debt. They started by bailing out the smallest and weakest countries to keep the contagion from spreading with bank runs and all of that bad stuff. But the truth is it will take much more than that if Spain or Italy and some bigger countries get to the point that they need bailouts.

The interesting exception is Greece, where they have written down the debt substantially. *That's* the right solution. But they could only do that because Greece is so small and so weak. And Greece is not pulling out of its endless decline, despite generous and early bailouts—it will need another bailout by late 2013, even though the last one was supposed to last until 2020. It just isn't competitive in world markets. Its wages and benefits are not justified. The euro and European Union allowed Greece and other southern European countries to borrow at lower costs and to spend more on imports from countries like Germany—a win-win until the world economy started to falter. Again, it just takes a trigger (like the U.S. subprime crisis) to expose the flaws.

You've got excess debt in these countries, and you have slowing demographic trends. It is not an accident that the worst debt crises are hitting in southern Europe. They have the fastest-aging populations outside of countries like Japan, eastern Europe, and Russia. But are you aware that Germany, Austria, and Switzerland have similar steep slides in demographic trends ahead, and that Germany hits its Demographic Cliff the earliest? No wonder Angela Merkel is balking at endless bailouts and a larger monetary union. Her voters support her in this.

This is where you can expect economies to slow the most. Slowdowns put pressure on government deficits, and, of course, where you have high government debt ratios, you'll have problems with your government debt. So let's look around the world and find debt. Then we'll show you that it's the *private debt* that is the biggest problem. It's an issue to which most economists and analysts are giving scant attention.

The United States Started This Crisis

First: The United States started this crisis in early 2008 with its subprime financial meltdown. Home prices had been dropping since early 2006, and all it took was a slowing of overall Baby Boom spending in 2008 and an increase in delinquencies and defaults on subprime loans to create a global financial crisis and stock crash.

The global crash of 2008 was triggered by a subprime crisis that was focused on just four states: California, Arizona, Nevada, and Florida. That's all it took in a global system so stretched with debt and stressed with slowing demographic trends for the first time since the late 1960s.

Banks made bad loans on the basis of very poor credit to a lot of households because the government was telling them to. Then they continued to do it because Fannie Mae and Freddie Mac made it easier with lower down payments and lower interest rates due to the government's implicit backing. The Fed pushed down interest rates, and Wall Street came up with securitized mortgages to fund riskier loans, making them look less risky. This sequence went on to the point that people's ability to borrow went up almost three times between 2000 and 2006.

Second: The global problem expanded in Europe with its sovereign debt crisis. We don't see how they're going to resolve this because they've got different interests. The southern European countries like Italy, Greece, Spain, and Portugal have higher government deficit problems, slower economies, and less competitive workers and industries. They also have trade deficits with Germany, France, England, and some of the stronger countries to the north; and high short-term and long-term debts to those northern countries, especially Germany.

The northern economies are staying stronger due to slightly better demographics, even though those turn bad in the longer term for many. The simple truth seems to be that the southern European countries put less emphasis on productivity and more on bureaucracy and government regulations. They generally have higher debt ratios in the government, although more often not in the private sector.

Germany and France are at the center of this whole European Central Bank (ECB) European Stability Mechanism (ESM), but even the countries trying to help their southern European neighbors look shaky. France has higher debt levels than Germany, especially private debt, and France's banks are more exposed to the southern European and eastern European debt crisis. Hence, France really wants these bailouts. They just want to keep these countries from melting down in order to keep the euro from breaking up.

Germany has very different interests. It has the strongest finances and the strongest economy due to globally competitive exports and more conservative borrowing rates, even though its demographics are very weak down the road and turn down by 2014. The euro has made Germany more competitive than it would have been with its own currency, which would have risen in value. Southern European countries have been able to borrow at lower interest rates due to their inclusion in the broader euro zone. They borrowed to buy German and other northern European exports, and, for a time, this was a happy formula.

Now, however, in the wake of economic challenges, Germany wants to see these "trouble" countries go into more severe austerity. For France and the rest of Europe, however, the more austerity, the more their economies slow down near term, the deeper the recession. In fact, some are in depression, like Greece, Spain, and Portugal. Their deficits will worsen, too, making this a Catch-22 situation.

Still, Germany wants these countries to get their budgets right, their expenditures down, and their revenues up so the deficits don't continue long-term. Germany doesn't want to see endless bailouts because Germany ultimately will have to pay much of the bill.

I would also add that countries that do go through austerity end up lightening their debt loads, increasing their competitiveness. Hence, they do benefit down the road. Austerity is something that should hurt in a trade-off of short-term pain for longer-term gain. Smaller countries in Europe like Iceland and Estonia that were forced to devalue and go through austerity went through a difficult few years, but are now rebounding, while most of Europe continues to languish in recession.

Obviously, the division between France, Germany, and the southern countries gets more severe as Germany starts to look at countries like Spain. Greece is easy to bail out; it's small. Portugal and Ireland? A little less so. But Spain and Italy are too big to fail and too big to bail out.

The Interest Rate Trigger

The trigger? In the countries that have the biggest debt problems, the bond markets raised interest rates. That started way back in the spring of 2010 with Greece. A ten-year government bond for the Greek government to borrow went from a 4.5 percent interest rate almost overnight to 48.6 percent at its peak in March 2012. That basically meant Greece couldn't borrow money. The country could not stimulate, the economy was down, and unbelievable deficits accumulated. Greece couldn't borrow at such rates; it would bankrupt the country. Greece needed bailouts and help from the ECB and Europe.

This is a European debt crisis, but it's going to spill over into the United States at some point, just as the U.S. subprime crisis spilled over into Europe. This will push the United States into another downturn, if we haven't already brought it on ourselves with stimulus that continues to escalate but with less and less effect. Then it will spill over into China because China exports so much to Europe and North America.

The European debt crisis will also affect countries in the emerging world as they export commodities to China, then impact countries like Canada and especially Australia, South Korea, Taiwan, and Japan, all of which export heavily to China. This debt crisis is going to bring down the whole world. That's why we have to understand the debt—public and private—and who has more or less.

Knowing something about the demographics, you can look at which countries have the strongest and weakest economies around the world. Of course, Japan was the first to see a demographic downturn in the 1990s, which triggered their real estate and debt bubble bust, and a stock market crash. That's what's happening now all over: slowing demographics triggering debt crises in one country after the next. But the biggest debt in the United States—and almost all countries—is not government debt. It's private debt.

In 2013 longer-term interest rates started to rise despite the Fed's intention to keep them lower than deserved. The Fed and central banks are finally losing control over interest rates and their printing presses! That is the beginning of the end, as I and authors like John Mauldin (*Endgame* and his new book, *Code Red*) have been waiting for, and suggests a downturn starting in the first half of 2014.

The dangers of high private debt increase when the economy actually slows down, hitting the financial sector debt the hardest. When the economy slows, the private debt will deleverage and deflate, just as it started to do in the United States in late 2008 to early 2009, when $4 trillion disappeared in a matter of months, triggering the banking crisis around the world. This was not just a government crisis, but a private banking crisis and meltdown like the Great Depression. Governments around the world put a quick halt to that debt deleveraging with their powerful new drug, quantitative easing (QE). This monetary tool has always been available, but previously it's been used only in real emergencies or wars. It is meant to bring liquidity into the system to keep a short-term crisis from mushrooming into a larger one—like the Japan tsunami in March 2011, or the Long-Term Capital Management hedge fund meltdown in late 1998.

The meltdown of Lehman Brothers and other companies was a good reason to employ quantitative easing. But what we have in Europe, the United States, and globally is a long-term structural crisis from the combination of massive debt levels and slowing demographic trends. I said it before: central banks should not be employing endless QE years after the financial meltdown. You end up perverting the entire financial system and allocation of investments. You end up killing the golden goose of free-market capitalism.

Who's Carrying the Heaviest Debt Loads?

In the pages that follow, I'll chart the debt of key countries around the world, citing the four sectors of government, consumer, corporate, and financial debt. It is the financial sector that is the most vulnerable to debt deleveraging. This sector includes banks, investment banks, brokerage firms, investment funds, and government-sponsored agencies that lend or buy mortgages.

The firms outside of the traditional banks are called "shadow banking." They don't lend against deposits. They borrow to lend or invest, and often they employ very high leverage, especially in a central bank–created environment of unprecedented low short-term interest rates. When investment firms leveraged at 30:1 or even 50:1 blow up, it causes huge disruptions and sudden market shifts in hours or days or months. This is a whole new level of debt and economic leverage that did not exist in past debt and financial bubbles like that of the Roaring Twenties.

Let's look at total debt country by country, starting with Ireland in Figure 4-9.

The Republic of Ireland made itself a major financial center for lending across Europe, a mini London that became a magnet for global exporters to park for low taxes. That's how it accumulated so much financial and corporate debt. Its total debt ratio was 727 percent before a major bailout and some private debt deleveraging. Its government debt is higher than average at 104 percent, its consumer debt is second highest only to Switzerland due to a

Figure 4-9: Total Debt to GDP Ratios in Major Countries

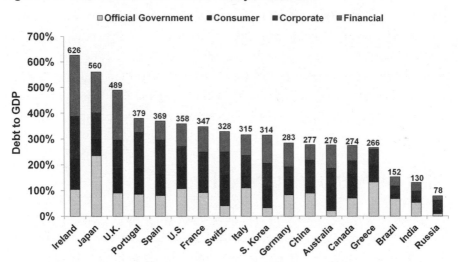

Data Source: "Measuring the Unfunded Liabilities of European Countries," Jagadeesh Gokhal, OECD, "The debtor's merry-go-round," *The Economist.* 9/29/2012. National Central Banks. 2013

Note that we move from the highest total debt-to-GDP ratios on the left to the lowest on the right. The measure is of total debt compared with their GDP, so it's relative to the size of the country's economy. The country with the most debt by this calculation is actually Ireland at 626 percent, Japan is second at 560 percent of GDP, and the United Kingdom is third at 489 percent (as of mid-2011). Those are the three countries in the deep red zone. Another global downturn would expose their weakness very quickly.

strong housing bubble. Its corporate debt (due to so many foreign companies) is the highest at 165 percent, and its financial sector debt is the highest by far at 240 percent. It is this sector of debt that tends to deleverage the fastest as it is all about leverage. Ireland has the best demographic trends of any country in Europe, pointing straight up into 2025 and plateauing into 2030 before turning down, and that may be the only thing saving it. But don't bet on Ireland's weathering another global financial crisis well.

We've looked at Japan in chapter 2, which has seen the highest run-up in government debt of any major country, as it has been running deficits the longest without dealing with rising costs and falling revenues. Japan is simply doing the same thing as the United States—it's just eleven years ahead of us. Government debt is at a whopping 234 percent of GDP as of 2011 and rising (now just over 250 percent).

The only way Japan can deal with this is to have the lowest bond rates of any country, even lower than Germany. This is both because Japan has had zero inflation on average and bouts of deflation and because Japan's financial institutions and its government buy 93 percent of its bonds, keeping rates very low (foreign investors would not take 0.5 percent returns on a ten-year bond from such a bankrupt country). Savings rates are plummeting as Japan ages, and that will make such bond flows impossible in the future.

On the other hand, Japan's consumer debt is on the low side at 64 percent, since it has had a long period where older mortgages from the bubble get paid down slowly and a smaller younger generation buys far fewer homes. The country's corporate debt is still on the high side, but it's the only sector that deleveraged somewhat. Financial debt has barely deleveraged at all and is very high at 159 percent. Japan is doing the same thing that the United States is: protecting the banks from deleveraging and failure—first, at the expense of the older consumers and average households that never got any substantial mortgage relief and get near zero returns on fixed-income investments for retirement (and stocks, too, for that matter); and second, by penalizing the younger generation, who do not have the jobs and benefits of their parents and are scared to buy homes.

Next comes the United Kingdom at 489 percent (see Figure 4-10). The United Kingdom has only modestly high public debt at 90 percent; higher-than-average consumer debt at 95 percent (London's expensive); and higher-than-average corporate debt at 109 percent. But its Achilles' heel is in the financial sector, with the highest financial sector debt of any country at 195 percent, more than twice that of the United States—and you saw how fast our financial institutions started to melt down in 2008!

Why so high? London is a major international financial center and the largest in Europe. Banks and financial institutions there have exposure across Europe and the world.

Japan, Ireland, and the United Kingdom are at the top of the danger zone:

Figure 4-10: U.K., Debt to GDP by Sector

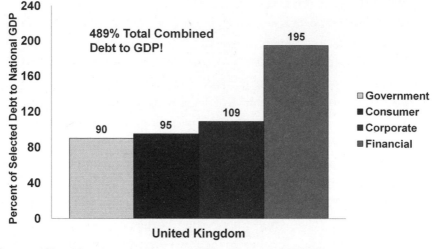

Source: "The debtor's merry-go-round," *The Economist*, 9/29/2012

Ireland has the best demographic trends to help offset the debt crisis. Japan has modestly rising demographic trends until 2020 and then goes off a deeper cliff. The United Kingdom falls off the cliff after 2013 or 2014 and has a substantial demographic slide into around 2025 before turning up and moving more sideways for decades. There is no way it won't pay a price for these massive private debt burdens in another global slowdown, or when its demographics finally turn negative as Japan's did after 1996 and the United States' after 2007. Yes, Britain appears more responsible given voluntary austerity and budget cuts, but that isn't likely to be sufficient.

Then we hit the next danger zone at around 350 percent to 400 percent debt-to-GDP, which includes the United States, Portugal, Spain, and France. I showed the U.S. debt by sector back in Figure 4-6 at 382 percent in total. But just for comparison, U.S. total debt peaked at around 190 percent of GDP in 1929–30 in the last great debt bubble. We're at double that.

Portugal's government debt is on the high side at 85 percent (see Figure 4-11); its consumer debt is high at 99 percent, as it had a strong housing bubble like Spain, but not as extreme; its corporate debt is very high at 140

Figure 4-11: Portugal, Debt to GDP by Sector

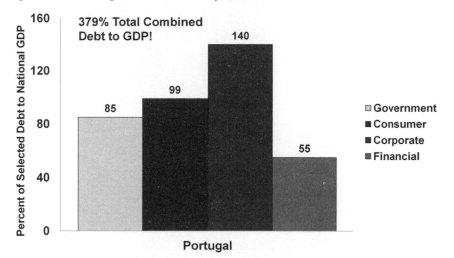

Data Source: "Measuring the Unfunded Liabilities of European Countries," Jagadeesh Gokhal, 2012; OECD, McKinsey and Company, 2012

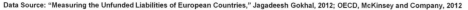

percent, likely dominated by real estate developers. But its financial sector debt is on the low side because the country is not a major banking center. Portugal has already gone through a first debt crisis and is still in recession, yet not nearly as deep as Greece or Spain. Portugal falls off the Demographic Cliff after 2018. With such high total debt ratios, its future is grim.

At 369 percent in Figure 4-12, Spain's situation is similar to Portugal's, with high public and high private debt. Spain had the greatest real estate bubble in Europe, fueled not only by its own citizens' super-high home ownership rates but also by vacation home buying from northern European countries like France, Britain, and Germany. This bubble was the largest in volume and second only to Ireland in degree. It extended three years past the U.S. bubble and went about 30 percent higher. Spain had 13 percent of its workforce in construction at the top of the bubble versus 6 percent in the United States. That's why Spain has such massive unemployment, especially given the multiplier effect in housing in sectors that feed the largest purchase that consumers make by far.

Spain's government debt is high but not that high at 80 percent, as is its consumer debt. Its corporate debt is very high at 133 percent, again due to

Figure 4-12: Spain, Debt to GDP by Sector

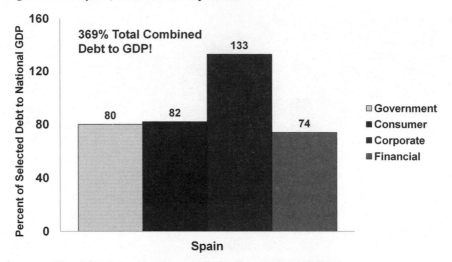

Source: "The debtor's merry-go-round," *The Economist*, 9/29/2012

high borrowing and leverage by developers. That has been the biggest banking problem thus far: failing developers. But as home prices continue to sink, the banks will get hit by failing mortgages more like those in the United States did in 2008 and 2009. Another global slowdown would be an outright disaster for Spain, and it is one of the more likely triggers.

France in Figure 4-13 has more than just a public debt problem, which is at 91 percent and growing. Consumer debt is low at 47 percent as the French don't live in large houses and condos as we do, and despite Paris's being the most expensive city in Europe on a price-to-income ratio. Corporate and financial sector debt is high at 110 percent and 99 percent, respectively. French banks have a lot of exposure to southern and eastern Europe. It's no help that France's economy keeps slowing, and its citizens are souring on the whole euro concept, despite their president's favoring bailouts for the south to keep the euro together.

Next we drop to a third level of debt risk and exposure with Switzerland, Italy, and South Korea. They are more at the three-times-plus debt-to-GDP level.

Figure 4-13: France, Debt to GDP by Sector

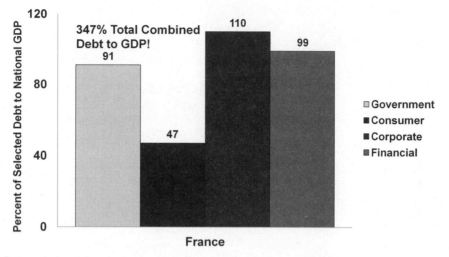

Source: "The debtor's merry-go-round," *The Economist*, 9/29/2012

Switzerland comes in at 328 percent total debt to GDP. That's lower than the United States and many countries, but consumer debt is almost 120 percent. I think I know why. Two decades ago I worked in Switzerland for four months and we used to go over to France to shop because everything was 50 percent cheaper (and France, by the way, isn't the cheapest country in the world to live in). Hence, Switzerland has high mortgage and high consumer household debt. But government debt is very low, a little less than 40 percent, so the country doesn't have a government debt crisis. Corporate debt is similar to that of the United States. It's high but not outrageous. The Swiss financial sector debt is a little surprising. I would've thought Switzerland would be more conservative. But after all it is a banking nation, like Britain, and its financial sector debt and leverage is a little over 80 percent. That's not quite as high as the United States and many countries. But a global financial crisis will not be good for major banking centers that deal globally, such as Switzerland and Britain.

Switzerland, Germany, and Austria all have very poor demographics going forward. As much as they look good today, because of their exports,

Figure 4-14: Italy, Debt to GDP by Sector

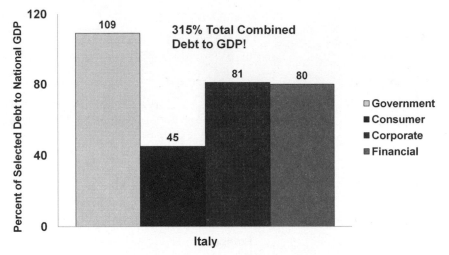

Source: "The debtor's merry-go-round," *The Economist*, 9/29/2012

they're going to weaken in the next global downturn, and they are the back-bone of Europe, along with France and the United Kingdom.

Italy's total debt in Figure 4-14 is 315 percent, lower than most would think with its very high public debt at 109 percent and rising, but, like France, it has only 45 percent consumer debt. Again, people in the Mediter-ranean don't live extravagantly (except for food and wine!). They don't have big houses, SUVs, or big appliances, so they don't have a big consumer debt, mortgage debt, or a big housing bubble. Spain has one—blame foreign investors—but Italy and the rest of southern Europe do not.

Italy's corporate debt is a little lower than that of the United States at 81 percent. Financial sector debt is higher than I would have expected at 80 percent. They're going to have some banking problems, but it's not going to be the consumer melting down. It's going to be more corporate lending and, of course, they have a big, big public debt problem. Their private debt is 204 percent, which in this bubble era is actually not unreasonable. If Italy can get over a public debt restructuring, its internal, private economic downturn is not likely to be as strong as those of many other countries in Europe, es-pecially the United Kingdom's.

South Korea is the up-and-coming major country in East Asia, the new high-end manufacturer to follow and compete directly with Japan. Its total debt is 314 percent, much lower than Japan's. Its population is aging on a twenty-two-year lag to Japan. But as I showed in chapter 1, South Korea will be the last developed East Asian country to go off the Demographic Cliff after 2018. Its government debt is its strong point at only 32 percent. It does have pretty high consumer debt for a country with its GDP per capita, which is a good bit lower than that of the United States. It's typical for East Asian countries to have very high corporate debt, and South Korea's comes in at 91 percent. The government encourages the country's export industries and its largest industries to borrow at low interest rates to help compete with Western companies. This does give them an advantage. But financial sector debt is higher than I would have expected as South Korea is not seen as a banking center. This means a lot of leverage in lending to the corporate and consumer sectors.

South Korea's Achilles' heel is also its greatest strength: exports are 50 percent of GDP, higher than Germany's and those of almost any major export leader including China. Even though its demographics are more favorable than most into 2018, a global downturn would hit South Korea hard, especially with a bubble burst and slowdown in China. Exports to China alone account for 20 percent of South Korea's GDP.

Germany has a 283 percent debt-to-GDP ratio (see Figure 4-15). Its government debt is 82 percent and rising as it bails out southern European countries. Its consumer debt is more reasonable than those of Britain, the United States, and most of the wealthier Western countries. The Germans are not as extravagant and didn't really have a housing bubble. Consumer debt is low at 59 percent.

Germany's 50 percent corporate debt is very low for an industrialized, high-export nation, though financial sector debt is on the high side at 80 percent. That's lower than in the United States, so Germany will probably weather the next downturn better than most of Europe, but not as well as most assume. It's doing better in the recovery because of its strong exports, and that is Germany's secret.

Germany's problem is actually the reverse. If we have a global downturn

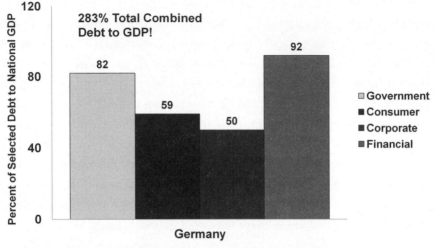

Figure 4-15: Germany, Debt to GDP by Sector

Source: "The debtor's merry-go-round," *The Economist*, 9/29/2012

and Germany exports 35 percent of its GDP—many European countries export near that level—Europe's going to feel the global downturn more than the United States will. We only have 10 percent to 12 percent exports as a percentage of GDP. And again, Germany will be the first major country to actually fall off the cliff after 2013, although many countries will follow. Germany could be the surprise in Europe, and its economy is already teetering on the edge of recession despite its very competitive export machine. A combination of global slowing and demographic weakness could wound the stalwart nation that is holding the euro together.

Australia is my favorite overall developed country in the world for vacation and for living, and it has the lowest total debt for English-speaking countries outside of Canada at 276 percent. It's also home to one of my favorite economists, Steve Keen, who has been a pioneer in charting the debt bubbles and their consequences around the world. Australia's government debt is an unbelievably low 21 percent! Hence, its government will have more room to cushion its banking crisis ahead.

Its consumer debt at 105 percent is higher than that of the United States and most other countries because it has the highest average real estate valuations among major Western countries. All of its major cities are on the coast, with very limited land for development as most of the country is very arid. Australia went through the first crash without a subprime or banking crisis. Housing prices didn't fall much, then went a bit higher. Now they're starting to crack on the high end and will finally fall in the years ahead.

No normal worker I've talked to in Sydney could afford to own an apartment in the downtown area. It's mostly international buyers and upscale households, as in London, Vancouver, and New York.

Australia exports a great deal to China and other countries: raw materials, commodities, and resources. Commodity prices are going to continue to drop, likely for the next decade, so we see Australia getting hit harder this next downturn. Banks will have to deal with failing mortgages, not because of subprime lending, but because they lent at valuations as high as ten times income, just like in California before its bubble burst.

Australia should weather this crisis better than any country in the developed world, but it won't avoid a crisis next time around like it did last time. That said, if I had a choice of anywhere to live for the next ten years in this kind of economic winter season and financial crisis—especially in the next two years, from 2014 to 2015—Australia would be my first choice.

Canada's total debt-to-GDP ratio is 274 percent (see Figure 4-16), one of the best in the developed world. It didn't have the subprime crisis the United States did, having had less risky lending by banks. Hence, the Canadians didn't feel the recession of 2008 and 2009 nearly as much, and home prices, which never crashed, have moved up to new, higher levels. Canada's only high-debt ratios are in its consumer sector at about 92 percent, but real estate is finally starting to crack in Canada, just as it has in Australia and it is now much more overvalued than in the United States.

Canadian public debt is substantially lower than ours, at about 70 percent of GDP. It's below that 90 percent danger zone, unlike in the United States and many countries. The corporate debt is much more reasonable than that of the United States at 52 percent, and the financial sector debt, typically the fastest to melt down, is only 60 percent.

Still, Canada will get hit harder by falling commodity prices, as they will drive down exports. Exports are around 30 percent of GDP (compared with

Figure 4-16: Canada, Debt to GDP by Sector

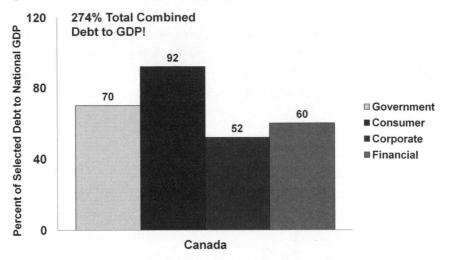

Source: "The debtor's merry-go-round," *The Economist*, 9/29/2012

12 percent in the United States), and they are concentrated in resources and commodities, which are falling and which we forecast to be down into the early 2020s. Overall, Canada's coming crisis still may not be quite as deep as in the United States, but, like Australia, Canada won't avoid a major crisis this time, and its home prices have farther to fall from higher highs.

Who would have thought that Greece would have the lowest debt to GDP of major Western countries (Figure 4-17), with total debt of 266 percent? Greece started the whole euro crisis, but it was also the biggest beneficiary with the first and the greatest relative bailouts. As later arrivals to the table, larger countries like Spain and Italy will never get the degree of assistance Greece did.

Greece's government debt was as high as 180 percent, but after the bailouts it is now 132 percent and climbing again, still higher than any country other than Japan. But here's why you have to look at private debt and not just public. Greece's private debt in total is only 134 percent, the lowest of major developed countries! The Greeks lead the simplest life with the fewest things and lowest debt to finance them. Consumer debt is 62 percent, corporate debt is 65 percent, and financial sector debt a mere 7 percent (Greece

Figure 4-17: Greece, Debt to GDP by Sector

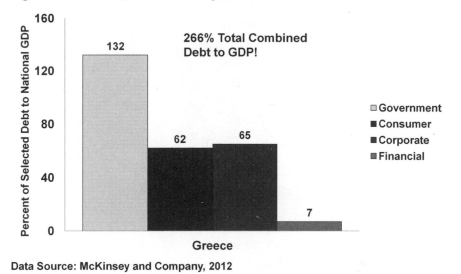

Data Source: McKinsey and Company, 2012

is definitely not a financial center!). When Greece goes off the Demographic Cliff after 2013, things aren't likely to get better there. Like all southern European countries, if it's in this much trouble now, how bad will it be when demographic trends are working against it?

Greece and southern Europe's crisis came from the imbalances in trade and borrowing created by the formation of the euro. The euro made German and northern European exports more competitive and more affordable. But it also reduced borrowing costs for southern European nations. Hence, they borrowed more to buy goods from countries such as Germany, creating trade deficits for southern European countries and less competitive exports for them than was the case before the euro.

But if Greece can continue to get its public debt written down and grind through the austerity, it will not have anywhere near the banking and financial meltdown that many other countries can expect because of its low private debt. As bad as Greece's situation has been—with an actual depression and over 27 percent unemployment—it will be better off down the road due to the fact that it got more bailouts than any other country is likely to get.

I've put China out of sequence because it's a special case. Emerging

Figure 4-18: China, Debt to GDP by Sector

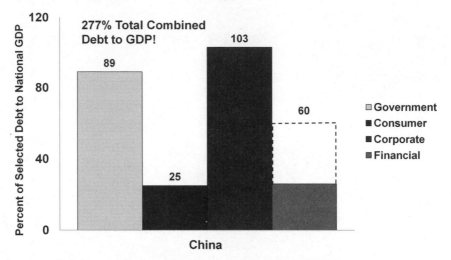

Source: "The debtor's merry-go-round," *The Economist*, 9/29/2012

countries always have lower debt ratios because their governments, companies, and especially their consumers are not as wealthy and hence not as creditworthy. But China has a massive debt level for an emerging country at 277 percent, which is mostly in the local government, corporate, and financial sectors. Its total debt ratio has actually risen to more like 320 percent since these statistics (from 2011), due to accelerating growth in its shadow banking sector.

We've been warning that China's massive debt and a real estate and overbuilding bubble promises an unhappy future, especially given China's aging population and a slowing global economy. The fall in commodity prices that is hurting China's best export customers in the emerging world may actually trigger the next global crisis before southern Europe does. Or China may be the last to fall, given such strong government investment and stimulus (with no one to answer to). Whatever the sequence, China will have a hard landing in the next several years.

In China people have to put 50 percent down and have five-year mortgages, but many save 50 percent of their income and the Chinese have much higher home ownership rates (89 percent) than in the United States despite a standard of living that is just 20 percent of ours. In China, a man stands little chance of getting married if he doesn't already own an apartment (albeit that means a very small one for most). Despite very high real estate prices, high down payments, and the fact that consumers are a much smaller part of its economy, consumer debt is at just 25 percent of GDP.

Corporate debt is high, as China's major export industries account for around 35 percent of GDP. East Asian governments tend to encourage corporations and export corporations to borrow at low interest rates, and they give them all types of incentives to compete with the Western world. This pushes corporate debt to very high levels for an emerging country. Meanwhile, in government most of the spending is done at the local Communist government level, where they're building public housing developments and roads and railways to keep growth and employment up.

China is already seeing signs of trouble, as exports are slowing with commodity prices. They have way overbuilt housing, with 24 percent of homes said to be vacant. The government won't report or admit to this, but independent surveys look at what percentage of homes hooked up to electricity are using it.

In 2013 China started ramping up shadow bank lending at the local level and that looks to raise financial sector debt, which was 60 percent, to in excess of 100 percent by 2014. So China's real debt will likely be more like 330 percent plus by the time you read this book. That is over twice the ratio of India and Brazil.

The private financial sector debt will rise even more as the Chinese government has a new plan to move 250 million people to cities by 2025. They are ripping people off farms and throwing them into high-rises. What happens when the global economy slows down and they can't provide jobs for all of those people who used to be self-sufficient, living off the land? I expect China will have civil unrest, possibly on an unprecedented scale, and a mass exodus back to rural areas.

That raises the question of whether China can react to a global downturn by building more infrastructures, housing, and factories that it does not need when it has already done so aggressively for the last decade. I see the answer in China's stock market. Since the 2008 global meltdown, China has grown faster than any major country, including India, yet its stock market has been the worst performer. The reason: If you overbuild, you get growth, but not profits, as overcapacity drives up costs. The stock market measures profits while the Chinese government's mandate is growth and jobs at all costs to keep its people happy. The truth is that China's economy is BS!

The countries that will feel China's hard landing the most in rough order are South Korea, Taiwan, Singapore, Japan, Australia, and Chile. Many of the emerging countries in Asia, Latin America, and Africa that are feeding China's manufacturing machine with raw material will also be hurt. They are already suffering from falling commodity prices for their exports—again, more on that in chapter 6.

Of the emerging countries, Brazil is one of the highest in total debt, yet it still comes to only 152 percent of GDP. It has almost 68 percent in public debt, which is very high for an emerging country, but its consumer debt is super low at 15 percent, despite its having a higher GDP per capita than China with 25 percent consumer debt ratios. That's low, too, as would be expected. Corporate debt is also modest at 34 percent, as the government does not support export industries as strongly as East Asian countries do.

Brazil's financial sector debt is a little higher than I would've expected at 35 percent but still low, so it does not have a private debt problem at a total of only 84 percent. But it does have high real estate prices in the inner areas of its largest two cities, São Paulo and Rio de Janeiro. There will be a crash there and defaults.

Brazil's big problem is the commodity price crash that will continue for perhaps a decade off and on. Brazil is very dependent on commodity exports. Its stock markets are weighted by resource exporters and the financial institutions that finance them, and by a strong energy sector. I don't look to invest in Brazil or its stock markets until the early 2020s, when we could see the greatest commodity boom in history into around 2040. Brazil doesn't start to go off the Demographic Cliff until the mid-2030s, so Brazil looks good from 2023 to 2036—but not now.

India's debt is even lower than Brazil's with 130 percent total debt to GDP. Of that, 53 percent is government, a mere 10 percent consumer, 34 percent corporate, and 17 percent financial. Lower consumer debt is explained by the fact that India has fewer people in its cities and very low income, way below China and further below Brazil. There are fewer people who can afford a home or a mortgage or a credit card. But the ones who can tend to be the new middle class of India, perhaps 5 percent–plus of the population, and the elite wealthy, who are very wealthy. Thus, 5 percent to 10 percent dominate the buying in the inner cities, and along with foreign buyers, drive the sky-high prices there.

Of course, India also has low financial sector leverage to feed that, so the country doesn't have a private debt problem. Instead, it has an infrastructure problem. India doesn't export a lot to the rest of the world as a percentage of its GDP so it's not going to feel the global downturn as much as China or Brazil or Russia or South Korea or Australia.

Better, India has the best demographics of any major emerging country. It's way better than China, growing at a high trajectory until a plateau between 2050 and 2065. We think, going forward, that India will be one of the countries to weather this downturn the best. And it'll come out of it fastest and the strongest. India is our number-one pick for a major emerging country to invest in after each global stock crash and especially in the next global boom from around 2023 forward.

There are caveats. Just as China overinvests in its infrastructures and major companies, India underinvests. India needs to become more aggressive in its infrastructure investments, and the government has started to do that in recent years. It also needs to cut the massive red tape in government. Businessmen in India tell me that the government bureaucracy is a huge roadblock. What I expect will happen is that global companies and investors will start to look at India when China has its hard landing and stalls for a decade.

Thus India is our number one emerging country for investment after each global stock crash, along with Southeast Asian countries such as Indonesia, Malaysia, Thailand, Vietnam, Cambodia, and Myanmar. We also like Mexico, which has become a major manufacturing exporter and is less dependent on commodities in the difficult decade ahead. Turkey looks to be the shining star of the Middle East in a decade of falling commodity prices where it has less exposure.

I don't know how much underground economy, *mafiya,* there is in Russia, so that's an unknown factor. Debt's probably higher than we're told, but

Russia does not have a major public or private debt problem, with total debt at a mere 78 percent. That's probably because Russia exports so much energy and other resources on which the government collects taxes.

Russia's government debt is a mere 9 percent, and its consumer debt is also very, very low at 12 percent, similar to India's. You can tell from these figures that, with so little credit, the average citizen does not live in high style. We've always said that Russia is like an emerging country with a first-world military (and that has been fading). Corporate debt in Russia is a not outrageous 40 percent. It is largely dominated by its large export industries for energy and minerals. The country also has low financial sector debt, so Russia doesn't have a private debt problem.

Like most emerging countries, Russia is a heavy export commodity country. In the next decade, that's going to be a problem, but debt is not going to be the biggest issue. For decades to come, Russia's poor demographics trends will be a significant drag. In fact, up until recently, Russia had a declining life expectancy, the only major country I know of to have that. Russia is not a country where I would recommend investing generally, as it will have a declining population and workforce for a long time.

All this talk of unprecedented levels of debt around the world today is key to anticipating which countries will have the biggest crises when the global debt and real estate bubbles finally burst between 2014 and 2019, most likely in the next two years. But we're not the first era to encounter debt bubbles, so next we'll gain the perspective of some three hundred years of modern history.

Perhaps we can learn how not to repeat the mistakes of the past.

CHAPTER 5

A BRIEF HISTORY OF FINANCIAL BUBBLES

There is no harder job in life than warning people about bubbles. I called it right when I identified the real estate bubble peak in the United States in late 2005, but no one would listen, outside of my newsletter subscribers, whom we had been preparing with evidence for a long period.

Bubbles are irresistible. They keep building beyond logic as more people are drawn in: "Come into my parlor," said the spider to the fly. Trader Jesse Livermore, who warned of the 1929 crash, almost went broke shorting it; he was several months too early and the market went up exponentially in its final "blow-off" phase. He stuck to his principles, though, and went on to short even harder, making the equivalent of $1.2 trillion in today's dollars.

As 2013 unfolded, I had to get into one debate after the next over the stock bubble, speaking for the most part to deaf ears. People who warn about bubbles almost always look like idiots as the black hole continues to suck people in. Ultimately, though, the bubbles always burst—there are no exceptions in history!

You can only understand our economy and its cycles if you look at long-term history, which offers a deeper perspective. As evidence of that, I'll begin this chapter with two overriding and undeniable growth principles that have been observed over the long term.

First: Growth is exponential, not linear. Two great visionaries to see this are George Gilder and Ray Kurzweil (along with many evolutionary scientists). It means that bubbles are inevitable, especially in the late stages of any long-term growth trend. We as human beings naturally tend to think more in linear terms precisely *because* we don't look very far back at history. We tend to look just behind us and just ahead. But the farther you go back in history, the clearer is the pattern of exponential growth and progress.

How do rabbits multiply? Exponentially. How has human population grown? For our entire existence, it's been exponential. How have technology and our standard of living grown? Again, exponentially.

Want an economic example? We've made more progress in our standard of living in the last century than in all of history. The learning curve of progress and evolution has its own momentum. Cells get together and evolve into greater organisms, towns grow into greater cities and countries, faster and faster. Our usual view is like looking at the ground and horizon ahead as we're walking. It looks flat to us, but from a higher view—from, say, a satellite—the earth is clearly round.

Second: Growth is always and only cyclical. Progress does not come in straight lines. It's exponentially up or down. The greatest booms and bubbles are followed by the biggest busts. People always forget this when things get really good and we want to think we have reached a new, better plateau as the economy bubbles up. But bubbles always burst, and the sectors or markets that bubbled the most? They burst the most, too. There are virtually no exceptions to this in history. Our instinctive model for forecasting is inherently wrong because our memories are short.

I presented what I call the Human Model for forecasting in the early 1990s and have never had to change the chart (see figure 5-1). There's a human tendency to project the future in a straight line in the direction it is going. We live and think as if the world is not exponential and cyclical, but linear and incremental. Why? We hate cycles and we are in denial about them. We don't want gains that are offset by losses. We want to think we can beat the casino. We are idealistic, not realistic, and that may be a good thing for our overall survival in many ways. But the reality is better represented by the rise and fall of the Human Model.

How do you know you're in a bubble? When people increasingly say that it's different this time, that stocks aren't really that overvalued when taking this or that into account, that the government or the Fed has finally figured

Figure 5-1: The Human Model of Forecasting

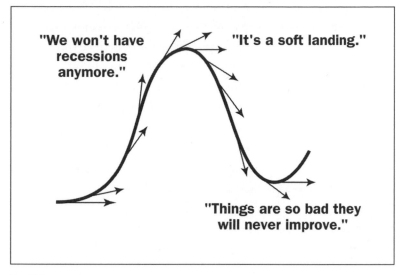

Source: Dent Research

a way to prevent economic downturns and stock crashes (like endless QE). No one, including me, wants the bubble to burst, since so many benefit so effortlessly. And we also want to believe in the "soft landing" logic.

Consider the hopeful arguments from experts like Nobel Prize–winning economist Paul Krugman. He says that there should be almost no limit to how far the government should go to stimulate the economy when it weakens. Does this really make sense? His argument is circular, that we need more stimulus and debt to fight excessive stimulus and debt in the past. Could you argue that to a ten-year-old? Has Paul Krugman ever run a business?

Human beings are endless suckers for the something-for-nothing pitch. That's what we're hearing now, and what we heard in late 2005 and early 2006 as the housing bubble expanded. We were in the same place back in early 2000 during the tech bubble and more recently in late 2011 in the gold bubble. When the bubbles finally burst or when we get a downturn in the economy, people feel foolish for believing in the bubble in the first place— the outcome always looks so obvious in retrospect. With the crash, the fear becomes that the economy will never recover. Then, when we finally boom again, we revert to loving the boom, at least until things start to stall and we go back to the soft landing argument.

There is another way to explain why a world that looks flat ends up being round, or how seemingly linear growth ends up being exponential: a mere 3 percent annual economic growth rate compounds into an exponential growth curve over time. This is the proven principle of compound growth, the "magic" that financial planners show you. And it is true that if you do save regularly from an early age, even in small amounts, you will grow rich. But most people don't do that, as they are overly optimistic and value today's consumption over tomorrow's wealth. Why? They need to spend more and more to raise their kids and buy houses. Too often, it's not the time to save.

You've heard about the marshmallow test for young kids? The kids who excel the most later in life will defer one marshmallow today for three in the future. But they're the exception: most will take the bird (or marshmallow) in hand.

Deferring gratification—that is, investing systematically in the future— is the surest way to build wealth. Taking higher risks, over and over, is the second way. The latter creates the greatest fortunes, but can also be the most painful way to get there, as there's the risk that you end up being the hare rather than the tortoise as in Aesop's fable.

Keep in mind, however, that many of the most successful entrepreneurs in history have repeatedly gone bankrupt. I know the hare path better; it is the one I have chosen, given my innate inclination to push the edge of possibility in my field. As the investor who first backed my newsletter in 1989 said to me, bold forecasting is "living by the sword, and dying by the sword." He was right: I succeeded greatly with my Dow 10,000 forecast in the late 1980s and saw the downside with my Dow 32,000 forecast in the late 1990s. Yet every failure allows learning opportunities. If you can keep going and not collapse, life brings you gifts.

When the second bubble shifted to real estate and emerging markets, I missed that 32,000 Dow forecast, but the misfire also led to the discovery of two new powerful cycles: the eighteen-year alternating Geopolitical Cycle and the thirty-year Commodity Cycle. That was worth the price of being wrong about the magnitude of the 2002–07 bull market. And, by the way, we still had our investors long for that boom altogether, including the strongest bull market of Asia (excluding Japan).

Figure 5-2 shows how simple growth rates become exponential rates due to compounding. Thus, all long-term growth is exponential, not linear.

Figure 5-2: The Power of Compounding at a Constant Growth Rate

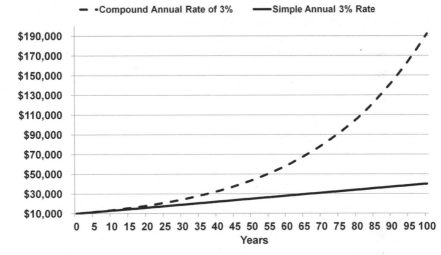

Source: Dent Research

A constant growth rate of 3 percent compounds over time (as the 3 percent is on an ever-rising value with the returns added, not a static one of taking the returns as income and spending it). This is how an apparent 3 percent linear rate of growth turns into exponential growth over longer periods of time due to compounding. This is how "flat" turns to "round," or linear turns to exponential. Compounding is like magic. But you have to take the long view to both understand and achieve it. It requires discipline to keep reinvesting, and not to overconsume for the short term. Most people have a short view, and that's why they are prey to bubbles and bursts.

The Bubble Booms

We experience major generational booms in innovation and spending about every forty years. In turn, we get a fall bubble boom every other generation, or every eighty years or so. When the bubble bursts, that leads into the winter deflationary season.

In studying the major bubbles of modern history (and earlier), I've identified ten summary principles:

1. All growth and evolution is exponential, not linear.

2. All growth is cyclical, not incremental.

3. Bubbles always burst; there are no exceptions.

4. The greater the bubble, the greater the burst.

5. Bubbles tend to go back to where they started or a bit lower.

6. Financial bubbles tend to get more extreme over time as credit availability to fuel them expands as our incomes and wealth expand.

7. Bubbles become so attractive that they eventually suck in even the skeptics.

8. No one wants the "high" and easy gains to end, so we go into denial as the bubble evolves, especially in its latter stages.

9. Major bubbles occur only about once in a human lifetime, so it is easy to forget the lessons from the last one.

10. Bubbles may seem fruitless and destructive when they burst, but they actually serve a very essential function in the process of innovation and human progress.

In looking for lessons, we'll start by marching back in history just over three hundred years to identify a larger cycle. Drawn from Robert Prechter's *Conquer the Crash*, Figure 5-3 puts together British stock prices before 1780 and U.S.

Figure 5-3: Stock Prices since 1700

Source: *Conquer the Crash* by Robert Prechter, with projection by Harry S. Dent, Jr.

stock prices after. It is clear that since the Industrial Revolution and the burgeoning of democracy came together in the 1780s—the Big Bang in economic history—stocks have had both exponential and cyclical growth. In fact, the progress is so exponential that charts like this are made on a logarithmic scale.

Logarithmic scales go from 1 to 10 to 100, not 1 to 2 to 3. Such scales reflect the natural exponential growth that is inherent but only shows up over the longer term. As bubbly as stocks look since the 1780s on this chart, they are even more so. Imagine rural people in small towns at the turn of the 1900s, before autos were common, not to mention jet travel. Could those people have ever envisioned the progress to follow for their kids and grandkids? Not a chance. Only the rare genius like Leonardo da Vinci sees such exponential progress in technologies that are way ahead of their time. Only geniuses like George Gilder, Steve Jobs, Tony Robbins, and Ray Kurzweil see such exponential changes ahead today.

Exponential progress also sees major cyclical setbacks along Elliott wave

Figure 5-4: Elliott Wave Patterns

Source: *Conquer the Crash* by Robert Prechter

In understanding the stock price curve (see Figure 5-3), it's useful to understand the Elliott wave. Here you can see how bull markets move in five waves, three up alternating with two down (the cyclical factor). You can see how the pattern unfolds, but know that in a bubble, the fifth wave peak tends to be the most extreme. Once markets move down after such a peak, corrections against the grain then move in three waves, two down and one up in between—an A-wave down, a hopeful B-wave up, and then a final C-wave back down into reality—or what I call the *Oh, crap* wave.

patterns as in Figure 5-4. First, look at the crash from 1720 forward in Figure 5-3, where stocks saw a sixty-seven-year bear market from 1720 to 1787. How can anyone possibly plan for long-term investing and retirement if that can occur? Such things do happen: Recall from chapter 2 that Japan had a bear market in stocks that lasted from late 1989 into early 2009, or twenty years thus far, and may see lower lows yet ahead. In fact, I expect that Japan's Nikkei will not go higher than around 23,000 by 2017 or 2020, in contrast to its peak near 39,000 in late 1989. I think it will be much lower ten or twenty or forty years from now. So we're talking up to sixty years or more ahead, not so different from 1720–87. What about the Dark Ages from the fall of Rome into the Crusades—five-hundred-plus years of a bearish economy where major cities disintegrated back into rural areas?

Now, look at the major bubbles and then the major setbacks. There's the first wave up into 1835, then a major crash and depression into 1843, and an on-and-off crash for twenty-two years into 1857. A third wave up follows, leading into 1929, then a sideways and down market into 1942. Next the greatest bubble in modern history—the one we're in. Do you doubt a sideways market will come from this, and possibly last for several decades?

Another major insight I've gained from looking at history in the long term is that there are always larger cycles that occur in four seasons, including booms and busts and inflation and deflation in economics.

So let's take another look, starting with the first great bubble in modern history, way back in the early 1600s, even before Figure 5-3.

Tulips were a natural fantasy in Holland. The first modern markets where you could buy such tulips before they were harvested started back around 1634. It was a progenitor of what we now call the "futures markets."

Tulip bulbs were not worth much until they started to become more popular. Along came the first market where you could put a little money down and speculate on the value of the harvest ahead. That launched the first major speculative investment bubble in modern history. As they developed, futures markets allow agricultural producers to lock in their profits at a certain price. But given the low price of doing so early on, futures markets also lead to speculation among the rich. In the case of seventeenth-century Holland, as tulip prices went up, more people bought such futures. The more they went up, the more people speculated. You can guess the outcome: yes, we are greedy bastards and want to get rich quick, with no effort when possible. So when everyone starts doing something, it starts to look more acceptable and less risky. It isn't. In the case of the Dutch, the wealthy speculators were caught off guard. The crash was extreme, partly because people back then had no history of such bubbles and went for it hook, line, and sinker. (See Figure 5-5.)

The next great bubble occurred in the early 1700s as the first trading companies developed around long-term sailing expeditions for trade in the East Indies (India and beyond), led by the East India Trading Company,

Figure 5-5: Dutch Tulip Bubble, 1634-1637

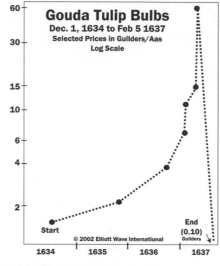

Source: "Conquer the Crash" by Robert Prechter, pg. 80

Bulb prices increased dramatically in just over a year, from 1634 into 1635, advancing 120 times in less than two years and then collapsing 99.8 percent! Though this was the greatest bubble in history, it was restricted to a very minor portion of society. One factor in its occurrence was that it came at the top of a five-hundred-year cycle of rising inflation into the mid-1600s when everyone expected commodity prices to go up forever (the fallacy, again, of straight-line forecasting). It had little reality to back it up—it was pure speculation, based not on rising productivity but just on higher prices.

founded in 1706. Investors could buy shares in such companies and share in the profits. Functionally, this was the beginning of stock markets. By 1719 to 1720 the first bubble was ready to pop, and the South Seas shares went up from 110 to 960, or 8.7 times in less than two years—and then collapsed 94 percent within a year as Figure 5-6 shows.

The story of the Mississippi land bubble in France in Figure 5-7 was even more telling, since it saw the first bubble induced by a central bank and its government. John Law had ascended to the top levels of finance in France after the long wars waged by Louis XIV had nearly bankrupted the country.

Figure 5-6: South Seas Bubble, 1718-1722

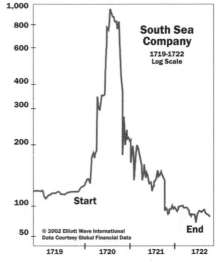

Source: "Conquer the Crash" by Robert Prechter, pg. 80

Figure 5-7: Mississippi Land Bubble, 1718-1722

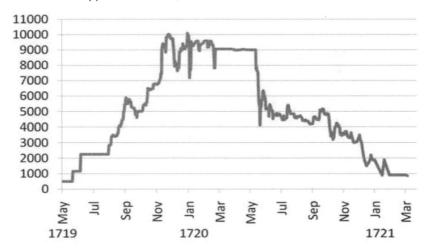

Source: François Velde, http://www.heraldica.org/econ/

He conceived the idea of having the bank of France raise money by selling shares in French-owned lands in Mississippi and Louisiana to pay off its debt. To do this, Law created the first central bank that could create money by loaning artificially created money against such speculative purchases in what turns out to have been swamp land in America. The interest rates were low and guaranteed by the government—does that sound familiar today? The Mississippi land bubble was much worse than the one produced by Fannie Mae and Freddie Mac, as the land being sold in North America was nearly worthless at the time but so far away that no one would know otherwise. To the investors, it all sounded like the future coming.

Of course the Mississippi bubble collapsed just as the South Seas bubble had (and all bubbles do). A long-term slowdown in the economy followed, with lower stock prices into the late 1700s. Only when the Industrial Revolution and the American Revolution took center stage did the momentum change, as the greatest "Big Bang" in history since the Agricultural Revolution, ten thousand years before, unfolded. The stocks and the economy spiked up again until the next great bubble peaked and burst.

What followed was the bubble into 1835. By then, investors owned factories, steamships, and shares in canals, but there was an even bigger bubble around real estate. The U.S. government wanted to induce settlers to move westward, which back then meant to midwestern states such as Ohio and Illinois. The government was selling land on the frontier very cheap and with low interest rates, which—of course—led people to buy and flip such land. The Great Lakes started booming from 1825 with the opening of the Erie Canal. That canal and others to follow made tiny Chicago an instant boom town of the Midwest.

Speculation created a land bubble into 1835 that peaked and then crashed. The bubble in Chicago is indicative (see Figure 5-8), as real estate prices went up 40,775 percent from $800 an acre in 1830 to near–New York prices of $327,000 in 1836, and then crashed 90 percent back to $34,000 in 1841. It was a fantasy that Chicago at that time could compete with New York that was much more massive and competitive as a port. New towns formed and boomed throughout the Midwest, especially between 1835 and 1837. Then there was the panic of 1837 with bank runs, especially in Chicago.

Figure 5-8: Chicago Real Estate Bubble, 1820-1843

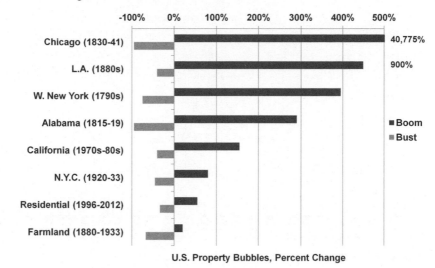

U.S. Property Bubbles, Percent Change

Source: "Betting the house," *The Economist*, 4/6/2013

The stock crash, first from 1835 into 1843 of 50 percent, and then the second stock crash from 1853 to 1857, represented a major two-wave down of the longer-term bull market from the 1780s forward after a one-wave up into 1835. At the time, it was the longest downturn at twenty-two years in modern history (like Japan today), but not as deep as the Great Depression in the 1930s to follow.

The railroad boom before and after the Civil War followed. This was a technology first innovated in England that would open up the entire American continent. The next bubble boom started in 1858 and mushroomed after the Civil War. Stocks peaked in 1872 and then crashed into 1877. The late 1800s was an on-and-off depression era on a larger five-hundred-year cycle (a longer-term winter season) as there was a major transition from the English empire to the American era.

Then came the greatest depression in American history (see Figure 5-9) and perhaps world history: 1930–33 to 1942 and World War II. Stocks went down 88 percent, and unemployment went up to 25 percent. There were dust

Figure 5-9: Dow, 1920-1942

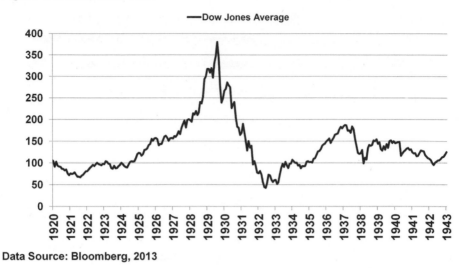

Data Source: Bloomberg, 2013

storms and droughts. Everything went down together, as in 2008. That's the hallmark of the winter season when financial and debt bubbles deflate. The next sustained bull market did not come until 1942 and after.

What did we do to deserve this? We invented the steam engine, high-productivity factories, steamboats, canals, the telegraph, railroads, electricity, telephones, automobiles, radios, and even the beginnings of home appliances and TVs. There was exponential growth in technologies and progress. But we forgot that progress is both *exponential* and *cyclical*, meaning the greatest booms create the greatest busts, then greater booms again. That is also a major law of physics: every action has an equal and opposite reaction.

Can we blame the newly created Federal Reserve for the greatest of depressions? There was great interest rate volatility in the deflationary 1800s, with long-term deflation cycles that began around 1820, bottoming around 1896, and to a lesser degree around 1933–42. The Federal Reserve was created in 1913 to help flatten short-term interest rate cycles by setting and controlling interest rates. The Fed's efforts did result in less volatility in interest rates, but, over time, its stimulus bias tended to minimize recessions and the natural shake-outs in debt and efficiency.

From my view, that's created a compounding curve in debt and finance that led to the bigger bubble of the Roaring Twenties, setting us up for the mother of all depressions. It's one of my fundamental beliefs that, when you mess with the market's natural mechanisms, you pervert the economy and create distortions.

The United States came roaring out of the Great Depression to become the greatest country and world leader since Great Britain in the 1800s. Why? What doesn't kill you makes you stronger! We didn't gloss over our debt and slowing demographic trends like today; instead, we eliminated most of our private debt. We allowed banks and companies to go under. It was a massive detox of the system, which made it more efficient and stronger in the end.

So is lower debt better than higher debt for the future? In a word, *yes*. Margaret Thatcher, and, to a lesser degree, Ronald Reagan, argued for such austerity in the early 1980s. And how did we come out of that? Again, we exploded out of the starting blocks. Since World War II, the whole developed world recovered unbelievably, and I credit that to the invisible hand and the concept of "creative destruction." We may not like cycles, but the dynamic of such changes is necessary for innovation and economic evolution. If there was any time in history that showed how unprecedented tragedy could lead to unprecedented progress, it was 1930 to 2007. You don't get booms without busts, or progress without challenge and innovation. The Fed's recent interventions in the economy to minimize recessions and endlessly stimulate counters the economy's natural mechanisms, slowing innovation and efficiency longer-term. The Fed is the enemy of such cycles at the expense of long-term innovation.

Bubbling in the Nineties and After

Major bubbles occur about once in a lifetime. However, as life expectancy has extended, so have economic cycles, so the old rule of fifty to sixty years between bubbles has lengthened to more like eighty years. But the bubble we're in now is different from earlier ones in that demographic trends are causing it to cascade around the world.

Figure 5-10: Bubble after Bubble

Data Source: Yahoo! Finance, Japan Bureau of Statistics, Bloomberg, 2013

In Figure 5-10 we can see that after Japan's stock market bubble burst in late 1989, the real estate market followed suit in 1991. Next came the tech bubble peak in early 2000. The U.S. real estate market peak in early 2006 was followed by the high point in global stock markets, with a bubble concentrated in emerging markets and China in late 2007. The next was commodities in mid-2008, followed by gold in late 2011. High-yield bonds appear to have peaked in May 2013 when we gave a sell signal there. Stocks will likely come last by early 2014.

The Japanese Nikkei peaked near 39,000 and fell 62 percent to around 24,000 in late 1992 before a strong rally as I showed in chapter 2. I predicted the long downturn in Japan in 1989 in *Our Power to Predict*. But unlike in the United States, Japan did not step in with heavy QE at this stage and its stock market never rallied past 23,000 in late 1996 before crashing to new lows into 1998, as it actually started falling off the Demographic Cliff after 1996. Note that the Nikkei has always fallen to new lows despite endless QE since 1997. Stimulus does not work long-term. It is a short-term measure and should be used to fight short-term liquidity crises, not to fight a long-term debt and demographic bubble bursting. Active debt restructuring should be the policy, as I will address in chapter 9.

As I pointed out in chapter 2, the world should be noticing that Japan's residential real estate fell over 60 percent and has never rallied twenty-two years later! Japan's peak in 1991 was right in line with peak spending on trade-up homes around age forty-two there. I explained in chapter 3 how a new trend is hitting with more dyers than young buyers. This trend worsens after 2015 in Japan again and after 2013 in the United States.

Then the most extreme stock bubble since the South Seas into 1720 hit: the high-tech and Internet bubble from 1995 to early 2000. I show the broader Nasdaq for tech stocks in Figure 5-11. It advanced from 750 to 5,050, or 6.8 times from late 1994 into March 2000, and then fell 78 percent to 1,100 in October 2002. The Internet index rose 9 times and fell 92 percent. This bubble was driven by the sweet spot of Baby Boom spending in the 1990s (which I predicted in the late 1980s) and the S-curve acceleration of Internet, cell phones, and broadband into the mainstream economy (much like the prior fall season boom from 1914 to 1928 when autos, electricity, phones, and radios moved mainstream rapidly, which I also predicted).

The 1990s was totally predictable as the greatest boom in U.S. history if you simply looked at projectable demographic trends and cycles of

Figure 5-11: Nasdaq, 1990-2013

Source: Yahoo! Finance, 2013

technology innovation and the S-curve projections of progress. But economists don't dirty their hands with such consumer fundamentals, which they don't consider as important as the intricacies of government policies. They totally missed the greatest boom in history.

The final boom in the United States and developed countries came into 2007 when the U.S. demographic spending trends peaked, and the economy has been very slow to recover since. In Europe, the trends have been toward mild recessions in most countries (and depressions in countries like Greece, Portugal, and Spain) since 2011 when they started to plateau in spending. As I pointed out in chapter 2, there will be more bad news when Europe actually starts falling off the Demographic Cliff after 2013, starting with Germany, the United Kingdom, Switzerland, and Austria.

The first bubble to peak in this final demographic boom was U.S. real estate, in late 2005 and early 2006 as I showed in chapter 3. Real estate fell 34 percent into 2011, more than in the Great Depression (housing in those early days didn't really bubble due to the lack of credit to fuel it, as consumers had to put 50 percent down and got a five-year balloon mortgage).

The bubble shifted more toward real estate and emerging markets after the punishing crash in tech stocks. That is something I didn't anticipate in the late 1990s and early 2000s when I was projecting a second bubble in stocks that could see the Dow go as high as 32,000 to 40,000 depending on whether it peaked in line with demographic trends in 2007 or other cycles around late 2009. As it turned out, U.S. stocks merely doubled from late 2002 into late 2007, going from 7,200 to 14,280 on the Dow. I expected the U.S. stock market to bubble to extremes again as it did in two bubbles from 1914 into 1929.

China's stock market in Figure 5-12 epitomized the emerging market bubble that was even stronger than the tech bubble in the 1990s. China's Shanghai Composite went up nearly six times to 6,000 in just two years and then collapsed 82 percent into late 2008. That was a bigger bust than in the United States, but China didn't even have a recession, though GDP growth dropped from 12 percent down to 6 percent.

Note that China's market rallied only modestly into February 2010 and was back near its 2008 lows in mid-2013. How could China be growing at 8 percent to 12 percent and its market perform so badly? As usual, the answer

Figure 5-12: Shanghai Composite, 2002-2013

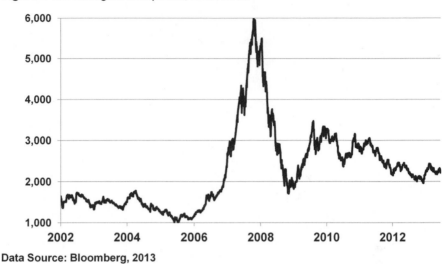

Data Source: Bloomberg, 2013

to that is that China is overbuilding everything. China's stock market tells the real story with its feeble rally into February 2010 and its decline to near 2008 lows since.

According to the Commodity Research Bureau Index (CRB), commodity prices were the next bubble to peak in late April 2011 (see Figure 5-13). Commodity prices had what is called in Elliott wave language a B-wave or bear market rally, and have continued to collapse slowly. Falling commodity prices create a vicious cycle of falling exports and profits in emerging countries, and that, in turn, creates lower exports for China. Silver peaked in that cycle at $48, rivaling its 1980 bubble peak. At Dent Research, we gave a sell signal on silver on that day in late April 2011 at $48.

Gold was the next major bubble to peak (Figure 5-14). The crisis metal market saw escalating money printing around the world, but gold had to start throwing in the towel when inflation was falling back toward a modest 1 percent rate in mid-2013, reinforcing my long-standing argument that money printing would not create substantial inflation in the winter season of debt deleveraging and deflation. Gold staged a rally into late 2013 as we expected, but this bubble looks to be over, and the next stop will be around

Figure 5-13: CRB, 2000-2013

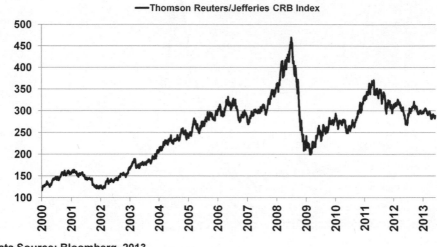

Data Source: Bloomberg, 2013

Figure 5-14: Gold, 1998-2013

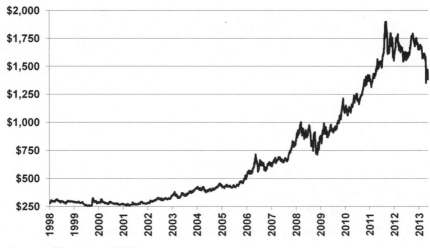

Data Source: Bloomberg, 2013

$700 to $750 after a rally into late 2013 or early 2014 back toward $1,420 to $1,520. Ultimately by 2023 gold is likely to fall back toward $250, its 1998 low from the last bubble burst.

Remember in 1980 when gold soared to $840 and was projected to go to $5,000? That's bubble logic, and we have heard the same wild projections for gold in recent years. But that is not going to happen.

In May 2013, the *HS Dent Forecast* gave a long-term sell signal in high-yield bonds. Bonds look to be the last bubble to burst before the whole world-wide stock market and economy bursts again from 2014 forward. HYG is an ETF index that tracks high-yield bonds and that does now look like it peaked in May 2013 at around 96 (see Figure 5-15). Corporate and Treasury bonds have seen rates rise into 2013, and ten-year Treasury bond rates look to be heading toward 3.5 to 3.8 percent, and possibly higher (see chapter 7).

The very last bubble to peak, global stocks, is *likely in very early 2014* between mid-January and late March. Figure 5-16 shows what is called a megaphone pattern for the U.S. stock market with each bubble seeing exaggerated highs and lows. I was predicting a peak over 16,000 on the Dow by late January 2014 after increasing volatility in late 2013. If we see the great crash

Figure 5-15: HYG, High Yield Bonds, 1998-2013

Data Source: Yahoo! Finance, 2013

Figure 5-16: Dow Megaphone Pattern, 1995-2015

Data Source: Yahoo! Finance, 2013

I expect into 2014 and 2015, then the Dow is likely to fall to 6,000 or a bit lower, the lower trend line of the megaphone pattern. If stocks take out the bubble that started in late 1994, then the Dow would ultimately have to fall to 3,800 or a bit lower. That is likely to occur into around late 2019 or early 2020 when our longer-term demographic and geopolitical cycles bottom.

If we don't see a major crash develop by mid-2014, then the greater crash and crisis is very likely to come by 2018 and develop out of an imploding European economy after it goes off the Demographic Cliff in full force after 2013 or 2014. Further demographic downturns from the more affluent sectors will lead to a tanking in the United States after 2014 or 2015 as well.

In chapter 6, I look at what could be the final trigger for the next global financial crisis: falling commodity prices. The emerging world is the future for demographic trends as developed countries will largely slow or move more sideways for decades to come. But these faster-growing economies depend strongly on exports to developed countries and on commodity prices—and both are falling. If the emerging world continues to slow as I see it, especially China, what is going to hold up the world economy? The answer is: *nothing!*

CHAPTER 6

COMMODITY PRICES: THE ACHILLES' HEEL OF EMERGING COUNTRIES

Commodity prices affect the fastest-growing sectors of the global economy—emerging countries—but they can't be considered in isolation. So let's begin with a little context, focusing on urbanization in particular.

Developed countries are already typically 80 percent or more urbanized, but it's a different story in emerging countries. Going back to the beginning of industrialization—that takes us to Great Britain in the late 1700s and early 1800s—we see the beginnings of large-scale urbanization. Britain led the industrial trend, as factories required larger numbers of workers in larger cities near ports, both to receive raw materials, produce the goods, and then ship the products efficiently.

Over the last two centuries, urbanization has spread to other countries in western Europe, the United States, and finally east to Asian nations, starting with Japan, then Taiwan, South Korea, and, more recently, China. Along with industrialization came profits, and Great Britain's early lead allowed it to create the greatest empire in modern times, despite working from a small island with limited natural resources (except coal, which was abundant and essential). The rest of western Europe quickly became more urban and more affluent, although early urban life was no bed of roses with sewage and air pollution rampant.

Only so many countries can dominate the highest value-added industrial products like automobiles, appliances, and computers or the new high-tech and information industries that are gaining dominance. Countries that come

Figure 6-1: S-Curve of Industrialization and Urbanization

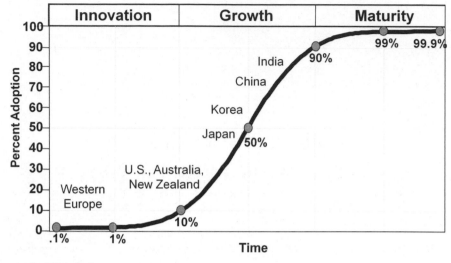

Source: Dent Research

later have to compete in what have become commodity markets at lower prices and margins; their means of doing so lower their labor costs (Figure 6-1). But that advantage starts to erode with higher urbanization and increased living costs, which leads to higher wages. This upward pressure on costs is the reason why industrial production has shifted more to East Asia. It also explains why Japan is a bit richer than South Korea, and China is not nearly as rich, even though it is the largest manufacturer in the world today. China produces lower-value goods like steel, clothes, shoes, and bicycles while Japan, Taiwan, and South Korea, as well as Germany and the United States, dominate higher value-added goods (like autos, higher-end appliances, and computers and components). Hence the lower standard of living in China and higher wages and comforts in Japan, Germany, and the United States. In the same way, India is not as rich as China as it is only emerging as a substantial producer of manufactured goods.

But back to urbanization. When people migrate from rural areas to urban areas, their incomes tend to nearly triple, as statistics from China, India, and Brazil demonstrate. Hence, GDP growth is most affected by rising

Figure 6-2: Brazil, GDP per Capita vs. Urbanization

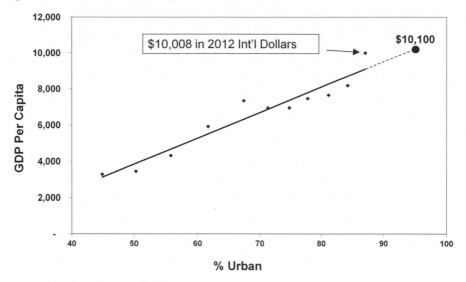

Source: Angus Maddison and World Bank

urbanization. The rates of such growth have an impact even greater than from demographic trends and, in most cases, GDP per capita rises in direct and linear relationship with urbanization.

I experienced an aha! moment a few years ago when I did some research for an interview with a Brazilian magazine. I was shocked to find that Brazil was already over 80 percent urban (see Figure 6-2), but still had a GDP per capita of only about $8,000 (now closer to $10,000). They were fully urban, yet had just 20 percent of the standard of living of the United States. That's when the lightbulb lit: Brazil and most emerging countries simply won't be as rich as the Western world unless they can upgrade to higher value-added industries. And I don't see Brazil competing with South Korea in high-end industrial products because, again, there is only so much room for countries to compete in that arena.

Only a handful of East Asian countries such as Japan, Singapore, Taiwan, and South Korea have been able to industrialize and transition from emerging countries to developed countries in the last century. Singapore did it in the information and financial sectors and, as a result, is even richer than the industrial countries (it is, after all, just one city with no rural sectors). I don't see how other candidates, such as China and India, can do the same; India is not that industrialized and, though China is, its strengths tend to be in the lower value-added sectors, which are not as profitable.

Malaysia is not quite fully urban yet is richer than Brazil and most emerging countries that don't compete in higher value-added industries. Malaysia is 73 percent urban and its GDP per capita would project to about $14,000 when it hits 80 percent urban in the next decade or so. That's about as rich as an emerging country gets without becoming an industrial giant like Japan or South Korea.

China was the first emerging country to fully appreciate the power of three times income and GDP from moving people from rural to urban areas. It has done this faster than any major country in history, and is now 53 percent urban (see Figure 6-3). China saw the greatest acceleration in the last bubble decade as its government pushed infrastructures and industry faster than ever with its own investment and backing of credit. Note that China's projection for GDP per capita at 80 percent urbanization decades into the

Figure 6-3: China, GDP per Capita vs. Urbanization

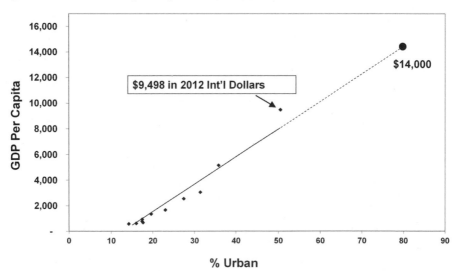

Source: Angus Maddison and World Bank

future from now will only be about $14,000, similar to Malaysia—and as good as it gets in the emerging world, falling far short of the United States and other Western countries.

China now has a new up-the-ante plan for accelerating urbanization even faster, aiming to go from 53 percent to 72 percent in just twelve years by 2025. That means 250 million more people will be uprooted from their farms and moved into high-rises. However, such overinvestment by governments can only result in a bubble and a burst, as in Southeast Asia from 1997 to 2002. China has already seen the largest shift of people from rural to urban areas since 2000 with massive overinvestments in infrastructures at all levels. In addition, China's timing is poor, as it is upping the ante just as global growth is slowing and its own demographics are slowing. If the world were going to continue to grow and China could continue to expand exports as fast as in the past, this plan might just work. But the plan calls for the rural migrants to build the very cities and infrastructures they move into. If they discover upon completing the construction that there are no jobs in the manufacturing sector, then the relocated workers will find themselves sitting idly in high-rises; they'll be unemployed and angry. Because I see the global economy slowing dramatically in the next six to ten years, this scenario may come true, the consequence of a disastrous policy.

China will not surpass the United States in GDP in the coming decades despite having a population four times our size. It will first very likely see the overbuilding bubble burst, and then grow more slowly as urbanization rates slow and demographic trends actually turn negative after 2025. However, China's economy will likely approach the size of the U.S. economy and will certainly be the second largest for decades to come, when it may be challenged by India many years hence, roughly by 2070.

Underlying all this is the fact that China will be the first emerging country to go off the Demographic Cliff, following a plateau in workforce growth between 2015 and 2025. China's population is aging faster than that of the United States and many northern European countries—few people fully realize this. All of this suggests that China will experience a hard landing economically in the years ahead, and it will likely grow much more slowly, say 3 percent to 4 percent in the next global boom. (Note that the China bubble is covered in detail in chapter 8 of my book *The Great Crash Ahead*.)

China has been the great hope for keeping up growth as the Western world and East Asia slow demographically. Many emerging countries export large amounts of commodities to feed China's manufacturing machine, making China the last support of the global bubble. When China's bubble bursts, the most overvalued real estate in the world will collapse, and the wealthiest 10 percent, who own most of the pricy properties and who drive 60 percent of China's consumer spending, will tumble with it. Everyday consumers will be hurt as well, as China's home ownership rate is very high at 89 percent, versus 64 percent (and falling) in the United States.

The Potential China Disaster: Government Planning Puts 220 Million in Hell

Mainstream economists are hailing China's model of growth as the new model of state-driven capitalism. That would imply that governments are better at driving the economy than the invisible hand of free-market capitalism. . . . NOT! And why not, as China's economy has urbanized faster than any emerging country in history and has grown faster than any major economy since the 1980s?

I'll give China one thing: it has realized how powerful it is to move people from rural to urban areas where their incomes and spending rise nearly three times. And China is the largest population and rising nation that has the national pride to want to be number one in the world, unlike many *mañana* developing countries.

But despite its meteoric growth since 1980, China has not proven to take over higher-end industrial and high-tech industries as have Japan, South Korea, Singapore, and Taiwan in East Asia—and many Western nations in Europe and North America before that. These "Tiger" countries have moved from emerging to developed country status in three or four decades on an S-curve acceleration of urbanization versus GDP per capita.

China has moved in a linear fashion instead, like almost all other emerging nations. But it has done so at light speed through the most aggressive government-driven expansion of infrastructure and export-driven industries in history. The Southeast Asian countries did the same thing in the 1980s and 1990s until they overexpanded and had a financial and currency crisis between late 1997 and late 2002. Their government-driven policies overshot what the free markets would have done.

Now China has expanded twice as fast and twice as long in the global bubble from 2002 to 2013. How could it not see a bigger crisis ahead, especially given that it is the one emerging country that now has demographic trends that are plateauing and will decline faster from 2025 forward, unlike other emerging countries that peak between 2040 and 2070?

The summary of China's unprecedented shift of rural workers to urban areas is that it has seen urbanization go from 28 percent in 1990 to 53 percent in 2012—that's 350 million people in 22 years, 210 million in just the last 12 years with plans to reach 72 percent (another 250 million) by 2025. That is an economy on steroids!

How can you shift that many people, uproot traditional cultures overnight, and create a massive urban underclass that fast without having something go wrong? How are these rural migrants going to compete? How are they going to afford an apartment there with the highest price-to-income levels in the world—higher than London or Tokyo?

The answer is they won't be able to compete when the government-driven gravy train of endless export and construction jobs slows down as the global economy continues to contract ahead. China's strategy is to have these rural migrants build their own new high-rise apartments at first and then hope that manufacturing jobs expand later, and consumer demand from these new struggling migrants also follows.

Hope is not a strategy!

This is the Achilles' heel of the "China Miracle." There are 712 million people, or 53 percent of its population, living in cities as opposed to rural areas. Out of that urban population, only 61 percent are registered urban residents with rights to education, health care, and any other social benefits— or 491 million. The other 31 percent, or 220 million, are basically "illegal migrants" from the countryside! They are not citizens, but are tolerated when things are good just as the United States tolerated illegal immigrants from Mexico to fill our unwanted jobs in the boom.

What happens when the boom turns to bust? These people are shunned and have no benefits. Illegal immigrants in the United States are now migrating back to Mexico as fast as or faster than new immigrants are entering, and that will only get worse if our economy plunges again as I expect from 2014 to 2019 and perhaps beyond. I see this as inevitable in China as these rural migrants are forced to move back to survive.

Does this lead to massive civil unrest in China and an even greater real estate bubble burst? How could it not, with unemployed people with no skills living in high-rises with nothing to do!

So here's the disaster scenario for China:

It has already built new homes at twice the rate of new households from 2000 to 2008. Now it is building them at 3.3 times that rate with rising speculation with investors now as high as 53 percent of home purchases. China has the most overvalued real estate in the world by far compared with incomes, as high as 35 times in Shenzhen, 30 times in Beijing, 28 times in Shanghai, and an average of 15.7 times. That's way more than London or Tokyo!

When global growth slows, these urban migrant workers with the lowest skills lose their jobs first with little ownership and benefits, and they then retreat to rural areas where they have family, self-subsistence agriculture, and often basic homes they do own.

Vacancy rates in cities in China are already 24 percent from overbuilding and speculation. What happens if up to 220 million of the unregistered leave? Overbuilt cities become ghost cities (like Ordos and many unoccupied cities that already exist) and real estate prices collapse 60 to 80 percent or more!

Everyday Chinese save 50 percent and the top 5 percent save up to 70 percent of their incomes and put most of it into real estate and bank accounts, not stocks and bonds, with over 85 percent home ownership. The top 10 percent save the most and control real estate assets, as well as 60 percent of income and the majority of spending.

If the China real estate bubble bursts, wealth will evaporate far more than in the United States and spending by the most affluent will evaporate even faster. Then real estate falls even more, and the economy collapses.

Let me give an analogy from the past. The United States was the rising emerging country from the late 1800s into the early 1900s as it overtook Great Britain in innovation increasingly from autos to electricity to the assembly line in 1914. World War I suddenly catapulted the United States into even higher growth and capacity as Europe went to war and needed its growing industrial and agricultural capacity. But after World War I Europe's capacity in all sectors came back on line and commodity prices collapsed with excess capacity and that caused the great recession of 1920–21. The boom in the Roaring Twenties was more on falling interest rates and higher speculation as well as rising demographic trends. From 1930 forward there was a global glut of capacity and trade tariffs that made that worse and the world saw a collapse of global trade. That also coincided with the peak in the Henry Ford generation spending cycle, augmented by its new immigrants before World War I. China is that new emerging industrial power today. Its slowdown and bubble burst ahead is most likely to trigger a depression and global currency and trade war in the years to come like the 1930s, rather than just another deeper recession.

China may be the last bubble to burst, but it will be the most lethal first to its citizens, and then to the global economy, just as its unprecedented pollution has been and will be. Don't look to China as the model for capitalism for the future. It will instead prove why top-down government planning and endless stimulus kills the golden goose of free-market capitalism that functions best only when governments provide a stable base of rules and a neutral monetary policy, as our friend George Gilder would recommend. The difference between the United States from 1914 forward is that we had rising demographics for decades ahead to bolster our new leadership position even after the Great Depression, and that shock made us stronger. China's demographic trends are already slowing and they have overengineered its urbanization and infrastructures such that its future urbanization will be in question for a while.

China is likely to go down in history as the greatest government-driven bubble and burst in modern history. It could take a decade or more just to absorb the overinvestment. But by then, after 2025, China will fall off a deeper Demographic Cliff and likely never be the largest economy in the world.

The other emerging national giant, India, is urbanizing, but later than and not nearly as quickly as China. It is now about 32 percent urban as Figure 6-4 shows, but as I've said before, India underinvests in infrastructures and key industries, while China overinvests. It is a bit too early to project,

Figure 6-4: India, GDP per Capita vs. Urbanization

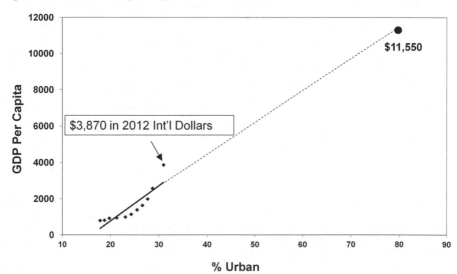

Source: Angus Maddison and World Bank

but if past trends continue, India will march up toward about $12,000 GDP per capita at 80 percent urbanization, which will take five or more decades to occur and, very likely, at a time when its demographic trends peak. India will look more attractive to foreign investors when China falls and slows down, and India's government is starting to invest more in infrastructures—but they need direct investment from foreign investors.

Kenya is an example of the low end of the emerging world (see Figure 6-5). It is only 24 percent urban and is advancing at a snail's pace. Its GDP per capita is only $1,448 as of 2011, even when adjusted for its lower costs of living and higher purchasing power. When you hear about large parts of the emerging world living on $2 a day, you may well be hearing about Kenya. In Kenya and other countries like it, corruption is a major theme: government leaders, tribal leaders, drug lords, and others all help themselves first. A few people have power and wealth, but almost everyone else is poor. High numbers of youth and strong demographics are more of a problem than a plus, with high levels of poverty and high unemployment.

Given present trends, Kenya can expect to reach only $3,100 per capita

Figure 6-5: Kenya, GDP per Capita vs. Urbanization

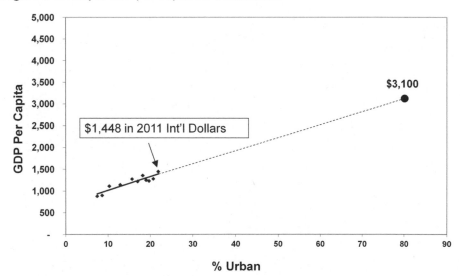

Source: Angus Maddison and World Bank

GDP at 80 percent urbanization eighty years from now. Until corruption can be curbed, Kenya is going nowhere. Most countries in sub-Saharan Africa, outside of South Africa and Botswana, fall into this camp. The Philippines, Afghanistan, and Bangladesh are other examples of low urbanization and very low GDP per capita. They have not joined the capitalist party yet. Until they do, they remain question marks despite very strong potential demographic trends.

Demographic Trends in the Emerging World

While urbanization is critical, demographic trends are also important drivers of growth in the emerging world. In fact, demographic growth will be dominated by emerging countries in the decades ahead, because almost all developed countries are trending flat or declining.

I have found in emerging countries that workforce growth is a better indicator of demographic trends than the Spending Wave on a forty-six-to-forty-seven-year lag. The explanations are several. For one, emerging nations do not have anywhere near the proportion of managerial, professional, and technical jobs that developed countries do and that dominate higher-value manufacturing and information businesses. They also don't have the steep income and spending curve we do. Hence, projecting workforce growth is a better means to reflect their demographic potential for growth.

Let's start by looking at Southeast Asia in Figure 6-6, which includes Indonesia, Thailand, Vietnam, Cambodia, Laos, the Philippines, and Myanmar. The data suggest that their workforce increases until around 2040, then slows modestly over time. These countries have a strong work ethic and robust tourism. They are not threatening East Asia in the higher-end manufacturing arena, but show strength in the light industries like clothing.

Dominated by India, South Asia in Figure 6-7 includes Bangladesh, Pakistan, Iran, and Afghanistan. South Asia's workforce grows into 2050 to 2060 and then tapers off only mildly. Given that India has the scale to become a beacon for foreign investment and the size to become the third-largest economy in the world, this region likely has the brightest future decades out as

Figure 6-6: Southeast Asia, Workforce Growth

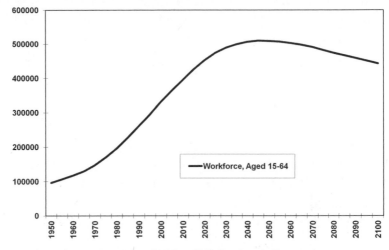

Data Source: United Nations Population Division, 2013; Numbers in Thousands

Figure 6-7: South Asia, Workforce Growth

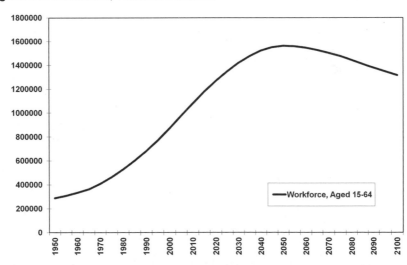

Data Source: United Nations Population Division, 2013; Numbers in Thousands

China's demographic trends continue to slow increasingly after 2025. India is also showing strength in movies and software, two key information/service industries now dominated by the United States. Tata, a very large company, is moving into automobiles with its acquisition of Jaguar and Land Rover.

Latin America grows until around 2040 (see Figure 6-8). Latin America has not made significant inroads into major manufacturing, with the exception of Mexico, which is becoming a major competitor to China in light industries and parts for heavier industries. Mexico has the advantage of being closer to the United States and Canada, as well as to South America, but the disadvantage of this region is that it is already 80 percent plus urban. The standard of living ranges from $5,000 GDP per capita to $15,000, with Puerto Rico, Chile, and Argentina at the high end and Brazil in the middle. Brazil peaks a little earlier than most Latin American countries, between 2030 and 2035. The easy gains from urbanization are over in Latin America, but the demographics are positive. A downward commodity cycle will work against most countries, especially Chile, Argentina, and Brazil, until around 2023 or so.

Figure 6-8: Latin America, Workforce Growth

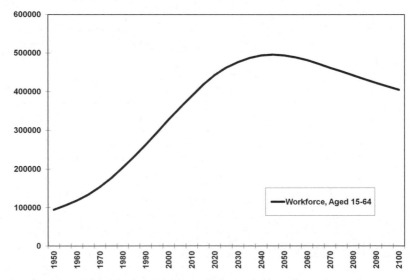

Data Source: United Nations Population Division, 2013; Numbers in Thousands

Figure 6-9: Middle East/North Africa, Workforce Growth

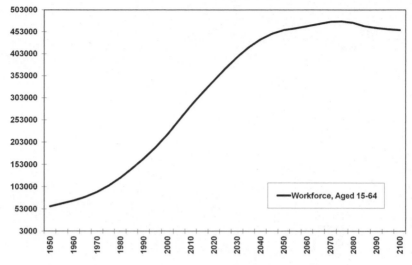

Data Source: United Nations Population Division, 2013; Numbers in Thousands

The region that includes the Middle East and North Africa in Figure 6-9 has even more bullish demographics than India and South Asia—workforce growth won't peak until around 2075. Dubai and the gulf countries are building leading-edge cities with their oil wealth and transforming themselves into major hubs for airlines and finance. Such major projects and investments are being made to counter long-term vulnerabilities due to the inevitable depletion of their oil reserves, and just as likely, the prospect that oil is replaced by alternative fuels from natural gas to carbon-free sources. The United States is already on the road to being a net exporter of oil, rather than an importer. I predict that oil prices could fall as low as $10 to $20, but average more like $40 to $60 over the next decade. This does not bode well for this region.

Thus, this region is a negative into around 2023 or so, but remains a question mark after that, depending upon how oil fares as a fuel and how successful their new industries are. The Arab Spring revolutions are likely to continue to create disruption and even chaos for years to come, but a difficult move toward greater democracy and capitalism would bode well for

Figure 6-10: Sub-Sahara Africa, Workforce Growth

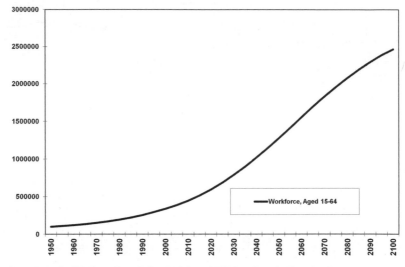

Data Source: United Nations Population Division, 2013; Numbers in Thousands

this region, especially in North Africa, Iraq, and Iran. On the other hand, a turn toward theocratic governments might ensure the opposite.

Sub-Saharan Africa in Figure 6-10 has the strongest and longest demographic trajectory of any region in the world, but most of its countries labor under two great disadvantages: not having joined the capitalist and democratic revolution, and being subject to out-of-control corruption, a drag on their economies that also limits opportunities for everyday people. These countries are among the most sensitive to falling commodity prices, and that bodes badly for the next decade. On the other hand, given political and economic reform, the upside is considerable, as workforce growth trends won't peak here until around 2100.

The Thirty-Year Commodity Cycle

To understand the twenty-nine-to-thirty-year Commodity Cycle, it is critical to realize that the present era (defined as 2008 to 2020–23 or so) is a unique period in history. There are three macro cycles that are pointing downward simultaneously, namely the Commodity Cycle, the thirty-nine-to-forty-year Generational Cycle (Spending Wave), and our eighteen-year alternating Geopolitical Cycle at Dent Research, which is explained in chapter 7.

The overlap of these cycles should create the perfect storm, economically speaking, with the Commodity Cycle peaking as it has peaked about every thirty years (in 1920, 1949–51, 1980, and recently between mid-2008 and early 2011). You can't get more clocklike than that in a long-term cycle, as I show in Figure 6-11.

What drives this cycle are the innovations in basic technologies that make things like commodities more affordable, which tend to happen after a time in which such goods are scarce and expensive. In other words, inflation drives innovation and, eventually, falling prices again. In other eras when the U.S. economy was more focused on food and basic materials, the four-season economic cycle covered in chapter 1 revolved around two twenty-nine-to-thirty-year booms in the Commodity Cycle. The mass production economy that

Figure 6-11: 29 – 30-year Commodity Cycle

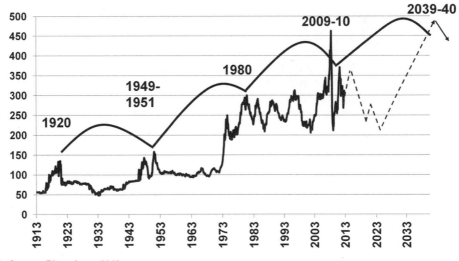

Data Source: Bloomberg, 2013

began with the assembly line in the early 1900s changed that longer-term economic cycle forever, shifting it to two forty-year Generational Cycles revolving more around growing productivity and the spending of new middle-class households. However, most emerging countries and a few developed countries that are major resource exporters, including Canada, Australia, and New Zealand, are still highly affected by this cycle.

Commodities prices are unlikely to turn upward again before the early 2020s, but then may undergo their greatest boom in history. Emerging countries around the world will drive the next economic boom, largely as a result of burgeoning demographic trends, as their citizens spend a higher percentage of their incomes on commodities than developed countries. Emerging countries will see the continued emergence of a growing middle class and the incorporation of larger numbers of female workers into the workforce, much as occurred in developed countries after World War II. But these workers will not have anywhere near the incomes of the middle class in the United States. Figure 6-12 shows the impact of female workers on both developed and emerging countries if they begin to equal the number of males in the workforce over the next decade. Countries such as Egypt and India

Figure 6-12: Impacts of Female Participation in Select Countries

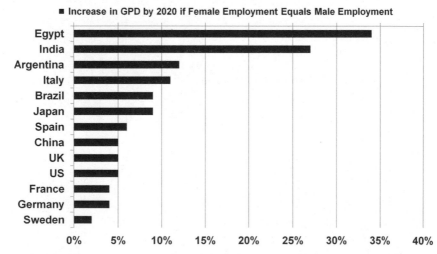

Source: Booz and Company, "Empowering the Third Billion, *Women and the World of Work 2012*"

will benefit the most, as they are young and behind on this trend. China and Brazil will not benefit nearly as much.

When I look at demographic trends and other factors like rising inflation and commodity prices, I see the next global boom from around 2024 to 2036 getting interrupted by rising inflation and commodity prices that are due to peak between 2038 and 2040. The United States will see a demographic downturn around 2037 to 2044, Southeast Asia and Latin America will start to slow, and China will be slowing more dramatically by then.

The years 2024 to 2038–40 should see the next commodity boom, which will strongly favor emerging countries that are major commodity exporters, and those same countries will have the strongest demographic trends. Then there should be a second surge from around 2046 into around 2055 with the second wave of Echo Boomers in the United States peaking in their spending and most emerging countries outside of Latin America and Southeast Asia still having demographic growth in workforce and spending. Global population and the broader emerging world boom will peak around 2065–70, and then we could see the next great depression globally after a fall bubble boom that peaks and surges into the 2060s led by countries such as India. The Demographic Cliff for emerging countries generally starts around 2040 with Latin America and Southeast Asia and ends around 2100 with sub-Saharan Africa, except for China's much earlier peak between 2015 and 2025.

The Commodity Index in Figure 6-13 (produced by the Commodity Research Bureau, or CRB) has fallen again ahead of most developed world global stock markets since late April 2011. The highest peak was back in mid-2008, around 465. A major A-wave crash to 210 occurred in late 2008, followed by a B-wave bounce to 370 in late April 2011; this was kind of a double peak as in 1949–51, but with a clear, overall fifth-wave peak in mid-2008. The first wave down in the C-wave saw a fall to 267 in June 2012 before bouncing a bit. The CRB Index has been up and down in a narrow range in 2013. A break below 265 should see commodities prices fall to at least 205 to 210 by early to mid-2015 and perhaps even lower. Ultimately, before this cycle turns upward again, as is likely in the next global boom from 2023 forward, prices could hit as low as 100 to 150 on this index.

China is the greatest current consumer of most industrial and energy-

Figure 6-13: CRB, 2000-2015

Data Source: Bloomberg, 2013

based commodities, purchasing between 37 percent and 51 percent as I show in Figure 6-14. Its biggest appetite is for iron ore, at a whopping 51 percent of global demand, followed by coal at 47.5 percent, lead at 44 percent, zinc at 42 percent, aluminum at 39.5 percent, copper at 38.5 percent, nickel at 37 percent, and oil at only 20 percent, which is still high. India and China together dominate gold demand in the world at 52 percent, with India at 32 percent (before its falling rupee caused a decline from 2012 forward), China at 20 percent, Europe and Russia at 13 percent, the Middle East and Turkey at 12 percent, and North America at 8 percent.

Economic growth for China has slowed, especially with regard to the massive level of exported goods manufactured in China from raw materials imported from emerging countries and from developed countries such as Australia and Canada. This slowing has caused commodities to peak ahead of major global stock markets this time around. Whereas the bubble for most stocks peaked in late 2007, commodities peaked later, around mid-2008, as growth was more buoyant for emerging countries than for developed countries during their banking crises. This time the rebound bubble in commodities also rose ahead of stocks, peaking for a second time back in late April

Figure 6-14: China Consumption of Industrial Metals

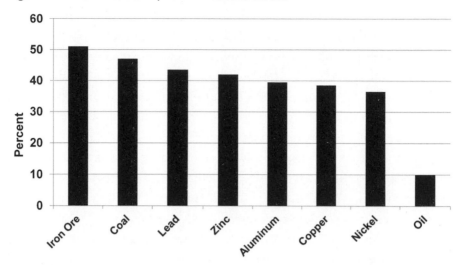

Source: The Economist; "A Game of Catch-up," 9/24/2011

2011, as did most emerging country stocks. But this suggests that developed country stocks will follow.

In looking at key commodities, the essential story is that industrial commodities are weakening the fastest due to the Chinese and global slowdowns; precious metals were trending upward as a "safe haven" in this evolving financial crisis, but now look to have peaked. Agricultural commodities are volatile and often countercyclical, given extreme climate variations. But continued high food demand in the emerging countries that have stronger demographics could cause agricultural commodities to buck weakening trends and head upward at times. Despite falling commodity prices in other markets, natural gas in the United States and agricultural commodities are likely to be the best performing and most countercyclical in the next decade.

A recent decline in iron ore prices has gone largely unnoticed. Needed for production of steel for many durable goods and construction, iron ore is the largest resource exported from Australia to China. Iron ore reached a very clear fifth-wave top in April 2011 followed by an A-wave crash to $85. Now iron ore is in a B-wave that looks likely to peak a bit higher, between

$120 and $130, and then crash to $50 or lower by early 2015 or so. Coal, a commodity in high demand in China, has been in a dramatic head-and-shoulders pattern that has included an extreme head top of $144 in April 2011, a dramatic crash to $40, and then a right-shoulder secondary peak at $84. A very dramatic crash is likely once the pattern breaks below the neck-line, at around $50. This market is likely to fall at least to $20 and possibly to $10 or lower by early 2015.

Copper is considered the classic industrial metal because of its wide use. Figure 6-15 shows a clear fifth-wave peak in copper around $460 in April 2011 followed by an A-wave crash to $300 in late 2011. The B-wave peaked near $400 and has fallen just below $300 in mid-2013. The C-wave crash will continue again if copper breaks below $295 and then will probably take copper to around $125 by early 2015, a 73 percent decline from the top.

The price of gold is highly dependent on demand in China and India, for jewelry and investment. Gold had a very strong surge into September 2011, then traded in a broad range between $1,525 and $1,800 until May 2013, when it broke down, ultimately landing at $1,179 before rallying into late 2013 as

Figure 6-15: Copper

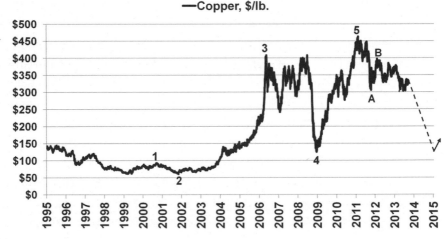

Data Source: Bloomberg, 2013

Figure 6-16: Gold

Data Source: Bloomberg, 2013

Figure 6-16 shows. Gold failed to break out after QE3 was first announced, and then again when QE3 was expanded, and again when Japan announced the most aggressive stimulus program in history. That suggests a shift, that the markets were viewing gold and other precious metals differently.

Two things changed for gold in particular. One was a drop in demand in emerging countries, especially India; the other was the failure of inflation to rise in 2013 after four years of escalating monetary stimulus. This discredited the hyperinflation camp that buys most gold outside of consumer needs. Ultimately we see gold breaking down to $700 to $740 in the next few years, and possibly to a low of about $250 before the commodity cycle likely bottoms in the early 2020s. Only if gold were to break above $1,525 and hold there would it have a shot at one more rally to new highs in the early stages of the next economic crisis. And that would occur only if there was an even bigger escalation in QE and stimulus programs than occurred in late 2012 and early 2013. Such a scenario is not likely at this point with the Federal Reserve's talking about tapering its QE for the first time.

Figure 6-17: Oil

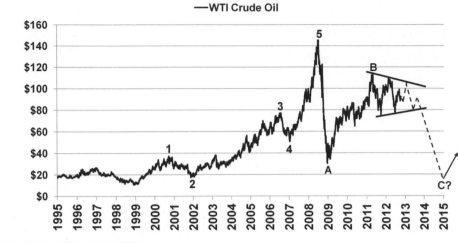

Data Source: Bloomberg, 2013

The bouncing ball among precious metals, silver, is at least twice as volatile as gold. We gave a first sell signal for silver and other precious metals when silver hit near $50 in late April 2011. Silver is likely to see $5 to $10 in the next few years and decade. Not a place for most investors.

Oil in Figure 6-17 had a very dramatic peak at $147 in June 2008 and then the most dramatic short-term drop I've seen, falling to $32 in October 2008. Hedge funds and speculators had been betting on the limited supply argument at high leverage but, when the United States and more economies started to slow in 2008, they dumped oil rapidly to meet margin calls, just as they did with gold in May 2013. Oil rallied back to $114 and has been in a sideways trading range since April 2011, as have many industrial commodities. It hit $109 at the top of the range in July 2013. If it breaks above there it should head higher, which looks less likely, in late 2013. A break below $80 for oil would mean oil is heading down again. Ultimately, I see oil heading back down to as low as $20 by early 2015 or so, and possibly as low as $10 by 2020–23. However, oil will likely trade more in the $40–$60 range for most of the next ten years. That does not bode well for alternative energies and even fracking for natural gas, which needs $48 a barrel in oil prices to be competitive.

As you can see from this quick survey of price swings, commodities have been leading the global downturn in this cycle rather than following as they did in 2008. If commodities continue to fall, then that affects emerging countries negatively despite their stronger demographic trends, and that affects growth around the globe, especially China's.

Emerging Country Exports Are Declining

In March 2013, I spoke at a Platinum Partnership conference hosted by Tony Robbins in Whistler, British Columbia, Canada. The attendees not only are highly successful, but also are creative, fun entrepreneurs, not boring business executives or economic analysts. Tony also has the ability to find the best experts in related fields, such as T. Boone Pickens, Ray Kurtzweil, and Marc Faber. Oprah Winfrey and Piers Morgan endorsed him in the past year. An S-curve in the making, Tony is moving mainstream and deservedly so after so many years of success in a niche market.

For the 2013 meeting, he invited Russell Napier, a consultant at CLSA Asia-Pacific Markets, to speak from England via Skype. Napier made the point that outside of Europe, it is emerging countries that are sucking wind, to the detriment of China, which now exports more to emerging countries than to developed nations.

My thinking had been that Europe was the area most likely to trigger the next financial crisis now that the U.S. economy is doing better (after triggering the last global crisis with its subprime crash). However, issues in emerging nations and falling commodities prices also could trigger a major crisis—before or after the next European crisis, which reared its ugly head in early 2013 again with the bank deposit confiscations in Cyprus.

Here are some thoughts to consider about the larger role of emerging nations, inspired by Russell Napier's talk and based on data from Dent Research:

1. One consequence of QE in developed countries is that it pushes up inflation in emerging-market countries (EMs), slowing such EM economies. EMs tend to be fighting inflation, whereas developing countries (DCs) are fighting deflation from slowing demographics and debt deleveraging.

2. QE tends to push EM currencies above where they would be otherwise, and that hurts their exports. And more recently the potential withdrawal of such QE is causing their currencies to fall against the U.S. dollar and hurt their imports and raise inflation—it's a revolving door!

3. Because of these impacts and falling commodities prices slowing world growth, exports and foreign exchange reserves are slowing and in some cases falling in many EMs.

4. Falling commodities prices are good for developed countries (DCs), because they lower inflation and imports, but bad for EMs, because most are major commodities exporters. Falling prices hurt their most profitable stocks, companies, and jobs.

5. Because China now exports more to EMs than to DCs, its exports are hurt by slowing in EMs more than by slowing in the United States or Europe, even though falling commodities prices reduce import and living costs.

6. China dominates many commodities, especially the industrial metals and minerals used to feed its high growth and its manufacturing export machine.

7. A vicious cycle is beginning wherein falling commodities prices hurt EM exports, which hurts China's exports, causing commodities prices to fall further, which hurts EM exports.

8. Declining growth in foreign exchange reserves means less demand from EMs for U.S. Treasury bonds, which could cause interest rates to rise despite QE, or could cause the Fed to have to buy more bonds to maintain low longer-term interest rates.

9. If long-term interest rates do go up, as our Treasury Bond Channel suggests, it would adversely affect the housing recovery, corporate borrowing costs, and stock valuations.

One disturbing trend is that the percentage of U.S. Treasury bonds held by foreign central banks peaked in 2011 at 38 percent and has since fallen to 33 percent, as I show in Figure 6-18. This trend is very likely to continue. The great majority of these foreign exchange reserves are held by EMs, mostly by China. Falling demand for Treasuries puts upward pressure on Treasury yields. If the Fed has to buy more bonds to keep yields down, the situation looks even more desperate.

Figure 6-18: Percent of Treasury Bonds Held by Foreign Central Banks

Data Source: Federal Reserve, 2013

Brazil has undergone the most extreme swings in foreign exchange reserves, with a peak growth rate of 136 percent in late 2007, followed by a fall to near zero in early 2009. As commodity prices rebounded in early 2011, growth rose back to 32 percent. More recently, growth fell to only 6 percent, which has a clear impact on Brazilian exports and foreign exchange reserves. Russia is another victim of these circumstances, with a peak of 75 percent growth in reserves that dropped to -29 percent in early 2009. Recently, growth slowed to near zero. India is another large EM for which growth swung between 57 percent in late 2007 and -20 percent in early 2009; growth recently fell to -8 percent. Growth in Indonesia swung from 36 percent to -13 percent recently.

As usual, China is the eight-hundred-pound gorilla in the room. China's reserve growth peaked at 51 percent in 2005 and fell to near zero in mid-2012, which is not good for global growth and certainly not good for U.S. Treasury bonds. Exports are slowing for many EMs as Figure 6-19 shows, as well as China in Figure 6-20, and are the reason for the fall in foreign exchange reserve growth. For a long time the deal has been that countries like the United States would run trade deficits with EMs like China, which then would buy U.S. Treasury bonds to balance that out. That trend is coming to an end.

China's exports to EMs have grown from 38 percent in 2001 to 51 percent in 2012, as Figure 6-21 shows. China now exports more to EMs than to DCs and thus is affected more by the slowing economic trends in those countries. Given how China dominates the global demand for commodities, especially industrial metals, a slowing in China's exports means lowered demand for

Figure 6-19: Exports for Select Emerging Countries

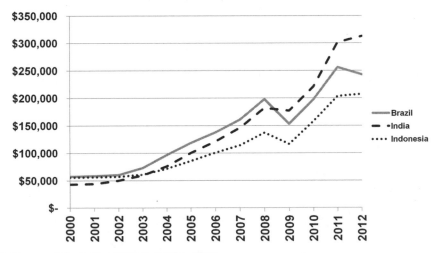

Data Source: International Trade Centre, 2013

Figure 6-20: Exports, China

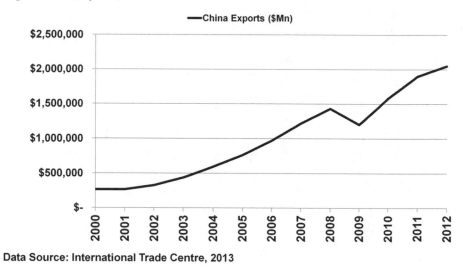

Data Source: International Trade Centre, 2013

Figure 6-21: Percent of Exports to EMs, China

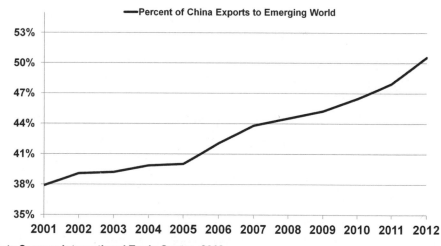

Data Source: International Trade Centre, 2013

Figure 6-22: Commodities as % of Exports for Key EEMs

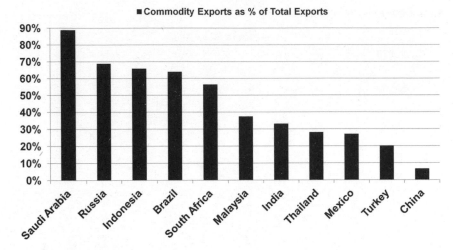

Data Source: World Bank, 2013

commodities imports. That slowdown will further reduce commodities prices, which will hurt the export industries of many EMs in a vicious cycle.

When looking at export commodity numbers for key EMs in Figure 6-22, note that China's are very low, at only 7 percent, to the benefit of Chinese consumers and export industry costs. Saudi Arabia has the highest level of commodities exports, at 89 percent, followed by Russia at 69 percent, Indonesia at 66 percent, and South Africa at 57 percent. China is affected indirectly (but probably to a greater extent) by falling commodities prices, which hurt the economies of its best customers.

We have not been recommending the stocks of countries in Latin America, the Middle East, Africa, and much of Asia because we think that the thirty-year Commodity Cycle has peaked and that prices will fall on and off for roughly another decade. Many emerging stock markets are dominated by commodities exporters as Figure 6-22 shows. After the next stock crash we will prefer countries that are less dependent on commodity exports, like India, Vietnam (and most of Southeast Asia), Mexico, and Turkey.

One final point is that QE in the United States has consequences for EMs. EMs are fighting inflation, whereas the United States is fighting deflation.

Printing money to fight deflation increases inflation in EMs. When inflation rises, EM governments have to restrain their economies with tighter monetary policies and rising interest rates. Because the United States is printing money and other countries (with the exception of China) are not, the currencies of these other countries tend to rise higher than they would otherwise, which hurts their export industries.

India has the biggest problem in this regard, as the inflation rate reached as high as 16 percent in mid-2010, though it fell to 5 percent in 2012 (see Figure 6-23). Now, however, inflation is 12 percent and rising, back into the danger zone. One reason is that India's currency has fallen, which raises the prices of commodities imports. India is the largest consumer of gold worldwide, a major reason that gold was flat after late 2011 and that total demand for gold actually fell substantially in 2012 and 2013. Russia's inflation reached near 10 percent in mid-2011, fell, and now is back to 7.3 percent and rising, again in the danger zone. China's inflation rate rose to 6.4 percent in mid-2011, fell to 2 percent, and is now back at 3.2 percent and rising. Inflation in Indonesia is at 5 percent and rising. Higher inflation rates are not good for emerging countries, especially when inflation occurs concurrent with falling commodities prices. So, yes, our QE has consequences for EMs!

Figure 6-23: Inflation Rates, Select EMs

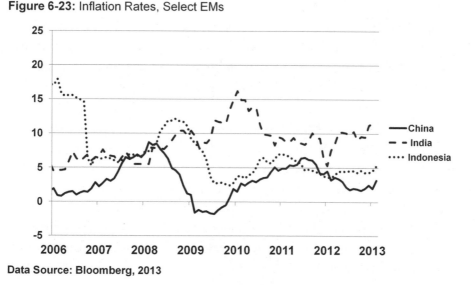

Data Source: Bloomberg, 2013

Figure 6-24: EEM vs. CRB Index

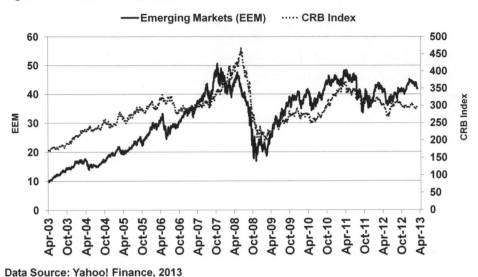

Data Source: Yahoo! Finance, 2013

To understand how important commodity prices are to emerging countries and their stock markets, look at Figure 6-24. EEM is a primary ETF (exchange-traded fund) for emerging market stocks, and the correlation with the CRB commodities index is very strong, stronger than the correlation with developed country stock markets like those of the United States or Europe. EEM peaked in April 2011 with the CRB, while U.S. stocks soared to new highs in 2013. The stocks of developed country resource exporters like Canada and Australia also correlate pretty closely with the CRB or commodity prices.

In addition to all of the trends covered here, George Soros is now warning that China's shadow bank lending is starting to look like the subprime crisis in the United States back in 2008. As Wall Street did in the last decade, China's private financial investment institutions are funneling loans and investments into real estate and corporate lending beyond the traditional banking system that China's government can more easily control. This sector's debt has grown to 60 percent of GDP since 2008 and is now most fueling China's escalating real estate bubble. Will the government lose control here? Will China's real estate bubble finally start to burst and help trigger the next crisis rather than be a victim of it?

While we have long assumed that Europe would blow up by early 2014, impacting the United States, the slowdown of DCs will also affect China's exports, which then would affect exports of commodities by EMs and create a further commodities crash. But it is increasingly likely that the combination of a global currency trade war and falling commodities prices will create a continued vicious cycle that will hurt EM exports, China's exports to EMs, and global exports altogether. It would be very interesting if the next global crisis emerges from China, EMs, and falling commodities prices rather than just from the blowup in southern Europe—or worse, if the coming crisis comes from both.

Now we see the possibility of either a blowup in Europe, especially in Greece, Portugal, and Spain, and/or a further deterioration in emerging markets and commodities prices triggering a crisis. There is also China, with the largest infrastructure and real estate bubble in all of history—she'll blow sooner or later, very possibly in response to a continued fall in commodity prices and slowing of emerging countries. Much of the Middle East is in a state of revolution and civil war that could escalate further any time, and U.S. stocks are bubbling up to the point that they look like they could start to crash. The U.S. stock markets look likely to peak by early 2014. With such strong and steady stimulus by the Fed and at most only a minor tapering ahead, it is likely that a global event will cause the next stock crash and recession.

As you can see, there are plenty of factors that could trigger the next global financial crisis, but next, having looked at the fragility of the global economy through the lenses of demographics, debt, and commodity cycles, let's consider investment strategies. I see what is to come as the most difficult period in U.S. history since 1930–33. The worst crash in financial assets is likely to hit in 2014 when I look at my best cycles, and the overall economic environment is likely to be at its worst between 2014 and 2019. So let's see what you can do to profit and prosper in the next half dozen years.

CHAPTER 7

INVESTMENT STRATEGIES FOR THE FINANCIAL CRISIS AHEAD

When stocks didn't bubble up as high as I expected between 2002 and 2007 from my study of the last technology bubble on the eighty-year, four-season economic cycle in chapter 1, I had to dig deeper to understand why. In the early 1900s there were two tech stock bubbles around automobiles, one from 1914 to 1919 and a bigger one from 1925 to 1929, as autos were progressing from 10 percent to 90 percent adoption in urban areas on an S-curve progression. What was different from the Roaring Twenties and Roaring 2000s bull markets on an eighty-year lag? Why was the second bubble not as strong in this cycle? The analysis produced two new powerful cycles. The first was the thirty-year Commodity Cycle as commodity prices were falling in the 1920s, but rising in the 2003–07 bubble (covered in chapter 6). But the global political environment was also very different. That insight brought the second phenomenon I now call the Geopolitical Cycle.

I can't explain why, but about every eighteen years stocks and the general economic environment wax and wane, bullish and bearish, shifting from favorable to unfavorable. I found that this goes back roughly two centuries, ever since the Industrial Revolution started. In the unfavorable cycles with high geopolitical risk, stock valuations (P/E ratios) tend to be significantly lower, about 50 percent. The last such cycle saw a favorable geopolitical environment with no major wars, or inflation shocks, from 1983 into 2000. Then, in 2001, the tech stock crash intensified and 9/11 happened. Since then

197

We've been in a negative cycle with one war after the next, one dictator after another causing problems, and the endless revolts that began with the Arab Spring. Plus we have banking crises all around the world and off-and-on deflation shocks.

Despite earnings rising as strongly as I expected in the 2003–07 rally, stocks barely made new highs as valuations came nowhere near those of the bubble from 1995 to 2000. When you look at long-term cycles in stocks, adjusted for inflation to get real trends (see Figure 7-1), you also see generational peaks that, over the last century, have come in every four decades (every thirty-nine years, to be more precise). Those major peaks are the result of predictable demographic cycles, with the peak of the Henry Ford generation in 1929 exceeded only in 1953, twenty-four years later. The peak of the Bob Hope generation in 1968 was not exceeded until 1993, or twenty-five years later. Buy-and-hold strategies do not work in these periods when the general trend is down and much more volatile. The past two such bear market periods were from late 1929 into early 1942 and from late 1968 to late 1982, spans of twelve to fourteen years.

Taking longer-term stock trends, not adjusted for inflation to capture the

Figure 7-1: 39 – 40-Year Generation Cycle in Stocks

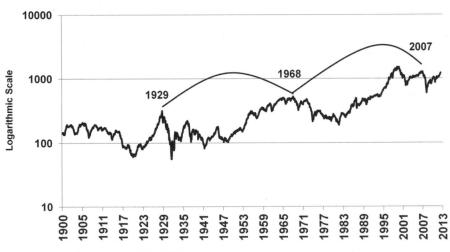

Data Source: Bloomberg; BLS, 2013

Figure 7-2: Long Term Stock Trends and the 18-Year Alternating Geopolitical Cycle

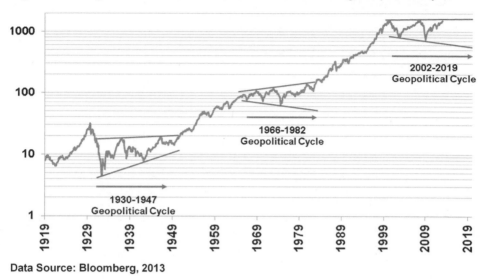

Data Source: Bloomberg, 2013

actual volatility of the markets, you can see when the adverse Geopolitical Cycles chime in, such as from late 1929 to late 1947, late 1965 to late 1982, and late 2001 into late 2019 (see Figure 7-2). Note that the first adverse cycle extended beyond the demographic bottom around 1942 through World War II (I think it is fair to say that World War II represented an adverse Geopolitical Cycle!). The second adverse cycle started a few years before the demographic cycle in late 1965, and then overlapped the downward Spending Wave cycle between late 1968 and late 1982. Stocks started to peak and slow down after 1965. The most recent Geopolitical Cycle hit well ahead of the demographic down cycle in late 2001. Stocks made little progress overall into late 2007 as the Geopolitical Cycle was adverse and pointed down.

That brings me to a critical point: the most dangerous periods for stocks and the economy come when the adverse Geopolitical and downward Spending Wave cycles overlap and point down together, as Figure 7-2 demonstrates. That happened in late 1929 to late 1942, late 1968 to late 1982, and again, currently, from late 2007, likely extending into late 2019.

Sunspot Activity?

I have been expecting a major top in stocks by early 2014 from patterns that suggested to me that stocks were getting bubbly in early August, but that they still likely had another rally or two before clearer signs of a top like 2000 and 2007 set in. Then, in early 2013, a sidebar in *Barron's* quoted fund manager Paul McCulley as saying that sunspot cycles could indicate a stock top between May and September 2013 or shortly thereafter. McCulley is not some wacky astrologer, but a past fund manager of $12 billion at PIMCO. McCulley said that he would have to see confirmation from divergences in stock indicators before he bets on the cycle, but he believes that sunspot cycles saved his fund the last time they peaked in early 2000. Oh, and by the way. That was the time when the tech bubble peaked and burst.

I wonder: Is there something real here? What could sunspot cycles have to do with stocks? All I know is that the solar radiation we receive from the sun is higher when there are more sunspots than when there are fewer, and that radiation is enough to interfere with satellite and communications in-frastructures. I also know that the magnetic pole of the sun totally reverses with this cycle. So, yes, certainly, high sunspot activity might affect human energy and emotions, just as anyone working in emergency rooms or police departments will tell you that full moons affect their activity.

I have heard of this cycle for years but didn't pay much attention as it was claimed to be an eleven-year cycle, which it is on average if you go back a few hundred years. I have never observed any correlations with stocks or the economy on such a cycle. But after reading this article I looked at the cycles for a hundred years back and found that the cycle actually averaged 10.2 years. Then I got very interested, because one of our most important intermediate cycles has been the Decennial Cycle from Ned Davis, a highly respected cycle analyst. Its pattern has played out pretty predictably every decade—until, that is, this one.

Look at how regular these cycles are (see Figure 7-3). They range from nine to twelve years, peak to peak or trough to trough. The upswing cycles are shorter and steeper, between three and five years; the downswings last more like six to eight years, more in a natural Fibonacci ratio. The first in-sight is that these cycles tended to peak right around the beginning of most

Figure 7-3: 10-Year Sunspot Cycle, 1900-2013

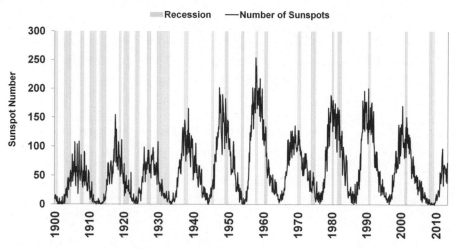

Data Source: NASA.gov, 2013

decades—until the most recent one. But look at some of the key periods when such cycles topped and declined in the past:

1. 1918 top and decline into 1924: There was a major stock and commodity crash and a deep recession between 1920 and 1922, and then a stock bubble after 1924 into the next up cycle.

2. 1929–34: A long-term stock and bubble peak happened in 1929; the Great Depression bottomed in stocks, housing, and unemployment by early 1933.

3. 1939–44: This was World War II.

4. 1958–64: Recessions and modest stock crashes occurred in 1958 and 1962. This was one of the milder down cycles during very positive Geopolitical and Spending Wave cycles.

5. 1968–77: A long-term stock peak occurred in 1968 adjusted for inflation, as did two major recessions and stock crashes in 1970 and 1973–75, an oil embargo, and skyrocketing inflation. This was more

severe as it hit at a time when both the Spending Wave and Geopolitical cycles were down.

6. 1980–87: Stocks crashed three times, with a major long-term bottom in late 1982, a major commodity crash from 1980 to 1986, and two recessions in 1980 and 1981–82. The 1987 crash was at the end of this down sunspot cycle.

7. 1989–96: The savings and loan crisis and recession occurred in the early 1990s; stocks had a mini-crash in late 1990.

8. Mid-2000–early 2009: The tech bubble started to burst in early 2000 right at the top, a recession set in from 2001 to 2002, stocks and commodities crashed between late 2007 and early 2009 right into the bottom of the cycle, and the largest real estate crash since the 1930s began in early 2006.

Note, too, that the two largest depressions of the 1800s fell within a downward sunspot cycle: the depression of 1873–77 in a downward cycle from 1871 to 1878 and the depression of 1835–43 in the down cycle from 1837 to 1843 (see Figure 7-4), which goes back to the mid-1700s.

This cycle simply is too good to ignore and now appears to be the reason for the Decennial Cycle from Ned Davis, which I have used for decades. He averaged stock cycles over the past one hundred years, finding that stocks tend to have their worst years in the first 2.5 years of each decade, for example at extremes between 1930 and 1932, 1980 and 1982, and 2000 and 2002; and that stocks tend to be weaker than average for the first half of each decade, as they were from 1990 into late 1994 before the tech bubble took off. The greatest stock advances and all bubbles have occurred or peaked in the second half of a decade: 1925–29, 1983–87, 1995 to early 2000, and 1983–89 in Japan. The 2007 peak occurred in the second half of the last decade. Consider that every sunspot cycle over the last century has pointed downward in the early part of each decade—except the present one!

Ned Davis long ago documented a widely recognized four-year presidential cycle wherein stock corrections tend to happen into midterm elections, as

Figure 7-4: Sunspot Cycle Back to the mid-1700's

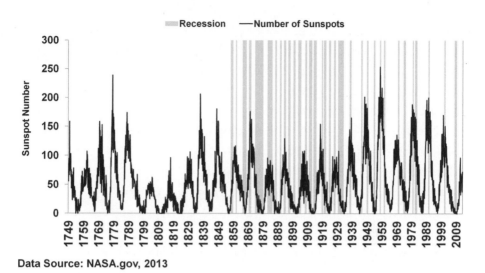

Data Source: NASA.gov, 2013

in late 1998, 2002, 2006, and 2010 (the next one would be in 2014). What I found was that major stock crashes and recessions tended to occur when both the Decennial and four-year cycles hit together, as in 1962, 1970, 1982, 1990, and 2002. The only major stock crashes that did not occur in these cycles were in 1973–74 (but the bottom in late 1974 was still in the weak in the first half of that decade) and in 1987 (which was at the bottom of the sunspot cycle).

These two cycles together seemed a good explanation for a lot of things—until 2010–12. After the demographic peak in 2007, we expected a second stock crash to follow the 2008 financial meltdown during that time frame, especially in late 2010 when the four-year cycle coincided. Stocks did start to correct and GDP fell back to slightly negative into the first quarter of 2011, but then the Fed stepped in with QE2. Stocks rallied with only a 10 percent correction in 2010. A 20 percent crash and a recession are the minimum I expect during a year in which both the Decennial and four-year cycles point downward. Note that the next four-year cycles are expected to hit into late 2014 and late 2018, two periods during which we see the markets as vulnerable to major crashes, and likely a bit beyond into late 2019 or early 2020, when most of our longer-term key cycles bottom together.

There is an obvious reason for the four-year cycle, as politicians will do what it takes to try to make the economy look its best before major elections (they're more likely to "take their medicine" in nonelection years). In the past, I knew of no fundamental cause for the very powerful ten-year pattern, but now I see a very high probability that the sunspot cycle is the reason. Because this cycle can vary from nine to twelve years, the current cycle in Figure 7-5 just happens to be much longer and even more irregular. The downswing from mid-2000 into early to mid-2009 was the longest in history, and that threw off the normal Decennial Cycle. In fact this cycle looks to be thirteen years from peak to peak if it comes in around late 2013 as predicted, which would be the longest up cycle over the past century.

NASA tracks and projects the cycle because sunspots create electromagnetic waves that can knock out satellites and other communications infrastructures. After the bottom or "solar minimum," sunspot activity rises for a few years, making it easier to project how the rest of the cycle plays. The NASA forecast is that the current cycle would peak around the summer of 2013. Experts who study the magnetic pole shifts that occur at the top of this cycle, like Todd Hoeksema of the Stanford University Solar Observatory,

Figure 7-5: Recent and Current Sunspot Cycles

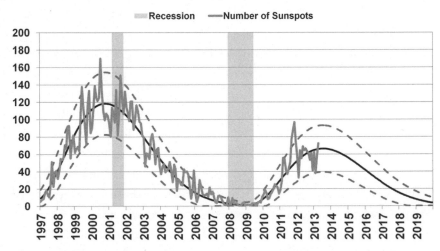

Data Source: NASA.gov, 2013

are forecasting a peak between November and December 2013, which looks more likely.

This cycle would explain why, for the first time in many decades, stocks did not correct in the early years of the decade; all other sunspot cycles pointed downward during such time frames over the last century. The forecast for late 2013 happens to be closely aligned with what I have been forecasting based on the patterns of the rally from early 2009 into 2013. As this book was nearing completion in September 2013, I saw a strong likelihood that stocks would peak between mid-January and late March 2014, more likely in late January. So, you should be looking to sell stocks soon after this book comes out in early January. If we don't see a substantial correction starting by April 2014 and intensifying by late summer, then a larger crash is more likely to come between 2018 and 2019. Like Paul McCulley, I will look for classic divergences to confirm such a top in my newsletters.

We expect a series of crashes, including at least one that is larger than the one in 2008, to occur between very late 2013 and very early 2020. The decline in the sunspot cycle projected from late 2013 into late 2019 increases the probability of our forecast for "The Great Crash Ahead" and that the Dow will fall to between 5,800 and 6,000 by sometime in 2015. We could see 3,300 to 3,800 by very early 2020. When we add in the four-year cycle, the times when stock crashes are more likely to hit are late 2013 to early 2015 and late 2017 into early 2020.

The deflationary scenario that we expect in the winter season will be critical to rebalancing our now perverted "bubble" markets and economy; there needs to be a major economic crisis and crash ahead. But, of course, governments and central banks are for the first time in history fully determined to prevent such a scenario. I just think the markets are bigger than they are. I think that the bigger crisis will come between 2014 and early 2015 as the markets are looking very bubbly in 2013, interest rates are rising despite massive QE to buy bonds and push down rates, there've been years of stagnation and recession in Europe, and China's bubble looks to be starting to get out of control.

Yet, if governments come in again and bring enough stimulus to minimize the next economic crisis, which is likely to occur later in 2014, then a larger crisis is very likely to start by late 2017 and to hit into 2018 and 2019 as demographic trends get much weaker for Europe and the United States in the second half of this decade. My view is the worst of the crisis is likely to hit in 2014 and 2015, and possibly last into 2016. All of that said, if we don't see a major crisis by late 2019, one is not likely to occur.

The QE Starts to Lose Its Punch

Take it as a truism: Ultimately, there will come a point when artificial stimulus just doesn't work. The drug-user metaphor is tried and true: if you keep taking more and more of the drug, you'll get less and less effect, until the side effects or the toxicity of the drug kills you.

The first sign I have been looking for of stimulus failure is the rise of longer-term interest rates despite escalating QE and near zero short-term rates. We started seeing that in early 2013 forward. I think this is the beginning of the end. If central banks can't keep pushing longer-term rates lower, then mortgages will become more expensive again, corporate buybacks of stocks will slow or stop, and stock valuations will be hurt by rising long-term rates.

The 10-Year Treasury Bond Channel (see Figure 7-6) is a tool I have used for many years now to gauge cycles in longer-term interest rates. Treasury yields have been falling with disinflation trends in a predictable downward channel since 1989. The last time we saw yields test the bottom of the channel and reverse back up was December 2008, when yields got close to 2 percent and we gave a major buy signal in bonds. Rates reversed back up to 4 percent in a matter of months. In late 2012 we got close to the bottom of the channel again, but did not quite hit it at 1.2 percent to 1.3 percent. The more such a pattern forms, the more traders are ahead of it. Ten-year Treasury yields bottomed at 1.38 percent in June 2012. In early 2013 yields started to head up again, despite an accelerated QE from mid-2012 forward by the Fed and then the most aggressive QE ever from Japan in early 2013 forward.

Figure 7-6: 10-Year Treasury Bond Channel

Data Source: Yahoo! Finance, 2013

I have been expecting ten-year Treasury yields to bounce up toward 3.5 percent to 3.8 percent into early to mid-2014, which will help trigger the next economic downturn and stock crash. That means investors should be out of longer-term bonds until we get near the top of this channel around 3.5 percent to 3.8 percent. Then we will look at buying bonds again, likely around early to mid-2014 or so, as yields will ultimately trend down again when the larger economic trends revert back toward recession or depression and deflation in prices instead of modest inflation. If Treasury bond yields break above this channel to 4 percent or higher, that will be an even greater sign of a financial crisis and a sign that central banks like the Fed have lost control of the economy.

In early May 2013 I gave a major sell signal in junk bonds, as a rising wedge pattern in junk bonds (ETF: HYG; see Figure 7-7) suggested a second major top was being put in with a crash in yields ahead, much as occurred into 2008. Thus far, that looks to be the top in the value of junk bonds, which could fall more than 50 percent in value as they did from late 2007 into early 2009. When higher-risk bonds see a recession coming, their yields rise due to default risks, not inflation risks.

Figure 7-7: Topping Pattern in Junk Bonds (HYG), 2007-2013

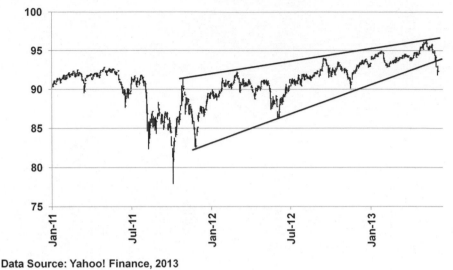

Data Source: Yahoo! Finance, 2013

A Dow Peak at 16,000 Plus?

The "megaphone pattern" is a simple topping pattern I've observed in U.S. stocks. Each bull market or bubble takes stocks to new highs, and then each ensuing crash takes them to new lows. Such a pattern occurred in the long topping process between 1965 and 1972. The classic example is seen again currently in the Dow Industrials (see Figure 7-8).

The first peak or A-wave was in early 2000 at 12,280, then stocks crashed in a B-wave into late 2002 to 7,200; then the higher C-wave peak in late 2007 reached 14,280, followed by a D-wave crash even lower to 6,442 in March 2009. The markets appeared to be closing in on a final E-wave peak around 16,000 or a bit higher into very late 2013 or very early 2014. There is a rising channel for the Dow in 2013 that would suggest a top as high as 16,700 by early 2014.

I believe the most likely scenario will be a top more like in late 2007 where economic growth and stock valuations were very similar to late 2013. Stocks first tested 15,650 in August, and we should see an extended sideways correction into October or early November around the debt ceiling debate

Figure 7-8: Dow Megaphone Pattern, 1995-2015

Data Source: Yahoo! Finance, 2013

and then stocks rally to a slight new high of 16,000-plus by early 2014, say around late January. Then the next great crash begins and it could bottom by early to mid-2015 (if it is like the 2008 crash), or it could last well into 2016 (if it is more like the 2000–2002 crash). In the latter case, the downside projection by early to mid-2015 is 5,800 to 6,000. That would be a 63–65 percent fall from a top between 16,000 and 16,700.

In Canada, the TSX stock index correlates more with commodities (CRB) than it does with the U.S. stock market, as many of Canada's largest commodity exporting companies impact the large-cap market (see Figure 7-9). The TSX clearly peaked back in late 2007 and has seen a secondary or B-wave peak back in early April 2011. I expect as large a correction, and perhaps larger in this market, as Canada now has a worse real estate bubble, not having seen the adjustment in prices in the last decade, and it will be more affected by falling commodity prices and more directly affected by China's ultimate bubble bursting in the next global crisis. The same goes for Australia's ASX market, which also clearly peaked in late 2007 and second-arily in April 2011 and will again sometime between late 2013 and early 2014. Australia also has a real estate bubble that is extreme and a higher exposure

Figure 7-9: TSX in Canada vs. CRB Index (Commodities)

Data Source: Yahoo! Finance, 2013

to commodity prices and China, despite having only a minor setback in demographic trends ahead.

What should be more obvious is the correlation of emerging country stocks with commodity prices (see Figure 7-10). These countries' stock markets are even more dominated by large commodity exporters and the financial institutions that finance them. Though emerging countries have the best demographic trends currently and for many decades to come, many will be adversely affected by adverse trends in the thirty-year Commodity Cycle (see chapter 6).

I recommend investing long-term in emerging countries starting around 2023, when we move into the next spring cycle with rising inflation and commodity prices again. In fact, we could see the greatest commodity bull market in history, as growth is dominated by emerging countries that consume a much higher percentage of basic commodities. But until then we recommend emerging countries, after each stock crash ahead, that are not as sensitive to the commodity cycle, in particular India, Mexico, Southeast Asia (including Vietnam, Cambodia, Thailand, Indonesia, and Myanmar), and Turkey.

Figure 7-10: EEM vs. CRB

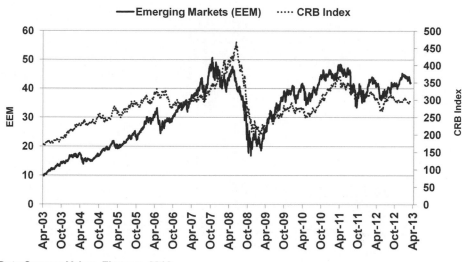

Data Source: Yahoo Finance, 2013

China's major stock market brings up an obvious contradiction: if China's growth is so strong at 8 percent to 10 percent, how come its stock market is doing so poorly? Its market not only crashed 70 percent, far more than in the United States, in late 2008 from a much larger bubble, but it only had a brief feeble rally into February 2010 and has generally been falling ever since back to near the 2008 lows in 2013. (See Figure 7-11.)

Why? China is overinvesting in everything with high debt, and that creates high fixed costs. That kills profits, as anyone in business knows. That's why governments don't tend to make the best investment allocations. I see China's markets falling to at least 1,000 again in the years ahead, and it will likely take the next decade for China to work off its massive excess capacity in housing, infrastructures, and industry.

Not only do I see a hard landing in China between 2014 and 2023, I also see high potential for civil unrest, with the government uprooting hundreds of millions of people from self-sufficient farmland and moving them into urban high-rises. A global downturn could create massive numbers of unemployed people with low skills and nowhere to go except back to the farms.

Figure 7-11: Shanghai Composite, China, 2002-2013

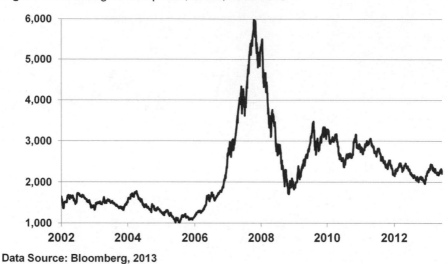

Data Source: Bloomberg, 2013

Let's take a look at the Euro Stoxx 50 in Figure 7-12, which is like a European Dow. This market clearly peaked back in late 2007 and has not seen new highs, although countries such as Germany and the United Kingdom have seen new highs in 2013—but those countries are about to fall off the Demographic Cliff after 2013. I expect this index to ultimately fall to somewhere between 1,000 and 1,400. Expect European markets to continue to underperform in the years ahead. This is not the place to reinvest when stocks crash, although they will bounce as every market will after a crash.

In general, the best investments in developed countries, especially the United States, after each successive stock crash are areas like health care and hospitals, medical devices, biotech, pharmaceuticals, vitamins and weight loss, recreational vehicles (RVs), cruise ships, life insurance and health insurance, and, last but not least, nursing homes, assisted living, and funeral home companies. These are the major sectors that will continue to boom with the aging of the Baby Boom generation, while broader sectors like housing, autos, furniture, food, and clothing will decline.

Figure 7-12: Euro Stoxx 50, 2007-2015

Data Source: Bloomberg, 2013

Starter and Vacation/Retirement Homes from 2015 Forward

The demand for housing is going to drop as dyers begin to exceed buyers in the demand/supply equation. As discussed in chapter 3, apartments and multifamily housing for rent have been the best part of the real estate market in the downturn since 2006. That will start to peak out for the first wave of Echo Boomers around 2017–18. In addition, major institutional investors from hedge funds and pension funds have been getting into the game, raising the costs of buying foreclosures and pushing down rents. It's probably too late in this game for most individual investors, and even the institutions started to slow their investments in the second half of 2013. But with rising foreclosures again in the years ahead, there will be opportunities for local investors who can find the best deals and manage the fix-up costs and rentals or flipping.

The next wave of housing demand will come from pent-up demand from Echo Boomers, who will want affordable starter homes in good neighborhoods. I recommend waiting until at least mid-2015, as I expect another wave of real estate and home declines ahead after the speculation-driven and low-interest-rate-fueled artificial boom from 2012 to 2013 as I show in Figure 7-13. It may take even longer than that for the next decline to play out. My golden rule is: *Buy in areas where home prices have gone back to where the bubble started in January 2000, or lower.* That's where you can feel like the bubble burst is getting close to over. Home prices need to fall by 55 percent from the top in early 2006, not the 34 percent we saw in the United States in 2010. Yes, home prices could fall 34 percent again from early 2014 into 2015 or later!

Since real estate is local and regional, use that golden rule. Ask yourself what your real estate was worth in January 2000 when the last bubble started. There or a bit lower is where you can at least feel like you can buy and not see prices continue to plummet. It's not a perfect mechanism, but it's the best I can offer in such a varied market that does not correlate as most stocks do. And recall from chapter 3: real estate may not grow faster than inflation for decades to come because of the shift from buyers to dyers in most developed country markets. That ratio gets worse in the United States after 2013.

Remember, too, the old logic of Monopoly: You buy real estate to live or

Figure 7-13: Case-Shiller, 10-City Index, 2000-2013

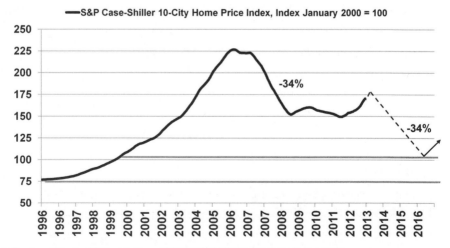

Data Source: Standard & Poor's Case-Shiller US 10-City Home Price Index, 2013

work in, or to rent out for positive cash flow—not for appreciation. If you get appreciation, that is a bonus.

The other sector of housing that should be attractive is vacation/retirement homes for Baby Boomers moving into a second wave of buying. They won't buy quite as broadly as in the last boom, but will tend to pay more and value higher-quality homes. Quality is the key, rather than size. Large vacation homes for show will likely be less in demand for older couples with fewer kids around, and, with the bubble having burst, people will be less conspicuous in their consumption. As I showed in chapter 3, that trend should peak around 2026. The trick is waiting for an even larger shakeout in prices in this sector, as it is more discretionary and a major downturn ahead will make people cautious for some time.

That means 2016 and after is likely a good time to look to buy your dream vacation or retirement home. Some of the best bargains are likely to come here, as this sector almost always falls the most when it finally does.

Large mansions were especially hot in the real estate recovery into 2013 as they were in short supply. However, I think that won't be so when the next wave of real estate finally sets in. It is that top 0.1 percent to 1 percent that will be hit the hardest when the financial bubbles finally collapse again and central banks won't be able to revive them.

Commercial real estate is the most sensitive to the economic cycle, and my demographic forecasts show slow workforce growth into around 2023 before it starts to turn up again. My general advice is to avoid commercial real estate, except to buy foreclosures priced low or below replacement costs, which can then be repositioned for positive cash flow rentals, starting in mid-2015 forward. Hotels will still be in a positive cycle into around 2021, but will also be sensitive to discretionary spending in a weaker economy off and on for the next decade.

Our Long-term Problem Is Not Inflation

One topic, perhaps more than any other, has misled investors. We've been told by the debt alarmists and goldbugs that hyperinflation is coming, that the dollar is going to go to zero and gold is going to go to $5,000-plus. Certainly, a crisis is building and it's futile to fight it by printing money for endless stimulus. With that I agree. But I'd suggest you park your ideology, hold your nose, and forget about gold and silver or any hard assets.

The lesson of the late 2008 meltdown was that the U.S. dollar is the safe haven.

All debt and financial asset bubbles are followed by deflation, not inflation or hyperinflation. The core theory behind the hyperinflation view is that governments, by endlessly inflating, create inflation. The argument is that this causes a debasing of currency, robbing you of your purchasing power and standard of living. This simply is not the case, and if you don't understand what actually creates inflation and why it is often not a bad thing, you will make bad investment decisions. Let's look at the why and the how.

Since its invention in 1971, the ever-multiplying microchip has created a revolution in human communications. The microchip's rapid evolution has also been both a clear sign of progress and a harbinger of a higher standard of living. So why would the multiplication of dollars not also be a sign of progress that similarly fosters a revolution in urbanization, a more complex and richer specialization of skills, and an improved standard of living? We're not talking about the recent QE here. We are talking about the story of economic history: more dollars per person and, more to the point, increasing urbanization that leads to rising affluence and the need for more dollars for transactions.

The one chart that every goldbug and fiscal hawk pulls out to prove that the government is destroying your life and our currency is the value of a dollar over time (see Figure 7-14). This may be the most misleading chart in economics history, as it actually means the opposite of what those who swear by it think it conveys. This chart is used to scare people into thinking that the U.S. dollar is going to hell in a handbasket and into thinking that their wealth is being taken away by governments and by never-ending inflationary policies. If we follow that logic, people should be much poorer now than they were in 1900 . . . *but they are not!* Let me tell you why this idea is borderline delusional and means worse than nothing—and why this is the last chart that you should worry about.

Figure 7-14: Value of a Dollar, 1900-2013

Data Source: Federal Reserve Bank of Minneapolis, Dent Research, 2013

Often a longer or broader view is required to see the obvious. I had one of my many great aha! moments back in the early 1980s, when I was studying three thousand years of Western history, from the rise of Greece and Rome through the recent era of western European and U.S. dominance. What I saw was that inflation over the long term correlates with a rising standard of living. In particular, I observed that inflation rises during times when population is growing, urbanization is rising, empires are being built, and the most powerful new technologies are advancing into the mainstream. Think of the Greek and Roman empires; the centuries following the invention of the printing press and gunpowder, and the discovery of America; the last century, during which electricity and automobiles became ubiquitous and mass production was perfected; and more recent times, with the information revolution and the Internet.

The major insight to be gained here is that about every five hundred years (one of our major long-term cycles), mega-innovations like the invention of the printing press, tall sailing ships, and gunpowder create huge expansions in technologies that lead to the spread of urbanization and greater specialization of labor.

Some examples: Two big surges occurred, the first from the late 900s into the mid-1100s, when Europe emerged from the Dark Ages and cities throughout Europe were repopulated. The second occurred from the late 1400s into the mid-1600s, with the discovery of the New World. Another, more recent big surge was the mass production revolution from the late 1800s forward, from which emerged the steam engine, electricity, automobiles, and phones—and more recently jet travel, computers, and the Internet.

How much have the later innovations changed our lives and standard of living in just one century? This revolution is likely to last into the mid-2100s as it expands throughout the emerging world, as further technological innovations are made in robotics, biotech, nanotech, and alternative energies, as our life expectancies expand dramatically again, leveraging demographics, and as a new network model is put in place for organizations.

When I first encountered the association between inflation and innovation, I was shocked. I always thought inflation was simply a bad thing. Period. And inflation has surely been bad during certain eras, as in the 1970s, when productivity was very low, or at the time of major wars, especially the years just after World War I for the Germans, when a costly, failed war led to bankruptcy, reparations payments, and, finally, hyperinflation.

Yet inflation has actually been a clear leading indicator of progress historically. So the question of the moment is: *how could inflation actually be good on a longer-term horizon?*

The answer is simple: through the specialization of labor, as I will explain. But first let's look at the simple evolution of the human family as one factor in why inflation tends to accompany progress, and why a successful and more urban economy creates the need for far more dollars so that each person can function at a higher rate of specialization and affluence.

Our economy actually needs and creates inflation for good reasons. Let's go back to circa 1900, when the dollar adjusted for inflation started falling (again see Figure 7-14). Back then our economy was still 60 percent rural, and it was 80 percent back in the late 1800s. Most people were still farmers, trappers, miners, and the like. It was a basic, commodities-based economy, not a complex industrial or service economy as is the case today in developed nations.

The typical turn-of-the-twentieth-century household wasn't so far from *Little House on the Prairie* circa 1870! Life was much simpler, but also much less affluent, much more difficult and risky. The bad-weather season could be life threatening, but a family in such a situation didn't need a lot of money; they were largely self-sufficient. They would build their own house; hunt, fish, and farm for most of their food; cook their own food and wash their own clothes; and raise and even educate their own kids. In such an economy and lifestyle, people didn't rely nearly as much on transactions with others, beyond the need for basic tools and farming supplies, pots, guns and ammunition, flour, and a plow, things a person mostly could buy at the general store. Many people would barter for needed goods. Towns had fewer government services to pay for and dirt roads didn't cost much to maintain. People did not need credit to buy things like homes or cars.

Fast forward to the highly urban, industrial, service economy of 2013. Compared with a family from roughly one hundred years ago, the typical household today has a much higher income and outsources a great number of tasks. Almost no one hunts, grows their own food, or educates their own kids. And who builds their own house? I don't even fix anything at my house, because I don't know how; instead, we hire plumbers, electricians, lawn managers, handymen, and so on. People have maids, nannies, and babysitters and use all types of local services, including dry cleaners, grocery stores, pharmacies, convenience stores, and gas stations. All types of utilities and services are delivered right to our house at a very low cost, including electricity, water, sewer, cable, Internet, and even pizzas!

We go to doctors, tax accountants, lawyers, dentists, financial advisers, mortgage brokers, real estate agents, and so on. What was health care spending in 1900? The answer is, almost nothing! Did people plan for retirement? No! We amass information from books or magazines or download it from the Internet. We borrow money to buy cars over the course of four or five years and houses over the course of thirty years so that we can afford what we need longer-term, especially while we are raising the kids and need these things more. Oh, I wish I had a time machine for all the people I hear say that they want to go back to the "good old days." I would send them there and they would beg to come back.

Technologies and greater urbanization allow us to create progress through a simple concept called specialization of labor. The more we focus on what we do best and develop specialized skills in that area, the more productive we become and the more we can afford to have others specialize as well, to do for us the things that we don't do best or are not interested in doing. That means exponentially more trade and dollars and credit to facilitate. We take this luxury for granted.

Specialization links back to the "invisible hand" written about by Adam Smith in the late 1700s (wherein markets are self-regulating); nations benefit from specializing and from trading with others. This concept increasingly is applied at the business and individual level as well.

If we are going to get paid more for our services and then delegate services to others, we need more money and credit. That's why monetary inflation is natural and inevitable. The costs of the goods you consume are going to be higher when you have to pay a lot of middlemen and specialists to produce and bring the goods to you. Over time, the higher wages from specialization more than offset the rising costs of living in a more urban, interactive, and specialized economy where we pay more and more people to do more and more for us.

Hand in hand comes a need for more government services and institutions to oversee and coordinate a complex, urban economy, much like how larger corporations have more levels of management and bureaucracy than smaller companies. Manhattan requires more government services than Mayberry. It's not that I don't think that government has gotten a bit too big, but I also don't think that we're ever going to be able to go back to the minimal levels of government and taxation of the 1800s and early 1900s.

While I agree wholeheartedly with the Republicans that our debt crisis is out of control, I don't agree that we can go back to their Camelot, the small-town and rural America of, say, *Tom Sawyer*. Urbanization, and the specialization of labor that comes with it, is the biggest single driver of rising affluence in history.

Let's look at a few of the myths about the past and present that should be dispelled right now:

Myth #1: Governments are purposely debasing our currencies and eroding our purchasing power so that they can spend recklessly and pay back their debts in lower dollars.

While most governments are recklessly spending and are promising entitlements that they will never, ever be able to pay for—that's true, no doubt—my research also shows clearly that urbanization, economic progress, and demographics (rather than intentional government policies) have both caused most of the inflation *and* delivered most of the progress throughout history.

Yes, governments let inflation get out of control at times, but no central banker or president would want to create inflation on purpose at the level of, say, the 1970s in the United States. That served no one's interest, in office or out. Creating inflation is excusable only when a nation is in a major war. And governments don't tend to pay back in cheaper dollars (unless they default), because the higher the inflation, the higher the interest that the government (and thus everyone) pays. Governments do have to pay back their debts with principal plus interest. (Did no one think of that?) The interest more than accounts for the inflation and the lower value of dollars paid back, thanks to our markets, which function well when governments don't interfere.

We use manufacturing wages to chart rising living standards, because we have data for these wages over a longer period than for any other measure of income. Average wages are even higher today, comparatively, because managerial, professional, and technical jobs have grown the most and pay the most. Increased earnings meant the standard of living went up, in this case by a factor of eight-plus since 1900, which is an increase likely greater than at any time in all of human history.

Myth #2: The falling dollar is eroding our store of value and capacity to save.

Even as the value of a dollar has fallen, your ability to preserve value has not, unless you are still living in the little house on the prairie and stuffing your

Figure 7-15: Real Manufacturing Wages, 1900-2011

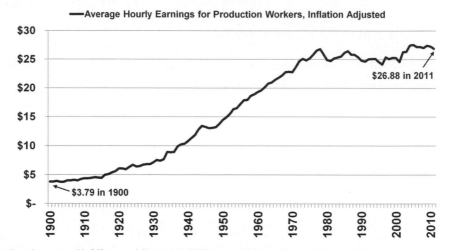

Citation: Lawrence H. Officer and Samuel H. Williamson, 'Annual Wages in the United States, 1774-Present,' MeasuringWorth, 2012, St. Louis Federal Reserve, 2013.

Are you better off than your great-granddaddy was? Indeed you are: after adjusting for inflation, wages are *7.1 times higher* than in 1900, the very period of rising inflation and the supposedly falling "value" of the dollar. Hence, it's not the "value" of a dollar but what your income in dollars will buy over time that counts.

money under your mattress. Now our money is held in financial institutions, and we get paid an interest rate on our savings largely on the basis of inflation rates plus a premium for risk. Since 1900, one-year government or risk-free interest rates adjusted for inflation have varied, though most have remained pretty steady and have averaged 1.31 percent over inflation, with long-term averages of 4.59 percent versus 3.28 percent inflation. Ten-year Treasury bonds are more volatile but have averaged 1.52 percent more than inflation (4.80 percent versus 3.28 percent inflation).

A person today can preserve the value of his or her savings plus a bit more with no risk and without being robbed of the savings value. However, in the last five years governments have pushed risk-free Treasury rates below inflation to save the banks and to stimulate the economy. In this case, the governments *are* robbing your savings capacity, now and likely for several years to come. So this is a temporary example where the government does make it impossible for you to preserve the value of your savings in the name of fighting a major financial crisis. They are in effect borrowing from you to fight a financial war that only stunts our economy's natural rebalancing mechanisms. Similar phenomena happened in the Great Depression and in World War II, times of severe crisis like this one. But that is not the norm over most of history.

Myth #3: The U.S. dollar and other currencies will decline to zero.

I just wish I had a dollar for every time I heard this statement about the dollar. The truth is that currencies trade relative to one another. Currencies don't have absolute values like stocks or bonds based on earnings capacity and projected inflation rates. Currencies are just a means of trading services and goods among people and countries. Since our economy is no longer commodities-based (as it was up until the last century), gold is no longer the best standard for money. And anyway, not enough gold exists in the world for it to be practical.

In addition, the value of gold is not growing as fast as that of the higher value-added goods and services that now drive our economy (health care, education, financial services, and even homes and autos). Gold was a good standard up until the late 1800s, when it was a commodity more in line with our commodity economy. If you print more currency for no good reason or just to stimulate your economy artificially as we do now in the United States, yes, you can devalue your currency. But what happens in a period (like now) when almost all major nations (thirty-eight at last count) are printing money and devaluing their currencies at the same time?

The Fed has printed nearly $3 trillion in QE out of thin air and has committed to print more until U.S. unemployment falls to 6.5 percent (in your dreams!). But the ECB for the euro zone, with a population roughly the size of ours, has printed more than $3 trillion, with more likely to come. That's why the dollar has gone up a bit in value against the euro since the crisis set in in early 2008, while the dollar is going down a bit against the euro currently as we have recently printed more than they have. Japan has done much the same, creating the equivalent of $4.5 trillion in QE over a longer period of time, adjusted for the smaller size of its economy.

Overall, when most nations are all printing money together, currencies do not just go down to zero; they appreciate or depreciate relative to each country's money printing, trade imbalances, debt, and economic progress. In fact, Figure 7-16 shows that, measured against the currencies of U.S. trading partners, the U.S. dollar actually has appreciated since the economic crisis began in early 2008, though only after depreciating 58 percent from its high in 1985 during the great boom.

Figure 7-16: U.S. Dollar Index, 1980-2015

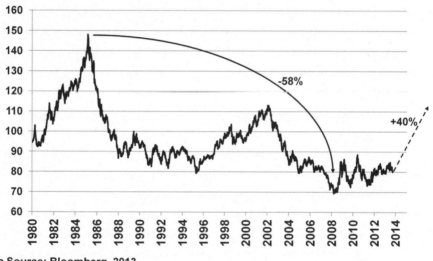

Data Source: Bloomberg, 2013

Which raises the question: *why has the U.S. dollar depreciated 58 percent against other currencies since the mid-1980s?* Because we created $42 trillion in private debt and $15 trillion in government debt (and foreign debt) at the peak of the debt bubble in 2008. The great secret is that the private banking system, not the Fed, creates most of the money and debt.

Although the Fed has printed substantial amounts of money in the recent financial crisis through QE, this is not usual. The point is that borrowing at the private or public level creates money out of thin air. That's what created the debt bubble that first peaked in 2008. QE has only been a desperate emergency response to that debt bubble bursting and deleveraging.

The United States led the debt bubble globally. The dollar devalued in the bubble boom largely because of private debt creation, which resulted from aggressive lending policies and government-led low interest rates and home-borrowing policies. The government did help initiate and accelerate the private debt bubble, but private banking and the shadow banking system took debt levels to unprecedented heights.

Deleveraging debt is the secret to restoring the value of the U.S. dollar and to rebalancing the economy. Lowering debt levels will take a huge burden off private sector households and businesses. In the natural, free-market systems of the 1930s, this happened violently; total debt levels fell from a high of 190 percent of GDP in 1929 to 50 percent! These days the Fed is actively preventing such a rebalancing by printing money. The government could more actively force banks to write down debts and free up cash flow for the private sector. Instead, the government is giving banks free handouts to keep them from restructuring and writing down debt that would greatly relieve the burdens of the private sector that can rekindle our economy again.

The truth is that we debased the U.S. dollar during the boom by creating debt at 2.5 times the rate of GDP growth for twenty-five years. Debt deleveraging in the downturn destroys such debt and thereby destroys dollars and makes them more valuable. We will restore the dollar only by allowing a massive restructuring of private debt—and the government is fighting that rather than facilitating it. In addition the United States has seen falling trade deficits since 2008 and that contributes to a rising dollar. In a deeper downturn ahead our imports are likely to fall more than our exports as we have consistently imported more since the 1970s.

Finally, we get to gold. I have been saying since 2008 that gold would be one of the last bubbles and that it would end up falling when deflation became more obviously the trend instead of inflation. Gold saw its final surge into September 2011 on ever-escalating QE and stimulus plans by one government after the next. Then Japan upped the ante even further in early 2013 with the most aggressive stimulus plan of all, and gold, escaping a two-year sideways channel, started falling.

There were a number of reasons for this. One was the declining demand in India when that country's currency weakened from 2012 forward (India had been the largest market for gold up until then). Second, inflation fell in the United States from 2 percent to 1 percent in the first half of 2013, allaying the hyperinflation fears once and for all. Third, hedge funds and leveraged traders were forced to start dumping gold ETFs to cover margin calls, much as they were forced to do with oil speculation in late 2008.

Gold in Figure 7-17 first broke very major support at $1,525 after trading sideways for almost two years. For a chart to surge as it did from late 2008 into late 2011 and trade sideways for so long is a slam dunk for breaking to a new high before peaking—but not in this case. Gold broke down to $1,179 in June 2013 before starting to bounce into the second half of 2013.

Gold is an inflation trade, not a deflation trade. Gold looks like it has made a major top in September 2011 and should be sold on any rallies back to as high as $1,420 to $1,520. The next support is around $700 to $740 and is likely to be hit by early to mid-2015. Ultimately I see gold going back to around $250 where the bubble started in 1998–2000 by 2020–23.

Figure 7-17: Gold, 2008-2015

Data Source: Bloomberg, 2013

Perhaps the most important insight for you to absorb is that we have not averted the next great depression. We will have to have a crisis in the years ahead to resolve our massive debt imbalances and to address the even larger demographic imbalances coming in the decades ahead. You have to have different strategies for the winter season and the summer crisis of the 1970s. Goldbugs and debt-crisis prophets are playing back the same old record from the inflationary crisis, but their core views on inflation are badly flawed.

I know that it is easier to respond to ideology than to face the hard facts and proven realities of the cycles we outline in this book (Walter Cronkite recognized such hidebound thinking, observing, "Facts change, but opinions don't!"). This is a dangerous time to operate on emotions and ideology. Too often we refight the last war, instead of confronting the next one. In this case, the next war is deflation, and the bursting of all financial asset bubbles, except for cash and the U.S. dollar.

Much as I respect their views on the debt crisis, the goldbugs were wrong in late 2008 when the last financial meltdown occurred, as all hard assets from commodities to gold to real estate fell along with stocks around the world. You can't afford to listen to them now.

I warn you that the two periods that are most likely to see another financial meltdown across the board are early 2014 to mid-2015 and late 2017 into very early 2020. Be safe, not sorry, in these time periods, especially the first half of 2014, and look to reinvest shorter-term if we see major targets like Dow 5,800 to 6,000 by early to mid-2015 and a Dow as low as 3,300 to 3,800 by early 2020—and only in the sectors that we recommend as most favorable in this chapter. If we don't see a major crash by August of 2014, then I may recommend getting back into stocks again earlier than expected.

(Please note that I have a free daily newsletter, *Survive & Prosper*, that allows you to keep up with my views on current events, changes in forecasts, and new research. Just go to www.harrydent.com to sign up.)

In chapter 8, we'll move to business strategies appropriate to the winter season that is upon us. The greatest payoffs will come to the companies that can simply survive the shakeouts in their industry. If you can grow in this period, then you will do even better.

BUSINESS STRATEGIES FOR
THE WINTER SEASON

Understanding the seasons of the economic cycle is critical for business: Companies and corporations require different strategies for different seasons, just as individuals (as discussed in the last chapter) require varied investment approaches to their personal finances. In this chapter I'll describe the four-season or four-stage cycle in individual product, technology, and industry life cycles, which more often than not operate on different time frames from the broader economic cycle. I will also provide a number of strategic tools for better anticipating changes and opportunities in this most challenging winter season and offer advice on how to reconceptualize and design your business for the ultimate competitive edge.

There are two drivers in the broad eighty-year economic cycle: first, technology innovations that occur over two generations; and second, a more specific generational productivity and innovation cycle (see Figure 8-1). The present cycle of technological innovation revolves most fundamentally around the computer, which was invented in the time span between late in the last winter season and in early spring. The ENIAC, assembled in 1946, was the first large computer.

In the spring season, the computer evolved into a mainframe for universities, research organizations, and larger corporations; then the minicomputer developed in the summer season into the 1970s. PCs and cell phones

Figure 8-1: 80-Year Four-Season Economic Cycle

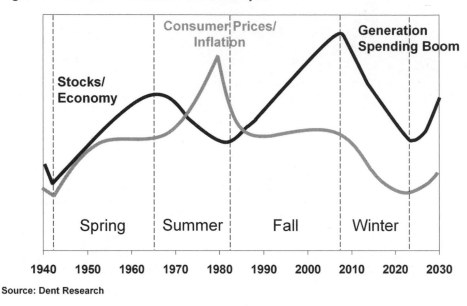

Source: Dent Research

were invented in the late summer season (1976 for the first Apple PC) and moved mainstream on an S-curve acceleration in the fall bubble boom season. The Internet and broadband were the accelerators, and more recently social media has been an important driver as I show in Figure 8-2. In the last fall boom, autos, electricity, phones, and radios moved mainstream on an S-curve. I show the auto S-curve in Figure 8-3. Cell phones and the Internet followed exactly eighty years later on this economic cycle in Figure 8-4.

Such new technologies elevate both productivity and our standard of living, especially in the fall boom when they rapidly move mainstream. They create whole new growth industries for decades to follow. The inflationary summer season is a sign that past technologies are waning in application and productivity, which creates the motivation for important new innovations, in this case PCs, cell phones, and operating software.

The second driver is the generation cycles of rising income, spending, and productivity I covered in chapter 1. The Bob Hope generation drove the boom from 1942 to 1968 on an exact forty-four-year lag on the birth index, as they got married a bit earlier than the Baby Boomers. Productivity rises as people

Figure 8-2: Evolution of Computers, 1946-2026

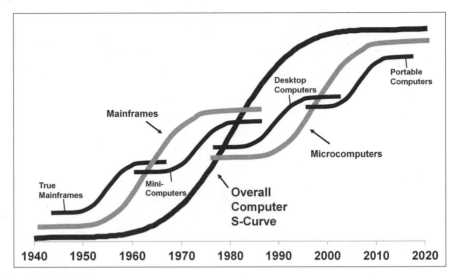

Source: Dent Research

age into their forties and then wanes after that. The recession came when the Bob Hope generation was slowing down, from 1969 to 1982. The massive Baby Boom brought the highest inflation rates in modern history, due to the costs of educating the Boomers and incorporating them into the workforce. But when they finally went to work, we had the greatest boom in history from 1983 to 2007, on an exact forty-six-year lag to the birth index (adjusted for immigration). Now the Fed is fighting the natural slowdown from 2008 to around 2023.

The great innovations occur in the downturns when the economy is challenged. The most radical new innovations, or what are called "basic innovations" by long-term economists (like the computer and jet engine), tend to occur in the winter season when the economy is at its worst. The most practical incremental innovations and applications, or killer apps like PCs and cell phones, usually occur into the summer season, motivated by rising inflation and costs. We will see basic innovations and breakthroughs in alternative energy, biotech, robotics, and nanotechnologies in the next decade, and those will create whole new industries and productivity trends for decades to come.

Figure 8-3: Cell Phone S-Curve, 1994-2008

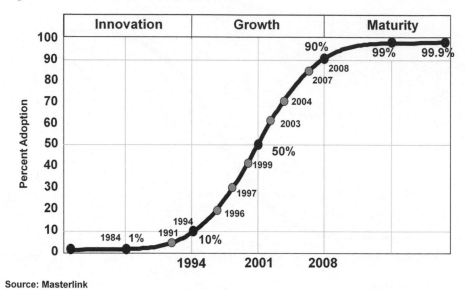

Source: Masterlink

The two booms in the four-season cycle are different, as are the two busts. The spring growth boom sees mildly growing inflation after the deflation bust in winter. This comes from a growing economy that raises inflation, but the rising productivity of the new generation tempers the inflation, which flattens out in the later stages of the boom. Then inflation surges into the summer season when expensive wars are common (like the Vietnam War and cold war in the 1970s and World War I and the Civil War in previous cycles), and the cost of the next young generation entering the workforce tends to be larger and exaggerated by rising immigration trends. Then inflation falls into the fall bubble boom as the productivity of the new generation combines with the highest productivity from new technologies as the killer apps move mainstream.

Inflation brings the seasonal flavor to the eighty-year economic cycle. Again, see inflation like temperatures: rising, but with mild inflation in spring; high and peaking in summer; and falling into fall; with deflation or actual falling prices into winter. From 2008 to 2023, we are in the deflation

Figure 8-4: Auto S-Curve, 1914-1928

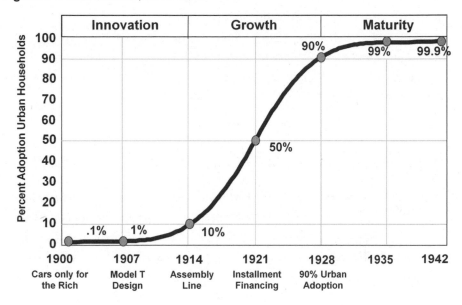

These two figures express in graphic terms the new revolution in productivity in the S-curve progression for cell phones (Figure 8-3), akin to that for autos from 1914 to 1928, eighty years earlier.

season, with debt deleveraging and falling financial assets, like those of the 1930s, eighty years ago.

Each season is necessary for growth and economic evolution. The seasons have different trends and economic/business impacts, thus the need for different business and investment strategies. The winter season deleverages debt and financial bubbles from the fall bubble boom season, and shifts market share to the strongest and most focused businesses, allowing them to increase their market share and scale and to further mainstream the new innovations of the fall into the spring season and beyond. Most important, it accelerates the adoption of the radical new business models that follow the architecture of the new technologies. It is the most advantageous season for the businesses that survive in older maturing industries and in new emerging ones.

The winter season proves most advantageous for the businesses that hunker down, focus, and make it through the survival-of-the-fittest challenge. This creates greater market share and advantages in scale and costs that pay off for decades in the spring, summer, and fall seasons to follow. The winter season is the most challenging and the most rewarding for the businesses that see it coming—and go on to survive and even prosper.

Strategies for Surviving and Prospering in the Winter Season

The current winter season will last until around 2023, with the greatest danger periods for stock crashes and recessions/depressions between late 2013 and mid-2015 and late 2017 and early 2020, and perhaps between 2021 and 2022. In between, the economy should be more favorable, with the next long-term boom starting by late 2023 or early 2024.

Given that the winter season is about shifting market share to the most focused, dominant, and efficient companies, your primary goal has to be gaining market share at the expense of your competitors. The winners will gain dominance for decades to come, not just years. In broader strokes, these are the nine most important principles for surviving and dominating in the years to come:

1. Cash and cash flow are critical to surviving the shakeout and having the resources to take advantage of unprecedented bargains in financial assets in the years ahead, especially around 2015 and 2020. The world will be on sale! "When times get tough, the tough go shopping."

2. Identify segments that you can clearly dominate, or where you need to focus more narrowly, and sell off or shut down others. If you don't, the economy will do it for you, more painfully and less profitably. Sell nondominant product lines or businesses now to generate a cash hoard to take advantage of the greatest sale in history on financial assets ahead. If you can't sell them, then cut them out to eliminate

fixed costs or cash flow drains now and in the future when things get tougher.

3. Develop a clear definition of your customers and their results to give your company direction, purpose, and focus. It's not what you think you do, but what your customers get from you that has meaning for them. It's not that you produce this product or service. It's about: do you save them time or costs; do you add quality to their brand; do you allow them to focus more by taking on nonstrategic functions for them; do you allow them to adapt to changing market conditions with your flexibility? Do everything possible to build customer loyalty in these times; it costs much more to acquire a new customer than to keep an existing one.

4. Be lean and mean, especially in danger periods like 2014-15 and 2018–19; cut fixed costs and overheads, and any variable costs, after allocating your fixed costs properly. To allocate fixed costs you first have to ask what causes them. For your accounting department, transactions would likely cause its costs, so allocate costs to different products by that measure, not the normal allocation by dollar sales of most accountants (more ahead). Then define your direct or variable costs of producing and delivering an extra sale and subtract that from your sales revenues. That gives you your contribution margin. Products with higher contribution margins are more profitable with growth and will increase your cash flow more in the downturn. After cutting your fixed costs to the bone and curbing your worst products, know your break-even level to cover your fixed costs. It's below that where your company will get into trouble and start to fail. You have to do everything to not get there.

5. Defer major capital expenditures—plant, warehouses, stores, major computer systems, real estate, or office purchases—until the next major crash and economic downturn, when you can acquire such assets at much lower costs when your competitors are in trouble. In the next financial crisis, banks will have more failing loans and will be looking

to offload those assets to companies like yours at twenty cents–plus on the dollar if you have cash and cash flow.

6. Focus on short-term investments that increase high contribution margin sales or cut short-term costs. This could mean investing in software applications that help you lower your marketing or production costs. It could mean direct marketing expenditures that allow you to get on Google's top listings in your keyword category and then only pay per click—and you know you can make cash flow gains on those clicks. Again, increasing cash and cash flow is critical to surviving and having the financial power to acquire assets at bargain prices ahead.

7. Sell nonstrategic real estate and lease instead, as there are likely to be losses in real estate and then little or no gains above inflation for years and even decades ahead; in other words, only own real estate if it is critical to your defined customer end results, your image, customer service, delivery, or other systems. Selling real estate at a profit while things are still good can add a lot to your treasure chest for buying more valuable and strategic assets in the worst years of the downturn ahead. Recall how hard it can be to sell such real estate or get out of the costs involved in a period like 2008–09. Leasing and renting is more flexible and allows you to focus on what is more strategic to your business and customers.

8. Identify in advance the competitors that you know are the weakest and the assets (customers, employees, business assets, real estate, product lines, and technological systems) that you want to acquire from them or out of bankruptcy if they fail or get in trouble. Estimate the cash you would need to do that. Be ready to move quickly and decisively when the crisis happens.

9. Look at your employees and identify who is weak and questionable. Fire them now, not only to cut costs, but to have the courtesy to give them a better chance of getting another job before the economy fails. Hire only employees who have a proven track record of creating results and are oriented toward a customer end-results focus. Reward

them if they create results in the downturn ahead, even if your company's overall profits go down.

The S-Curve and the Product Life Cycle: Microseasons and Strategies

The first dramatic S-curve I observed at Bain & Company in my early consulting years in 1979–80 was for radial tires, which went from 0 to 10 percent of tire unit sales in seven years and then from 10 percent to 90 percent in seven more years (see Figure 8-5). Firestone totally missed that opportunity, as did most major American tire companies.

The S-curve explains the 80/20 rule in business: namely, that 80 percent of the progress happens in 20 percent of the time. It unfolds in five stages: innovation, growth, shakeout, maturity, and decline. The innovation and decline stages overlap, between the old and the new, to create a four-stage or four-season cycle overall.

The economic cycle is a bit different: innovation (practical, not basic or invention) corresponds to summer; the growth boom with fall; the shakeout

Figure 8-5: Radial Tire S-Curve

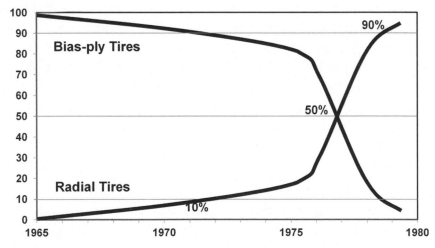

Source: Dent Research

Figure 8-6: S-Curve and 4 Stages

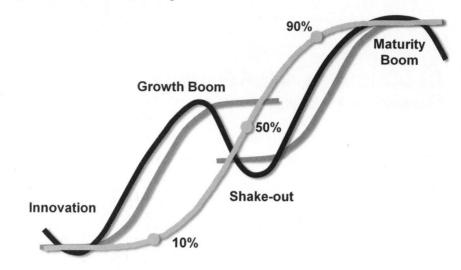

Source: Dent Research

with winter; and the maturity boom with spring, when the next new technologies emerge (see Figure 8-6).

The innovation stage occurs after invention from commercialization at 0.1 percent adoption on the S-curve toward 10 percent adoption. The products move into niche markets and first appeal to "opinion leaders," who first adopt products (the first 1 percent), and "influentials," who are higher-income or more sophisticated users who make up the next 9 percent. The product is shaped in this stage by what these discerning customers want and need; hence, product innovation is the most critical aspect of this stage. The growth boom comes as the product proves it can move mainstream and does so rapidly, growing from 10 percent to 90 percent adoption in the same time span it took to go from 0.1 percent to 10 percent, making, in short, nine times the progress in the same time period. You can see why it is so important not to miss this stage.

The growth boom is the big phase of that S-curve progression. It progresses first until competition gets so stiff from many entering competitors that overcapacity develops and the exponential growth rate starts to slow. Between 40 percent and 60 percent on the S-curve you get the shakeout stage. Companies have to cut prices, leading to a survival-of-the-fittest shakeout, during which many companies go under. The companies with the highest market share and lowest costs tend to be the winners. Then the few surviving companies duke it out in the maturity boom from 60 percent to 90 percent plus, after which growth slows and the product starts to mature. Cash flow becomes higher with larger market share, low costs, and lower investment for future growth required.

At Bain, they had a four-stage model for business strategy, which I will translate into the S-curve progression from my experience (see Figure 8-7). The first stage was called the Question Mark (innovation 1 percent to 10 percent) in the lower left quadrant. If such new innovations succeeded and moved mainstream on the S-curve from 10 percent to 40 percent, they became new Stars with high growth and leading market shares. Then the ones that survived the shakeout from 40 percent to 60 percent became Cash Cows from 60 percent to 90 percent. Then growth slows as the markets mature, creating Dogs (90 percent plus and decline). The strategy then is to maintain market share and cut costs by employing economies of scale and efficient management, but to stop investing in these maturing markets and to invest

Figure 8-7: Bain Strategy Matrix

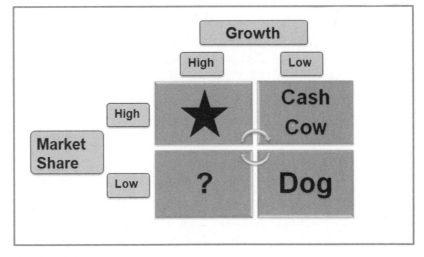

Source: Dent Research

in new stars to create growth again. There is a second shakeout in this stage that narrows the field to even fewer leaders in a declining industry. Those few leaders can still make money, while the others start to lose.

The greatest historical example of this was Ford versus GM in the car industry. The invention stage (before the S-curve starts) was 1886–1900. The innovation phase was 1900–1914 with the Model T and the assembly line innovations from Ford. The growth boom phase was 1914 into 1928 as the assembly line made cars broadly affordable in urban areas and saw the first acceleration on an S-curve into the mainstream. GM started gaining market share after Alfred Sloan's turnaround strategy and a superior marketing and business organization model from 1921 forward. By the top of the growth boom in 1928–29, GM had caught up with Ford. The shakeout phase was 1928–42, during which GM's superior marketing, financial controls, and organizational efficiency allowed it to pass Ford in market share. Then GM dominated and became the greatest company in history in the maturity boom from 1942 into the 1960s. GM's greatest competitive weapon ended up being the new, decentralized corporate model that Alfred Sloan innovated in the early 1920s. History proves that, in the end, superior organizational innovation (GM) trumps technological or product innovation (Ford).

The present shakeout or winter season will set the leaders in newer and older industries for decades to come. That means huge opportunities for those that survive and dominate. As GM proved in the Great Depression, superior organizational design, financial controls, and marketing are the key to surviving, dominating, and gaining market share in the treacherous shakeout stage. Such S-curves come at different times in different industries, but all businesses will feel the effects of this broader economic eighty-year cycle in key technology and generational cycles driving the economy. Here are the strategies for each stage:

1. In the innovation stage, invest in question marks or new products in niche markets and look for those that make it to 10 percent penetration and dominate, since most of the new question marks will fail by then or shortly thereafter; product quality and innovation are most

critical in this stage. The early-stage customers are more discriminating and demanding, and sudden product innovations can cause shifts in preferences. That's why this stage is so risky and a Question Mark. Your best assumption is: *I don't know which product or refinement is going to work here. I will just keep testing and innovating until I see what works best and makes it to the 10 percent level.* Then invest heavily in those products for the mainstream acceleration of the S-curve ahead.

2. In the growth boom, build systems for growth and expanded distribution for the Stars in the first 10 percent to 40 percent mainstream acceleration phase; the challenge is now rapid scale of growth and incremental innovation, no longer radical innovation, the most important features of the product having been established in the innovation stage. Now products just need constant incremental innovation and refinement and ever lower costs to penetrate markets further. Bain & Company used to advise companies to price below costs in this 10 percent to 40 percent stage to gain market share faster and lower costs in order to survive the shakeout stage when it comes. Entrepreneurs, who are by nature radical innovators, need to step back and bring in a CEO or CAO (chief administrative officer) who is an incremental innovator and systems person, but still stay involved to drive the vision or research and development. You also must have a superstar to drive marketing and distribution, as those functions become more important than product innovation.

3. In the shakeout stage, get mean and lean, and continue to gain market share at the expense of competitors who are failing as the product moves into the 40 percent to 60 percent stage and exponential growth slows after too many competitors enter and overinvest. Only a few are going to make it to the next phase, and your goal must be to be one of those—at all costs! As with GM, focus, financial efficiency and low costs, better marketing, customer loyalty, and—most important—organizational innovations that increase all of the above, are critical. This is the most important stage for long-term success

and market share dominance, and that is what, in the end, brings the lowest costs and highest cash flow.

4. In the maturity boom, start to harvest cash from dominant positions or "cash cows" in the 60 percent to 90 percent stage and beyond as investment for growth slows down and margins from higher market share dominance increase and lower costs. Look for the early stages of invention and innovation in new products, monitoring them for investment in new niche markets for the next innovation stage that will emerge. That often literally means splitting off a new entrepreneurial unit that can focus on more radical innovations and niche markets again, but one that can access the distribution and marketing systems of your more mature divisions.

5. In the decline stage when the next innovation period is emerging, aim to be the low-cost and volume leader and gain share at the expense of competitors as in the earlier shakeout stage. But don't overinvest, as eventual decline is inevitable. If you don't think you can survive this second shakeout to become one of the last survivors, sell out to someone who can and cash out. This is where investments in new question marks and innovative niche products and sectors will pay off. If you do sell out, as the entrepreneur you can look to create a new business in the next S-curve emerging in your industry or in related businesses.

In summary, you must have different strategies for each stage of your industry and individual product life cycles. When products shift to the next stage, many companies start failing precisely by continuing to do what they did so well in the last stage. For example, in the growth boom from 1914 to 1928, Ford kept cranking out Model T's at lower costs, while GM started to develop trade-up car lines (Chevrolet, Pontiac, Buick, and Cadillac) for aging, more affluent consumers in the fall boom of the broader economic cycle. You must also understand that aging and the arrival of a new generation of consumers will affect your product cycles. Even if you don't sell directly to consumers, your down-line customers do. If you can anticipate how consumers change in each cycle, you can prosper and survive rather than be blindsided by predictable changes.

Consumer Life Cycle and Microdemographic Opportunities

As generations age, successive product cycles grow and ebb in different waves from the overall economy, as the broader family cycle creates microdemographic cycles. But don't miss the greatest consumer information available in history, only available since 1980 in annual surveys.

Economists see the world as ever more complex and changing, hence less predictable. I see the economy as more predictable, thanks to better information in the great information revolution of the last forty years.

We have information on the consumer life cycle—from cradle to grave—via the annual Consumer Expenditure Survey (CE) from the Bureau of Labor Statistics, made available annually since 1980. These numbers matter more than in past centuries when there were no middle-class consumers like those who so dominate our economy. If you understand the consumer life cycle of spending from cradle to grave, your business can anticipate by decades changes in consumer spending that will drive trends in your industry or products for years, just as I can predict macroeconomic trends years and decades ahead.

Note that you need to adjust your forecasts for individual product trends for broader trends in the economy and for inflation/interest rates that will influence them to a smaller or larger degree, depending on your product's sensitivity to these economic trends.

To review: As I described in chapter 1, at the first stage of the consumer life cycle people are entering the workforce between ages eighteen (after high school) and twenty-two (after college)—on average around age twenty and rising toward twenty-one for the Echo Boom generation. Baby Boomers got married on average around age twenty-six, and the Echo Boom at more like twenty-seven currently. Then people have their kids on average around

Figure 8-8a: Early Consumer Spending Life Cycle

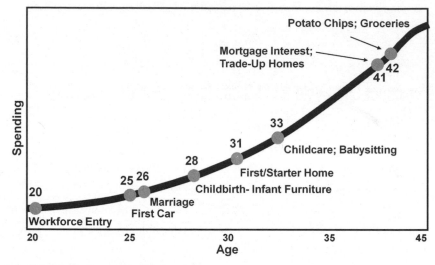

Source: U.S. Census Bureau, Dent Research

age twenty-eight for Boomers and twenty-nine for Echo Boomers. They buy their first home at around age thirty-one. Add about a year plus for every statistic we quote from here forward for the Echo Boom.

Babysitting peaks around age thirty-three when the kids go to elementary school. Trade-up homes peak between ages thirty-seven and forty-one; food and calorie intake for the kids peaks at parental age forty-two.

The midlife stage follows as we continue to furnish our homes, peaking around age forty-six, right at the overall peak in spending for the average household. Spending on motorcycles, sports cars, and boats peaks in the late forties or early fifties. The first wave of vacation home buying comes here, around age forty-eight, as does rising spending on vacations and overseas travel into ages fifty-four to sixty. Spending on hospitals and doctors also peaks around ages fifty-eight to sixty, along with life insurance and financial planning. People weigh the most and spend the most on weight-loss products in the age range of fifty-five to sixty.

The retirement stage follows, from age sixty-three forward. Savings and net worth peak around age sixty-four, health insurance around age

Figure 8-8b: Mid-Life Consumer Spending Cycle

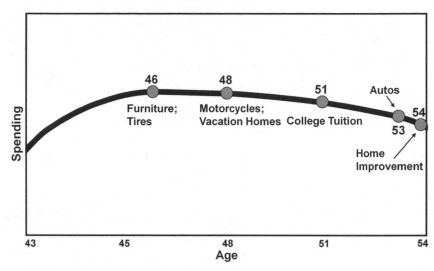

Source: U.S. Census Bureau, Dent Research

sixty-eight. After people tire of jet lag and international travel, they are more likely to vacation on cruise ships, between ages sixty and seventy. Medicare payments peak around age seventy-four, funerals at ages seventy-eight to seventy-nine (the average age of death), especially for males. Prescription drugs peak at ages seventy-seven to seventy-eight, and nursing homes (more for women) peak at age eighty-four.

There are always sectors booming, despite the overall economy, but the broader economic trends affect various sectors in differing degrees. The best way to do demographic research is to survey and collect data on your own customers, as different sectors by income and lifestyle may vary in their levels of spending and the ages at which they peak. In other words, your customers may be a bit different from the average statistics we document from the CE.

Real estate is the largest and most leveraged industry, but it will never be the same, as the product lasts more or less forever and a larger dying genera-tion will outpace a smaller buying generation in supply versus demand (see chapter 3). The major sectors of real estate are also age related, from

Figure 8-8c: Retirement Consumer Spending Cycle

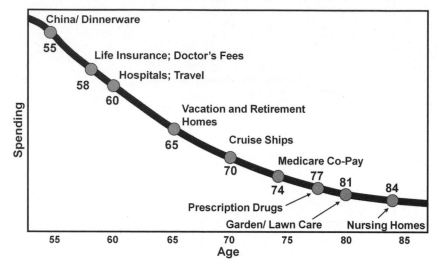

Source: U.S. Census Bureau, Dent Research

apartments/shopping centers (ages twenty-six to twenty-seven), to starter homes (ages thirty-one to thirty-two), trade-up homes (ages forty-one to forty-two), resorts (ages fifty-four to sixty), hospitals (age sixty), vacation and retirement homes (ages sixty-three to sixty-five), and nursing homes (age eighty-four). Apartment rentals and affordable starter homes will be the best sectors of real estate in the decade ahead, along with, selectively, vacation homes and retirement communities. In the years and decade ahead, the greatest opportunities will be first in hospitals and health care facilities. The best down the road will be nursing homes and assisted living facilities.

(Please note that I have a special research report, *Spending Waves*, that has taken ten years of data from the Consumer Expenditure Survey and that shows the cycles in more than a hundred key consumer categories of spending by age. You can find out more about this report at www.harrydent.com/spendingwaves).

The top consumer markets ahead for the larger, aging Baby Boom generation are:

1. Discretionary health care and wellness

2. Nursing home and assisted living facilities

3. Health and life insurance

4. Retirement and financial planning

5. Home maintenance services

6. Convenience stores and drugstores

7. Pharmaceuticals and vitamins

8. Downtown townhomes/condos

9. Active retirement communities

10. Recreational vehicles (RVs)

As the winter season shifts into the spring boom from around 2023 forward, look to bring upper-end products and services into mainstream affordability as inequality of income and wealth reverses. SaveDaily Inc. is a company that I invested in that is bringing self-directed financial planning and affordable investment options to small accounts through totally automated financial transactions, prospectuses, and reporting. They offer a flexible system at costs that financial firms can't even believe, so that everyday people with smaller 401(k)s or investment accounts can afford investment and financial planning at credit unions, community banks, and smaller business 401(k) plans. LearnVest is another company bringing affordable, personalized financial planning (with a real adviser and detailed financial plan) to the masses, backed by major venture capital investments.

The share of the top 1 percent and 10 percent (Figure 8-9) varies over the eighty-year economic cycle, with the highest proportion at the top of the fall bubble boom season and the lowest into the summer season, like the mid-1970s. The middle class should resurge in the coming decades and the top 1 percent to 10 percent to 20 percent will not grow as fast as they did in the 1990s and 2000s.

Figure 8-9: Income and Net Worth Share of Top 1% and 10%

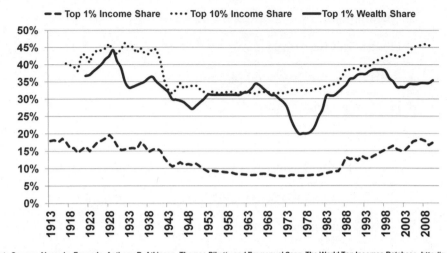

Data Source: Alvaredo, Facundo, Anthony B. Atkinson, Thomas Piketty and Emmanuel Saez, The World Top Incomes Database, http://ig-mond.parisschoolofeconomics.eu/topincomes, 2013, Edward Wolff, as printed in *Wealth and Democracy and New York University, 2010*

The greatest growth markets will come from businesses that make up-scale products and services more affordable to upper-middle-class and middle-class households. They will never be as rich, but their incomes and wealth will grow faster than the top 1 percent to 10 percent that so domi-nated the bubble boom of the 1990s and 2000s.

Immigration, Migration, and Local Demographics

The movers are younger families, ages twenty to thirty-four, and especially twenty-five to twenty-nine (see Figure 8-10). These are new families looking for career opportunities and the best places to raise families, and their mo-bility affects the growth of local and regional markets.

For decades younger families have been moving from the Northeast and Midwest into the Southeast and Texas. They have also been moving from California into the Southwest and into the Rocky Mountain states. The motivations are largely lower costs of living, better weather, better places to raise kids, and more job growth. These patterns will continue, but at slower

Figure 8-10: Out-of-State Movers by Age

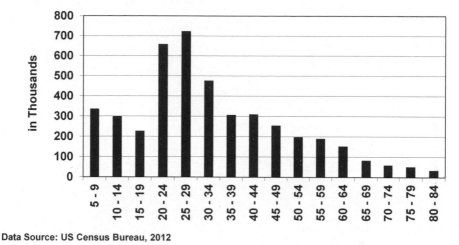

Data Source: US Census Bureau, 2012

rates as there are fewer young people in the Echo Boom generation. More people have also found it harder to sell their homes and move as many are underwater on their mortgages.

Of the top ten states for growth from 2000 to 2010 in Figure 8-11, Nevada tops the list at 35.1 percent. The strongest growth rates come in the Southwest with Arizona, Utah, and Texas. Idaho is the top state in the Rockies, followed by Colorado. Southeastern states come next with North Carolina, Georgia, Florida, and South Carolina. (The best source we have found at Dent Research by which to track movers out and in is United Van Lines.)

The biggest trend change in the top five inbound and outbound states in the last decade has been the shift away from Florida (see Figure 8-12). After Florida's real estate bubble, more people found it attractive to move to other southern states, and some Floridians started moving to Georgia, North Carolina, and South Carolina. These people, often called "half-backs," move from the north to Florida then move halfway back.

Immigrants have been a major factor in U.S. growth (as well as in Canada and Australia/New Zealand). They tend to concentrate between ages twenty and thirty, peaking around age twenty-three. Immigration peaked in 1991, and as we forecast decades ago, it's been dropping like a rock since the

Figure 8-11: Top 10 States for Growth, 2000-2010

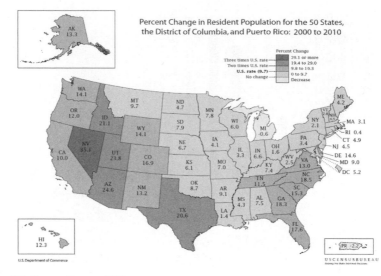

Source: U.S. Census Bureau, 2012

Figure 8-12: Top 5 Inbound and Outbound and Trends by Region

State	% Inbound (2008-2012 Average)	State	% Outbound (2008-2012 Average)
Washington, D.C.	64.1%	Michigan	62.6%
Oregon	59.2%	New Jersey	60.4%
Nevada	57.2%	Illinois	58.7%
North Carolina	56.8%	North Dakota	57.5%
South Carolina	55.4%	Pennsylvania	56.0%

Source: United Van Lines, via Unigroup, Inc., 2013

economy peaked in 2007. Net immigration from Mexico is recently near zero, as births peaked as well for the Echo Boom and have been falling since 2008.

Economists and international organizations such as the United Nations are forecasting growth in the United States to 420 million in 2060, from 311 million in 2013. That assumes much higher birth rates and immigration than we are likely to see during the winter season and beyond (birth and immigration rates plummeted in the 1930s during the last winter season). Thus, we would estimate more like 360 million and a growth rate of less than 0.27 percent per year. Immigrants tend to come into key states like Texas, Florida, Arizona, California, and New York, but immigration has already come to a halt from Mexico and will slow more from other areas, like Latin America and Asia, as the economy goes into a deeper slowdown and debt crisis over the coming decade.

The biggest impacts are from migration among key states (see Figure 8-13): out of the Northeast/Midwest into the Southeast and into Texas; and from California and the West Coast into the Southwest and Rocky Mountain states, especially Colorado and Idaho. Texas captures both sides. Canada is

Figure 8-13: Migration Map

Source: Dent Research, theodora.com/maps

seeing similar shifts from eastern Canada into Alberta and British Columbia, as well as immigration from Asia into British Columbia.

International Trends: Emerging Markets Will Dominate Growth

I repeat here a summary of the Demographic Cliff, over which one wealthy country after another tumbles (see chapter 1 for a more detailed discussion).

It started with Japan in 1989 and will end with Spain and China around 2025 in Figure 8-14. This is the first time in history that a smaller generation follows a larger one in most developed countries, as urbanization and wealth have caused birth rates to drop dramatically everywhere in the world, especially in the wealthiest nations.

Europe overall drops like a rock after 2013–14; it hasn't seen anywhere near the worst yet. Then Japan drops further after 2020 (after two lost decades and a brief rebound), along with Singapore after 2010 and South Korea after 2018.

At best, wealthy countries move sideways in the decades ahead, with a few minor exceptions like Australia, and it moves more sideways for a decade

Figure 8-14: The Demographic Cliff around the World

Country	Peak Spending
Japan	1989-1996
United States	2003-2007
Germany	2010-2013
United Kingdom	2010-2013
France	2010-2020
Italy	2013-2018
South Korea	2010-2018
Spain	2025
China	2015-2025

Source: U.S. Census Bureau, United Nations Population Division

before moving modestly higher along with most of the Scandinavian countries (but they, like Australia, are small potatoes in the larger picture). The developed countries that will fare the best, in rough order, during the next global boom from 2023 to 2036 are: Australia, Norway, Sweden, Finland, Denmark, the United States, Canada, New Zealand, the United Kingdom, and France. The laggards will be Japan (after 2020), South Korea (after 2018), Singapore, Greece, Italy, Portugal, Spain, Germany, Switzerland, Austria, Russia, and most of eastern Europe. China will still benefit from continuing urbanization after suffering a near decade-long hangover from the greatest bubble in history. But its demographics will plateau from now until 2025 and then start to work against its extreme growth since 1980.

The emerging world is driven most by urbanization, as that creates up to three-times the growth for urbanites versus rural workers in income and GDP per capita. Investors and businesses should be most focused in emerging markets after the series of global crises and crashes ahead in this arena. The best countries in rough order are India, Southeast Asia (including Vietnam, Cambodia, Thailand, Indonesia, and Myanmar), Mexico, Colombia, and Turkey.

Latin America is already 80 percent plus urbanized, so will see less leveraged growth ahead; Southeast Asia is 50 percent plus; China 53 percent; India 32 percent. The greatest potential in a large economy is India, as China's population is aging with slowing workforce growth and urban migration as a result. In the next global boom (spring season) and the next up cycles for commodities from around 2023 forward, emerging countries in South America, the Middle East, Asia, and Africa will be very compelling again.

If you are a smaller business and don't plan to market overseas, look at selling to companies that do the best in such areas and/or partner with companies in such countries; or focus on bringing higher value-added products and services.

The New Customized Economy

Customization and real-time, personalized service are the megatrends in business in the new economy for decades to come, carrying through the next

Figure 8-15: Standardized vs. Customized Economy Progression

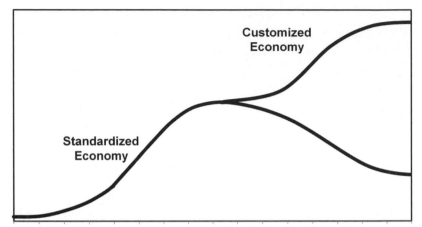

Source: Dent Research

I produced this chart in the late 1980s to show how new information technologies would allow the emergence of a new customized economy over the standardized ones of the past. This is what always happens throughout history, but it takes a long time and accelerates on the same S-curve principle I introduced earlier in this chapter—slowly at first and then rapidly—and then maturing as the next exponential growth technology or trend emerges.

long-term four-season cycle, which will next peak around 2065–70. This trend began more in the affluent, developed world and will spread to the emerging countries down the road, outside of their small, affluent sectors today (as I show in Figure 8-15).

In the early stages of this transformation to a new customized economy, discount models emerge using new technologies to make the maturing standardized sectors more efficient. Ultimately, however, the new higher-end, more customized models become more mainstream and eventually eclipse the older models. The greatest growth will increasingly come in the new premium sectors that move mainstream, just as the automobile did—it was a luxury in the early 1900s but became more widely available from the 1920s

Figure 8-16: Premium, Standardized and Discount Strategies

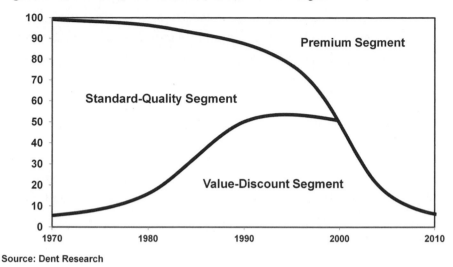

Source: Dent Research

forward. As customized products and services become more affordable in this new economy, who would want standardized versions?

Examples of discount models using such new technologies to make the older industries more efficient and lower costs are Walmart and other big-box stores, along with Charles Schwab in brokerage and financial planning (Figure 8-16). But many leaders in bringing the old standardized products into lower costs, particularly big-box stores (think Borders in books, Circuit City in appliances) are now failing in the face of Amazon, which can deliver such goods online at cheaper costs, often with better information. Is RadioShack next to fall? Amazon represents the new premium strategy rapidly moving mainstream at the expense of failing discount models. Barnes & Noble will likely survive, as will Best Buy in electronics and appliances—but that's likely to be about it.

This will continue. Amazon is experimenting with delivering produce and grocery items online with home delivery in Seattle and New York, potentially succeeding where Web Van failed in the late 1990s, and Fresh Direct is also currently succeeding. Higher-definition computer screens and the greater ability for returns and service are giving these new

Internet-based companies a growing advantage in more products and services. I know I order more and more products from Internet retailers—many I never thought I would—but when I can read online reviews and then send the products back at no cost if I'm not satisfied . . . what is there not to like?

Direct Response Marketing Is the Leading Edge

The first step in making older, more standardized products more affordable and toward customizing new or premium products has been to cut major layers of marketing and distribution costs and to deal more directly with customers. Fewer layers of distribution mean lower costs, as the distribution chain gets closer to the end customers with better knowledge about them and the ability to deliver better service.

Four direct marketing models have developed over the last several decades, as I show in Figure 8-17:

Figure 8-17: 4 Direct Strategies for the New Economy

Strategy	Example
Direct Producer to Consumer	Dell
Direct Warehouse to Consumer	Amazon
Peer-to-peer	eBay, Tupperware
Front-line Customization	Independent Financial Planners

Source: Dent Research

1. *Direct Producer to Consumer.* This works with higher-ticket items or services that are less complex and that can be easily shipped directly or delivered electronically, thereby cutting out the wholesale or warehouse and retail levels of distribution. By dealing directly you also know your customers and can track them better. Dell was the first to do this in the PC industry, but many mail-order and Internet

firms deal with customers directly and ship direct. At Dent Research, we market and deliver economic research and newsletters to our customers with no middlemen. This is the ultimate model that cuts the greatest amount of marketing and distribution costs and allows the most direct and intimate relationship.

2. *Direct Warehouse to Consumer.* This model works best with small-ticket items that can't carry the marketing costs of going direct or individual shipping costs. They need to have a warehouse level. But in this case you skip the retail level as Amazon does, with the Web site becoming the store. If local retail is required, the local store morphs into a larger warehouse, typically with much wider selection and fewer store design frills. Costco, Walmart, Best Buy, and Barnes & Noble are examples of this strategy.

3. *Peer to Peer.* This model works for low- to moderate-ticket items (and sometimes higher ticket) that require personalized sales and application. Network marketing organizations have been doing this for decades with a high concentration around health and wellness products and weight loss. People who have used the products and believe in them make great salespeople and can help customize to customers' needs. People can leverage the friends and business associates they know and skip a lot of marketing costs. Tupperware is the classic model where everyday people sell to people in their local area by throwing Tupperware parties or giving presentations locally to demonstrate the products. The obvious Internet model is eBay, which has created a Web site that facilitates online garage sales and allows people to sell products to others from their homes. Airbnb is my recent favorite, where people around the world rent rooms, apartments, or houses directly to one another with high trust based on the information sharing its Web site allows. It is the size of a major hotel chain and growing rapidly.

4. *Frontline Customization.* This model works best for higher-ticket, complex products or services, such as those offered by independent

financial planners and computer systems integrators. It is the other ultimate model for the new customized economy and premium segments moving mainstream, where customers get the most personalized applications, often where they need and value them the most. Doctors are already shifting in this direction, as they have to have very specialized facilities and staff to meet the critical health needs of very different patients.

Specializing (or "strategic focus") is the first way to bring better service and lower costs, since it avoids the complexity of dealing with very similar clients. Automating as much of your expertise into software is the second way to make these costly services more affordable. Again, medicine offers a paradigm: there is a new trend toward "concierge doctors," who take fewer clients, charge more, but spend more doctor-to-patient time. Business consulting firms like Bain & Company are another example of this. Small teams of highly educated consultants focus on a business and help them make very high-impact decisions in return for high fees. Computer systems integrators adapt a broad array of technology systems to meet the needs of their business or consumer clients. Architects and interior designers are examples at the consumer level.

Know and Measure Everything about Your Customers

Direct marketing strategies have been around for a long time now, but they will not be enough to ensure your competitive edge in the new economy and the winter season. In their place many companies have adopted the leading-edge model, what's called "direct response marketing." It is this model that, like the direct producer-to-consumer model above, allows you to save the most costs and have the most intimate relationship with your customers, delivering personalized real-time service at increasingly affordable costs.

Direct response marketing starts with a concept called "relationship marketing." The first rule is: *Never trick or confuse your customer.* That was clearly the inclination of most in the past, in order to drive sales or feed the assembly-line process. But how can you grow intimacy with your customers if they don't trust you? Let them get to know you, at first giving away free information and trials with no strings attached; that is the new function of marketing and PR: to build trust first, based on your strategic focus and superior customized products/personalized service or super-low-cost value. This concept was first broadly introduced by Seth Godin in his 1999 book *Permission Marketing*.

The more you deal with your customers directly, the better you can get to know them and personalize, customize, and build trust. Find ways to capture potential customers' interest and offer them something free for getting a taste of your products or service. Give them more and more, until they fall in love with you—or not. When they trust you, then the salesperson helps them select the best product, or in many cases, employs user-friendly software that allows customers to be better informed and choose what they want, driving their orders directly into your software and delivery systems. As they build greater trust and you continue to deliver, they become "raving fans" and lifetime customers. That's what every business ultimately wants.

I will draw on some experience from my own company and what I have learned from Sovereign, our marketing partner, which is a leader in this field (a publishing division of Agora, marketer of many authors and newsletter writers); and most of all from Aaron Halderman, a longtime business associate who has worked with Infusionsoft, a great source of software for direct response marketing for small businesses; and with one of the greats in this direct response marketing industry, Dan Kennedy.

To deal with customers directly, you must first get them to respond to you directly with no costs or risks. So "response" obviously is the key focus— you need to get potential customers or customers to take action. The key to that is good copywriting that has effective "calls to action"—*Call now . . . Send in this response form to get your free report . . . Enter your e-mail here for a free sample,* and so on. Since more companies are doing this now, you need to focus on developing very compelling free offers.

I was totally ignorant of this in my own marketing until 2008. My book *The Roaring 2000s,* published in 1998, sold more than 800,000 copies worldwide, and I could have easily built a list of 150,000 or more from those readers, but I didn't think of offering something free to readers in order to get their names and build such a list. A subscriber who was a direct-marketing professional enlightened me when we met in Florence, so I offered free periodic updates to readers in *The Great Depression Ahead* in 2008. I captured about 20 percent of the readers, just as he predicted. I can now have ongoing communication with those readers directly and educate them on new ideas and other services we offer.

There is obviously a broad array of media you can use to communicate with potential customers directly and elicit direct responses, among them TV, radio, magazines, newspapers, mail, e-mail lists, Internet ads and banners, search engines, social media, and even retail stores. And these are always changing and evolving. Smaller businesses have to be more creative and stay ahead of the trends as larger companies can outbid them, getting lower rates on the popular media of the past and simply outmarketing their smaller competitors.

The more innovative businesses moved early on into e-mail lists, but that has gotten more saturated and spam filters have gotten better and better. The strategy of getting higher on Google's lists has been another focus, by doing videos and putting information on the Internet and focusing on keywords (the latter is called SEO, or search engine optimization). This is free but you have to create content that will be picked up—and that is where the cost is. Google also has programs where you can be featured and then pay per click for the visitors you get. Amazon is doing that in their network, too. But that is getting harder as more companies do it. Social media, from LinkedIn to Twitter to Facebook, is the new frontier.

The most important step in any strategy is, once you get your customers' attention with a compelling free offer, to drive them to a landing page where they are greeted with effective headlines and copy that gets their attention and provokes an online response within fifteen seconds, or a call to a real person on a toll-free number if they will likely need a little more information or help to make a decision.

Test, develop, and use multiple media. You'll reach more customers and build scale to lower costs and prices, and also maintain flexibility; while any one medium can be effective today, things change, often overnight (like spam protection for e-mails), potentially leaving you with no way to market or grow. Start with the best potential media, but keep testing others to find ways to diversify your approach.

The great advantage of direct response is simply that you can test different ad copy in different market segments *before* you make large commitments of money. You can also measure every step of your customers' response: how many opened the e-mail on this offer versus that offer, how many responded and took the next step, and the next after that. How much did the customer buy in the first thirty days, sixty days, ninety days, or the first year? What percentage renewed the product if it is a subscription or traded up to a higher offering (that's called the conversion rate)? The most important measure over time is to determine the average lifetime value of a new customer—how long customers tend to stay with you and how much they buy over time after the direct costs of servicing them (your contribution margin)—then to measure that finding against your marketing costs. And of course, this should be broken down into relevant customer segments.

Don't measure the profitability of your marketing costs and efforts based on your first sale. When you calculate your profits over the average customer's lifetime, then you know your marketing budget—how high it can go while you make profits or a return on investment over time. Most companies don't spend enough or reach as many customers as they could. If you knew that the average customer stays with you for three years and spends $3,000 after your direct costs for servicing them, why would you say, "I don't want to have to pay more than $250 for a lead"? The cheaper the better, yes, but how much more could you do to create more and higher-quality customers if you spent more?

Most companies are too timid in their marketing. They think: *I don't want to mail them too often.* Aaron Halderman disagrees, saying, *Hammer them until they object or leave.* You want customers who love you and want to hear more from you and buy more from you (hence you also want quality, not just quantity). The direct marketing consultant who got me to start using this form of marketing in the first place told me the same thing: the typical customer wants to hear from you every three weeks if they like you. I would have thought three to six months.

Don't just build a larger list of customers, build a data-rich list, and build better, more loyal customers. Measure demographics, lifestyle or psychographics, personal preferences, buying behavior; know what products they favor, what price ranges, and how often they buy. That way you can keep segmenting your customers and deal with them more personally. Survey your customers in nonintrusive ways and get them to give you more information about them and what they really want and value.

Once you have names and e-mails or addresses, you can go to databases and service companies and augment your list, adding phone numbers and demographic and lifestyle data. A zip code will tell you their likely lifestyles and income if you don't know that already. Conversely, your customers' lifestyles and income will tell you which zip codes to focus on. There are companies that can take your list and tell you what other lists you can purchase that best match your customers.

Partner with other companies that have complementary, noncompeting products or services. Swap lists, pay to mail to their lists, or share profits from mailing to their lists. That's been a major strategy for my company, as I have a compelling message to many other investment-oriented businesses that can be delivered in a webinar and add value to their clients—after which we split revenues if they sign up for my newsletter or other services.

Study companies that are much larger, or are already the best marketers in their arenas. See what works for them and model their best practices. Study the strategies of people like Dan Kennedy at GKIC (www.dankennedy.com). Examine the copy you get from direct response marketers in your mail or on the Internet. What seems to work? What are the most compelling offers and calls to action?

You need good systems to manage, track, and deliver products and services at each level of interaction with the customer. Measure the quality and execution at each step as you deal with your customer—marketing, ordering, order status, delivery, returns, and warranties. But your business needs to stay focused. Much of this can be subcontracted to an array of firms that do individual functions better or at lower cost than you can. The most important function to focus on in-house is content and copywriting, and if you don't have the scale to do that get the best outside firm to do it.

The shift to direct response marketing is the leading-edge area today.

But it will not be enough in itself as competition intensifies and the new economy steamrolls forward. Customization and real-time personalized service also require organizations that operate like networks, organize around customers, and operate from the bottom up, not the top down. This will become the forefront in the next decade and beyond—the most powerful competitive edge and barrier to entry for businesses.

The New Network Model for Business

The last several decades have seen radical innovations in the use of new technologies to streamline organizations, cut costs, get closer to customers, and eliminate marketing and distribution layers. But the one thing that has not changed is that our organizations still run from the top down, not the bottom up. Only that, too, is changing with the new network approach. I'll start with an example today of a real-life network in business that I observe every day: the stock exchanges.

Where's the management? Some poor guy runs up, rings the bell at a set time in the morning, then gets the hell out of the way. All types of chaos and trading occur in real time, with immediate results and no bureaucracy. Everyone knows what price they got and how much profit or loss they made. Statements are updated in real time. Prices for zillions of stocks, bonds, commodities, and options fluctuate mildly or wildly. Then the bell is rung at the close of business and the chaos stops until the next morning.

That's a network organization. It operates in real time with no apparent management or bureaucracy. The management, transactions, and bureaucracy are all in the software that functions at almost no cost and at virtually the speed of light. This system is totally driven by the users who buy and sell as they wish, when they wish, all in real time.

Why aren't all of our organizations this way? The first reason is that stock exchanges have no real hard products to be produced, stored, and transported, unlike makers of cars, TVs, and books. But what happens when you convert books to electronic versions—now you can deal in real time and customize at low costs. I dream of the time when I can have a book that is largely electronically downloaded and I can make major updates in real time, and those can be passed to past readers and new readers. Over time, all products will become more information intensive and more likely to be managed increasingly in network logic.

The other reason the old model survives is we simply don't think in network logic when it comes to business because we've been in top-down hierarchies forever—and most managers and supervisors love bossing people around, interfering in their work, being on top and in control. Yes, and do people like that? Is nature like this? Is the lion really the king of the jungle or just the most successful predator? Where's management in nature? You don't see it. It's invisible. We tend to call it God. Adam Smith called it the "invisible hand" in economics. The Zen saying is "The grass grows by itself."

Inevitably, then, there is an emerging new model for business and organizations, like the innovation of the assembly-line model of the early 1900s, but very different and with even greater potential. Its design follows the architecture of networks and information technologies, just as the factory system followed the architecture of the steam engine. Again, this model is about organizing around your customers and operating from the bottom up, not the top down. Who knows more about your customers—your frontline workers or your top management and back-line bureaucrats? Who can respond faster and more appropriately and more efficiently, if they only had the information and structure to do so?

This is about producing to demand, not inventory, and delivering real-time, personalized service in what I call the new customized economy. Its functions have less environmental impact, with reduced inventories, energy, and distribution costs. This economy has been emerging slowly for decades in higher-end markets, but now is starting to move more mainstream and will do so for decades to come. And this is where the greatest growth will come in the winter season and spring boom ahead.

The new network model is the secret to bringing higher-end, more customized products and services mainstream as it is the opposite of the standardized, mass-production model of the past. It offers efficient customization at a time when information technologies allow it and more affluent customers increasingly demand it. The new customized economy innovates in the summer season, emerges in higher-end niche markets in the fall season, and then goes increasingly mainstream from the winter season into the spring, summer, and fall seasons to follow.

The five principles for designing network organizations for delivering real-time, personalized service at lower and lower costs are as follows:

Principle #1: Strategic Focus: Do Only What You Do Best

The winter season is the shakeout season and is all about forcing companies to emphasize what they do best and where they can dominate. Only the strong and focused survive, so the new model starts with strategic focus. Focus on your strengths and subcontract everything else to strategic partners. Invest in and remain only in products and markets you can dominate.

Analyze every product line, department, and function in your company and decide whether what you do is as good as or better than anyone else. That means taking a hard and honest look at your direct and indirect competition. If there is someone else who does what you do better, in a more customized way, and/or at lower costs, then you are cheating your customers if you continue to do it your way. They will eventually leave you for a better solution.

At Dent Research we were never good marketers. We tried many new approaches and outside consultants, but we finally merged with Sovereign/Agora as marketers so we could focus solely on economic research and forecasting, which, over time, we had come to understand is our greatest skill. We are now twice as focused as before and let Sovereign do what they do best: marketing up-and-coming authors and research firms like us. As a result, my partners and I are looking to quadruple our business over the next few years.

Principle #2: Determine Which Customers You Serve Best and Break Them into Unique Segments

Any business should start by clearly defining its ideal customer: *Who is it that you best serve, or could best serve? Where and how can you add the most value to that customer at the lowest costs so that you have little or no competition?* Define your product or service, not as what you do, but in terms of the actual end result that the customer feels and most values.

In my firm's case, we deliver timely economic research to help investors and businesses see opportunities they wouldn't see otherwise, in order to avoid costs or losses when economic trends change. In other words, we increase the profits of investors and businesses by helping them anticipate changes in the economy and trends. If we're not doing that, it doesn't matter how good our research is.

In the case of, say, a carpet installer, the priority should be to provide greater aesthetics in a commercial customer's retail environment to help them attract better customers. Notice in this case that the carpet installer is not dealing with everyone. They are focused on the needs of retailers, not offices, not homes that can have very different priorities.

Consider an instructive example here: I read about a carpet company that redesigned its role with the customer. They don't sell and install carpet in a one-time transaction anymore. They charge an annual fee for maintaining their customers' carpeting. Their ongoing annual fee includes installation, maintenance, and repair, and replacement over time. Their role is to keep their clients' carpets looking good and to take over that function entirely so that their clients never have to think about it and can focus on functions that add more value to their clients.

Ask the key questions of yourself: *Do you save your customers time or costs? Do you take a nonstrategic function off their hands so they can focus more on what they do best? Do you add quality to their brands with your components or services? Do you bring specialized expertise, innovation, and adaptability to their process? Do you simply bring convenience and provide something when they need it without their having to take on overhead they don't need?* Find concrete ways to measure those end results from customer behavior, interactions, and/or nonintrusive surveys.

The next step is to separate your various customers, and newly targeted customers, into unique segments that share similar needs and priorities. Some want higher quality and more customized solutions; some have more occasional needs; some have constant needs; some want the lowest costs and don't need high service; some need rapid delivery; some make their own decisions with a little good information; some need a lot of hand holding.

The variations are many, but learn to recognize and differentiate them where it makes a difference to your customers.

Start by dividing them as finely as you can into segments that have distinctive needs that make them unique. The art comes then in regrouping them into a smaller number of segments that are more practical to serve based on the scale, affordability, and personnel realities of your business. Not every customer can have his own "butler" (though in some very high-end services this is the case). As your customer base grows and your technology systems get more sophisticated, you will be able to segment more finely in the future—and in this process you have already thought about that and know the next finer segments that could make sense.

Once you have defined the most relevant unique segments of your customers, you need to literally organize around each segment's unique needs. And, yes, that means each customer segment gets its own team to serve it, its own butler, or what I call frontline browsers.

Principle #3: Organize Each Unique Customer Segment into Frontline Browsers and Back-Line Servers

Computers have allowed networks—principally the Internet—to develop around browsers and servers. Browsers are the gateways by which users find and link to the key information, products, or services they want and need in real time. A principle that makes this possible is integral to networks and to the example of the stock exchanges I gave earlier. If you simply *think* in network terms of organization—that the ultimate principle is organizing around your customer and operating from the customer back or the bottom up, not the top down—you'll find the need for less management, supervision, and petty bureaucracy. That will liberate your employees and delight customers. Strive to make decisions on the front lines wherever possible and in real time.

My motto is: *management is the problem, not the solution*. Real-time communication and personalized service simply don't align with bureaucracy or top-down systems.

Essentials of network organization are, first, the automation of management and bureaucracy, and, second, real-time systems that feed the front lines and the customer the information needed to drive the decision-making process from the bottom up, even directly by the customer where possible.

What are computer, software, and Internet networks, other than browsers and servers? Your network organization should be designed first around frontline human browsers, namely, individuals or small teams that focus on a narrow group of customers with unique needs and deliver customized products/services at low costs by accessing back-line servers to coordinate and meet their customers' needs (Figure 8-18).

Chart 8-18: Network Organization

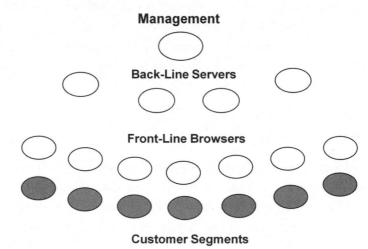

Source: Dent Research

Wherever possible, information and decision making should be put on the front lines for instant, personalized service, but there remain larger-scale, more costly functions that require specialized expertise that cannot yet be put on the front lines. This means there are certain functions that still have to be put on the back lines, at least today. All such components, products, and services that are needed to customize and deliver the full range of products or service are organized into back-line servers. But the most important principle here is that such units are driven by the needs of the frontline browsers, who are in charge of the real end customer and their end results. The organization always operates from the customer up, not the top down!

Determine the information needed to make as many decisions as possible on the front lines, using the minimum number of people to understand and meet the needs of a narrow group of customers. The questions should always be along these lines: *Why do we do this on the back lines? Why does this decision need to be approved by a supervisor?* Or *why can't this information or approval or supervisory function or expertise be programmed into software and made available in real time on the front lines?* Things that can't be done on the front lines today will be possible in the future, thanks to technology and software that just grows exponentially in power and applications. The people in your frontline teams obviously need to multitask and be relationship oriented if they are going to meet the needs of customers.

Only the expertise that is too complex to be programmable with simple rules and approvals, or functions that require too much scale to operate, should be put into back-line teams or outsourced to outside service firms. Back-line teams should also act like real-world consultants who see the frontline teams as their customers. Their mission is to provide service in real time, where possible, and in customer-friendly language and with courtesy and respect, not bureaucracy and arrogance. The people in back-line teams will naturally tend to be more technical and more specialized in their skills, and, quite likely, a bit less relational.

The ideal is that your customers never have to deal directly with your companies' back-line people or "servers"; the latter are coordinated like a butler by the frontline browser units, which are the ones most sensitive to the targeted customers' real needs and know them personally.

Principle #4: Make Every Frontline and Back-Line Unit Accountable as a Business Down to a P&L

There are two important dimensions in delegating decision making to the front lines. The first is simply that if you delegate such decisions without control, feedback, and accountability, you could make many bad decisions and create huge losses. The second is to make everyday workers more like the local dry cleaner—a responsive and accountable businessperson, not just an employee.

Your local dry cleaner does not have to be sophisticated or have an MBA, but he or she does need to know his or her customers intimately. Dry cleaners have to know their costs, what they have to make every week to cover overheads, how much they make every time they make an additional sale. They have to respond to customer complaints or special demands. They have to deal with fluctuations in sales and costs. Their business depends on their being informed and responsive. If they don't perform their business will not, their business and income suffers or even disappears. They don't earn salaries and benefits, except what they create.

Accountable people become more decisive, more creative; sometimes, these folks are aptly called small-business entrepreneurs. But there is a big distinction between the entrepreneurs who are what I call "radical innovators" and everyday small-business people who are what I call "incremental innovators." Radical innovators tend to think outside the box and create technologies, products, or services that did not exist before—you know, like Steve Jobs! They take big risks and have big failures. Some take an approach that worked in one city or country and expand it into other major areas. These are the people who truly create new jobs and products that would not otherwise exist. These are the people who drive advances in our standard of living and progress in our economy, just as George Gilder has stressed for decades. These are the people most likely to usher in innovations, like the network organization I am talking about here, that represent something really new, not just an improvement or a further streamlining. The United States leads in this arena, and Israel is a big up-and-comer. Governments need to encourage and support such people.

Most people will not be radical innovators, who are an eccentric and rare breed. Most people don't want a high-risk life or to be a lone wolf—most of us are more social than that. And if too many people were like this, we would have constant disruption and change and fewer tangible, enduring benefits. In contrast, the local dry cleaner and most small businesses are providing something that already exists or would exist even if they weren't there.

If your local dry cleaner died and went out of business, another one would pop up to meet demand in your area. But the difference between the small-business person and most workers in companies is that the former are more responsive, more innovative, always improving things for customers, always cutting costs, always tracking customer response.

A key benefit of the network organization is that it makes everyday workers as responsive and accountable as a small business owner. Most people would rather be running their own business than working for an employer. But they don't have the skills or the capital or the means. Information technologies allow you to give them such a network with financing, relevant information, and the accountability to do what they really want to do in a lower-risk environment, a win-win for most people.

The key to delegating responsibility down to frontline decision making with accountability is real-time goals and performance measures at every level possible; delegating without accountability leads to disaster sooner or later. I did a lot of consulting to new ventures and small businesses early in my career. They were often trying to delegate decision making to be more responsive to customers. But if you delegate without giving both the necessary information to make good decisions *and* accountability for results and profitability, then such decentralization can create disasters. It would be natural for frontline employees to do things for customers to please them, but in the process they may also be causing the company to lose money. In fact, one bad apple can bring down a company through bad decisions or even theft that remains undetected for too long. This is where information technologies perhaps create the greatest value-added impacts.

Information and Internet technologies increasingly allow you to put the best information right on the front lines, and for those decisions and services that have to be put on back-line server units, information and measurements can be put there as well for accountability to both the front lines and management. Create measurable productivity measures for each frontline or back-line team that relates to creating the end results for the customer; for example, orders booked per day, customer mailings per week, and the like. Every frontline and back-line unit should be a real business, with goals and measured results. You're not a real business without a profit-and-loss statement (P&L).

You need to reconstruct P&Ls in total and individually for each frontline and back-line unit to reflect the real nature of your business, in which fixed costs have to be covered before profits accrue, and variable costs must be monitored, as they determine how much cash flow each sale generates. This is not how accountants do things for financial reporting and taxes. But your accounting needs to reflect accurately to management and business units how your business actually works.

Bain & Company did this with its clients. I did this with my small business clients. By discriminating between fixed and variable costs, allocating fixed costs properly, and determining your variable costs for sales, you can see which products, teams, or divisions are profitable and which are not. You can understand the actual dynamics of your business and how much profit or loss you make at different sales levels.

Most businesses tend to think along these lines: *We have profits of 10 percent on sales on average.* That's the wrong approach. The truth is your profitability will vary greatly if your sales are substantially higher or lower because a large part of your costs are fixed regardless of sales—so you may have as much as 90 percent cash flow profits for every extra unit you sell after your fixed costs are already covered! If you don't understand such realities, you and your frontline employees will make bad decisions and miss profitable sales.

My favorite example of this comes from traveling. Sometimes I arrive at a hotel late at night and ask what the rates are. The front desk clerk will quote the standard rate. If that is too high, I will walk out and try another hotel. If it is late and the hotel has rooms open, that employee should not let me walk out that door. The truth is that it will only cost, say, $15 to clean and service the room. If I walked out at $100, why not offer $75 or $50 if you have to? Even at $50, the hotel is still making $35 that it wouldn't have made—and which goes straight to the bottom line. The point is that frontline employees may be missing opportunities to add to their company's profits and to create new customers or add to their sales and satisfaction.

So picture your business this way: There is a bucket of fixed costs—rent, accounting, management and administration, utilities, business licenses, research and development (R&D)—that have to be paid whether you have any sales or not. You have to fill up that bucket from the direct profits on sales until you recoup those costs. After that, every sale contributes to profits after its direct costs. When you make a sale, there are variable costs beyond your fixed overheads to fulfill that sale (such as sales commissions, product production and packaging costs, delivery costs, credit card fees). These costs can be a high or a low percentage.

The most profitable companies are those that have low direct costs because profit margins accelerate rapidly once they cover their fixed costs. Software companies are the classic example. It takes a lot of R&D (fixed costs) to develop a software application. But it costs very little to print out a CD or to electronically deliver such software. If such companies can get up to scale, they make very high profits as each sale drops mostly to the bottom line. My company is another example. We do economic and demographic research, which requires a very substantial ongoing overhead of several people. But when we sell newsletters, most of which are electronically delivered, the variable costs are near zero. It's effectively all profit after our fixed costs are covered.

Subtracting variable costs from sales creates a new critical measure called contribution margin; this is what you contribute to cash flow and ultimately to profits every time you sell an extra dollar's worth of goods. This is the most important accounting figure that everyone needs to know—from management to frontline sales and service people—and for every product or service.

An example: If your contribution margin is 70 percent and your fixed costs are $10,000 a month, then it takes $14,286 of sales to cover your fixed costs and break even. If a new business or business unit cannot get to this point fairly quickly, it will either go under or require massive amounts of capital at great costs of equity and much higher risk. In fact, keeping fixed costs low in the early stages of a business is often critical to a business's survival. After the break-even point, however, every $1 contributes 70 cents to your profits; at $20,000 in sales your profit would be $4,000 a month, or a 25 percent profit margin; at $30,000 in sales your profits would be $11,000 per month, or 36.7 percent; at $40,000 in sales your profits would be $18,000, or 45 percent. In this case a 50 percent increase in sales created a 175 percent increase in profits, and a 100 percent increase created a 350 percent rise in profits—because profit margins were quite different at each sales point. When contribution margin is high, small increases in sales can cause large jumps in profits.

When teams and employees at all levels understand their contribution margins, fixed costs, and profit dynamics, they make more profitable decisions. They can also respond to customer demands or needs and price changes in ways that are win-win for the customer and the company. The key is to enable frontline customer service teams so they can make real-time, profitable decisions without having a supervisor approve every creative decision they make and only add costs and delays in service.

In any business that has multiple product lines or business units, it is essential to allocate actual fixed costs to product lines and units. Rather than arbitrarily assigning cost as a percentage of sales, you might use the number of transactions of each business unit or product line to allocate accounting costs; or allocate office costs by the square footage used; or research and development expense by the time key personnel spend on different products. Other approaches would track actual usage of phone, Internet, and computer services where possible for direct allocations; or allocate key management salaries and their office overhead by the time they spend on different projects, products, or divisions.

In allocating costs properly, you will probably find that some products, divisions, or units are not as profitable as you thought, while others are more so. In the network organization, strive to allocate fixed and variable costs to all frontline and back-line units and create a P&L. Bill out internal departments like accounting or human resources at market-based rates comparable to what an outside service would charge.

Back-line servers should have their time charged to the frontline servers at market or near-market rates. If the frontline units feel they can get better services from outside consultants or firms, they should be allowed to do that, or to argue for better terms to management. That serves constantly to hone your strategic focus in Principle #1. In this way, the frontline units are responsible for the costs they incur from the back-line servers; the back-line servers are more accountable to their customers; and the back-line servers are accountable for results for the prices they charge, just like any outside business doing the same thing.

Measuring profitability down to individual units means you can have an accountable profit-sharing plan with each team that gives them a share of the profits they generate, which can be larger or smaller depending on how much value management the company invests in their systems and capacities and how much value they add.

The ultimate benefit of making every individual or team a real business is that you will attract the best employees and retain them longer. Who wouldn't want to have their own business, see their own direct results, and get a share of those measured results without having to take the larger risk of starting a business on their own? You should have people from your competitors knocking on your door—and bringing their customers with them!

Principle #5: Management Becomes the Vision, the Architect, and the Legal Arbitrator of the Network

That brings us to your role as management. Start with the reality that more and more people, especially the most talented and creative, don't like management, supervision, and bureaucracy. It makes them feel like second-class citizens, like the serfs of this era.

By following principles #1 through #4, you can create a clear vision and focus for the company. You will have designed a network organization with little or no bureaucracy and a clear focus on the end customers and the measurable benefits they get from your company. The needs of the customer become a first priority, and the frontline browser units are in charge of those customers and needs; the back-line servers serve the front lines, rather than management or the customer directly. You will be the architect of the network that allows all of this to happen with little management and with much more customized, personalized service and increasingly in real time.

Once it is in place, you must constantly work to maintain and improve the network and make it even more real-time and responsive. Ultimately, you are also the political and legal system. In any human system or network, there will be disputes. Customers have complaints, but perhaps the frontline team feels this is just an irrational or bad customer. Management has to decide who is right. Sometimes you have to fire customers who abuse your frontline people.

Frontline teams may feel that back-line servers are charging too much or are unresponsive. Management needs to arbitrate and decide whether that frontline team can go outside or whether this back-line server should be further automated or outsourced as a result.

A back-line unit may feel that a partner company is not performing as well as it should and propose to take over that function. Management has to decide what's best. A frontline employee sees a new market opportunity and wants a new unit to exploit it, perhaps with resources from management or added incentives if he or she cracks the new market. Those are management decisions.

From the higher political level, management has the vision and keeps the strategic focus until some bright entrepreneur within the organization finds a new arena that works to expand it. Management has to have the wisdom to support and give that person some rope with limited capital to prove such a new direction. Overall, management designs the network and organization with the goal that it becomes ever more self-managing, so that it doesn't need you anymore. Your job is automating your past functions, therefore automating management. Instead, at the operating level, management becomes the legal system, arbitrating disputes between units and outside partners, demonstrating fairness and maintaining the vision and the architecture. But the true measure of management's success is merely the summation of all other key measures from sales and profit growth, return on investment, and customer satisfaction. The ultimate measure is that management is seen as the visionaries and leaders, not the bosses and bureaucrats.

Two qualitative measures are to what degree the employees are happy running their own businesses, and their rate of turnover. Just as with customers, it's harder to find a new employee than to keep a good one. With your employees making decisions for customers and more intimately entwined with them, keeping the best employees becomes more important than ever (not least because if they leave, they could take their customers with them). Ultimately, the best sign of a well-run company is the absence of bureaucracy and politics. Customers will knock on your door if you offer excellent service at affordable prices; in the same way, highly qualified people will flock to work for you, too. Together, these mean lower marketing and human resource costs.

If you hunker down and follow the principles we espouse here, you can succeed at a time when many businesses are failing. Your competitors' blindness and weakness become your strength and triumph. You're delivering what the natural economic cycle wants, reaping the rewards for advancing our economic evolution into the future.

The most successful businesses that survive this shakeout in the winter season will bring greater innovation and lower costs to most consumers. That will cause the economy to advance through higher productivity, which also means consumers will earn more and spend more. Network organizations of the future will contribute and share more in profits and develop more inspired, motivated, and productive workers—not the bored assembly-line workers of the past.

Again, we are witnessing the dynamic of the invisible hand, which drives long-term progress and growth. The United States and many developed countries may not grow as fast as they have in past decades or centuries due to slowing demographic trends. But we don't have to lose our competitive edge if we adapt first to the new technological and network models of business. We don't have to lose our higher standards of living even as many countries in southern Europe and Japan have already begun to do.

Governments can become more accountable and follow the network organizational principles as well. And we need that more than ever in an increasingly complex global and urbanized world.

CHAPTER 9

GOVERNMENT STRATEGIES FOR FACILITATING FREE MARKETS

The free market needs rules to ensure effective and efficient competition. Why? Because we are essentially greedy, taught by evolution to protect ourselves and our kith and kin and to conspire (intentionally or not) for unfair market advantages when possible.

That means the real question is not whether we need Republican- or Democratic-leaning policies, or even whether they ought to be stimulating or restrictive. We need the best balance *and* the good sense to know when to lean more one way or the other.

Free-market or survival-of-the-fittest policies (Republican) reward merit and give greater wealth and income to the strong. That stimulates innovation and allocates capital to the proven leaders to continue to advance economic evolution. George Gilder argues this better than anyone in his recent book *Knowledge and Power*. The political war between countries like the United States, which tends to be more free-market, and countries like the former Soviet Union (more socialistic or communistic) was decided a long time ago when the more capitalistic free world outperformed Communist countries during the cold war of the 1950s through the 1980s, helping bring down the Berlin Wall in 1989. The Soviet government simply could not keep up in the arms race because of a superior U.S. economy (they also couldn't bullshit their people anymore about how bad the West was when they started getting

Dallas on their satellite dishes). The failure of one philosophy has shifted the issue. The question before us is: *Which capitalistic model is the best?*

Should we favor the more free-market models like the United States, Hong Kong, and Singapore? Or the more socialistic free-market models like those in Scandinavia and northern Europe? Or Japan's model, which occupies the territory somewhere in between? And what of the new state-driven capitalistic model of China, a top-down social and economic planning system on steroids?

My first prediction is that China is going to demonstrate that the state-driven capitalistic model doesn't work with its governmental overstimulation and overbuilding (China has trumped every other emerging country with this model!). And it's not just overbuilding, misallocating capital, and creating bubbles and inefficiencies. China's pollution internally and its contribution to global pollution are off the charts. Plus China's debt bubble is immense; that's not healthy and doesn't bode well.

Southeast Asian countries went this route, too, overbuilding through government-driven plans. They saw a major financial crisis from late 1997 into late 2002. And I predict China's unprecedented bubble will burst over the next six years, likely beginning in 2014.

Within the more capitalistic and democratic Western world and newly wealthy East Asian countries (Japan, Hong Kong, Singapore, Taiwan, and South Korea), there are many degrees of the free-market model—some more capitalistic (Hong Kong, Singapore, the United States, Australia, Canada, and the United Kingdom), some more socialistic (Sweden, Norway, Finland, France, Italy, and Greece), and some occupying the middle ground (Germany, Switzerland, Austria, Japan, South Korea, and Spain). And many of these variations work well.

The Scandinavian countries, for example, are very democratic, but also the most socialistic with greater safety nets for welfare, health care, and retirement. They have some of the highest standards of living in the world, low income inequality, and the top ratings for happiness.

Why do these models work as well as they do? There are two main reasons. First, these are high work ethic countries with little demographic diversity and immigration; second, they voluntarily sacrifice a bit of innovation and higher incomes for the broader goal of less income inequality, which results in higher social cohesion and lower crime. The result is higher happiness with little sacrifice in average standard of living. But again, these are high-innovation, high-achievement societies that have been so for centuries.

The most capitalistic models are in major countries such as the United States, Australia, Canada, and Israel, and city-states in the East such as Hong Kong and Singapore. These countries have the greatest income inequality, but also the highest average incomes and wealth due to higher innovation, entrepreneurial activity, and investment. These countries tend to have less traditional culture. They were immigrant-driven from the beginning, ever changing due to constant innovation and immigration. Live by the sword, die by the sword, and no risk, no gain are, in effect, the mottos in these more dynamic countries. Let the average person or immigrant have the same opportunities as the elite! Many average people support this system because they believe their kids have a chance to become more wealthy, even if they have not.

Models characterized by cultural and ethnic diversity also must deal with the tensions that naturally come with it, as well as with the higher income inequality that is the price for this more free-market model. As an entrepreneur, I would rather be in the United States than Canada, Britain than France, Australia than New Zealand, Singapore than Japan, or Dubai than Saudi Arabia. But then the Swedes and the Canadians, despite living in a much more adverse climate, are happier than Americans. Individual and collective cultures factor here, too.

Through democratic processes, countries choose their priorities, and different strategies have different outcomes in overall happiness versus innovation, higher average incomes, income inequality, and cultural cohesion. What works best for a given country depends upon its cultural history and makeup. Again, the United States, Canada, Australia, and New Zealand were immigrant countries from their beginnings, and they thrive more on radical innovation and entrepreneurial tendencies. Japan and much of western, central, and southern Europe thrive more on tradition, culture, and incremental innovation.

The result has been that more socialistic versions of free-market capitalism function well in much of Europe and East Asia, and more entrepreneurial models have worked better in the United States, Australia, Hong Kong, and Singapore. Canada and Britain are more in between, leaning more toward the free-market side. Then there's the original wild card, England, which was the most innovative and risk-taking country in the world from the 1500s into the 1800s, much like the United States in the last century.

In the longer term, world leaders tend to emerge more from entrepreneurial and innovative countries. Greece was the leading edge of scientific, philosophical, and business innovation from the 500s into the 300s B.C. Then Rome took the lead into A.D. 150. Western Europe, with Great Britain leading, was the avatar by 1800, then the United States into 2007, and, increasingly of late, Israel. Greece would not be called the cradle of innovation today, nor would Italy, outside its high-end sports cars and fashions.

Recall from chapter 5 that the Big Bang in modern history was the marriage of democracy and free-market capitalism. Democracy is socialistic in nature because it gives everyone a say—*All men are created equal, that they are endowed by their Creator with certain unalienable Rights, that among these are Life, Liberty and the pursuit of Happiness.* That's democracy chiming in and giving involvement and motivation to the everyday person. But the invisible hand was conceived around the same time by Adam Smith in *The Wealth of Nations*, wherein bottom-up markets allowed the best to rise to the top and improve the whole system—survival of the fittest and rewarding the most fit—without excessive regulation and government interference and planning. Darwin came several decades after and found similar principles in nature and the process of evolution.

In modern-day terms governments are increasingly fighting the invisible hand and natural forces, as David Stockman argues even more thoroughly than I do. Although I expect China's bubble to burst badly between 2014 and 2019 from such massive intervention in its economy, thereby destroying the credibility of their approach very quickly, at present we have central governments in ailing Western countries mimicking some of China's governmental strategies. In effect, the Fed is doing what China does with its strategy of endless QE.

That raises a big question. *Why is it so bad that governments and central banks are bailing out the economy endlessly with monetary injections?* It has prevented a great depression thus far, the very one I projected both in 1989 in my first book and, in 2008, in *The Great Depression Ahead.* I maintain the answer is that taking more and more of a drug (in this case, debt and stimulus) to keep from coming down off a bubble high is delusional. Addiction and denial never work out well in real life, personally or collectively. Endless QE and stimulus keep the economy from rebalancing and innovating again.

Denial: The Nine Consequences of Endless QE and Stimulus

In late 2011, the head of the European Central Bank (ECB), President Mario Draghi, single-handedly drove a two-day surge in stock markets around the world with his simple statement, "The ECB will do everything possible to preserve the euro and, believe me, it will be enough." Markets were sliding on rising short-term interest rates in southern European countries and lower and lower growth forecasts when his statement changed the game.

This story has repeated itself since late 2008. The economy slows due to falling demographic trends, excessive debt burdens, and deleveraging, then governments step in with more aggressive monetary and fiscal stimulus. The stimulus works for up to a year, after which it wears off, and the economy slumps again. Then governments stimulate again, upping the ante.

How long can this go on? My answer: Given slowing demographic trends and ever higher debt burdens, governments will have to continue upping stimulus programs for another ten years! Does that sound sustainable to you? How about a U.S. government debt of $26 to $30 trillion by 2023? Or a Fed balance sheet of $15 trillion, versus $4 trillion today?

Furthermore, each additional stimulus plan has less and less of an effect (see Figure 9-1). We have gotten less and less GDP response in GDP per dollar of debt added since the late 1960s. We've already approached the near-zero point of diminishing returns. Can governments do this forever, or is there a point where stimulus just doesn't work at all and the economy dies from the side effects, as with any drug? I am certain there is.

Japan has used stimulus for about a decade and a half, but it faced its

Figure 9-1: Incremental GDP per Dollar of Debt

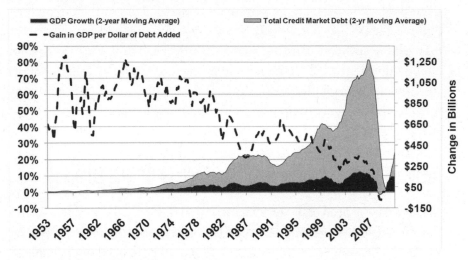

Data Source: St. Louis Federal Reserve, 2013

crisis alone in a global boom, which made things easier as its export industries were still expanding and mild global inflation offset its deflationary tendencies somewhat. Japan also came into that crisis with budget and trade surpluses and has had more stimulus capacity over a longer period of time. But I am convinced that most major governments around the world simply do not have the luxury of continuing to push endless stimulus in a deteriorating global environment.

Japan's recent and extremely aggressive QE program—it was 2.5 times the rate of the U.S. QE in 2013 when adjusted for the size of its economy— saw interest rates on its ten-year government bond rise at first rather than fall. Even though the government's aggressive buying should drive rates down, private buyers are looking at a new target of 2 percent inflation versus 0 percent. Rates have to rise just to adjust for expected inflation. And Japan is saying it will go as far as it takes to create 2 percent inflation! That means such bond rates should be 2.5 percent to 3 percent, which would only give a real return of 0.5 percent to 1 percent. If that occurred, Japan's interest payments on its enormous debt (250 percent of GDP and rising) would quickly bankrupt it.

We have economies and markets addicted to QE since 2008. After first setting short-term rates at near zero, central banks have injected new money into the banking system at unprecedented rates. This injection is meant to keep the banks from imploding, bolstering their reserves to cover losses and reserve ratio deficits. Then the rest of the money gets invested, often at high leverage, to replace the profits from past lending. In effect, our financial institutions have become gambling casinos. What happens to them when the next financial crash hits? Common sense says this is clearly a something-for-nothing scheme and a means of denial.

The government and the major banks advising them, such as Goldman Sachs, are simply trying to avoid the consequences of past excesses in leverage and very bad lending. We all know that real life doesn't work that way. However, governments do not seem to have understood this simple principle. They haven't had to abide by it, as households and businesses have, because of money printing, QE, based on Keynesian economics.

Endless stimulus has kept the bubble from bursting, but the system will continue to get more stretched due to more debt and overcapacity until some major event triggers an out-of-control meltdown, as occurred with the subprime crisis in the United States in late 2008. I see a high likelihood of such an event occurring in the first half of 2014.

This meltdown may be a bank run in Spain or the final exit of Greece or Portugal from the euro—some event that triggers other bank runs and exits. Or we could see the China real estate bubble start to burst, torpedoing its most affluent consumers. Or the U.S. real estate rebound ends with the combination of rising mortgage rates and speculators' backing off. Then it'll be deflation and debt deleveraging with a vengeance! This new crisis is most likely to start by early 2014, but it will almost certainly come by 2019.

A new book published in mid-2013, *Why We Should Leave the Euro*—the "we" in this case being Portugal—outsold bestselling novels like *Fifty Shades of Grey* (in Portugal!). As austerity grows and riots against it build, don't underestimate the odds of Portugal or Greece or Spain choosing to exit the euro rather than being forced to (also a growing possibility), especially in Spain with its deteriorating real estate bubble, far greater than any other real estate bubble in Europe except Ireland's.

Figure 9-2: Impacts on Interest Rates

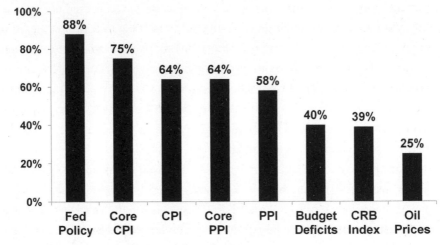

Source: Business Insider, 6/21/2012, Haver Analytics, 2012

Monetary policies like QE have an impact on interest rates by pushing down inflation rates and natural market levels; in fact such policies are seen as having the greatest impact by 88 percent of economists (see Figure 9-2), but there are a number of other factors. Core inflation is next at 75 percent and so on, down to 40 percent for government deficits and 39 percent for CRB (commodity prices). In the real world of business and personal finance, rising debt and deficits would be number one, but governments apparently live in another universe, in which money can be created out of nothing in seeming violation of natural laws.

At some point, however, the rising debt ratios and deficits must overwhelm the system, as shown by the economic downturns of Greece, Ireland, Portugal, Spain, Italy, and increasingly France. At the same time, spiking government bond yields can take such nations out of the debt and stimulus game, forcing them to rely on bailouts from other countries and investors—as happened in 2011. Why? The "printing presses" no longer had the ability to devalue their currencies to rebalance trade once they agreed to membership in the broader euro. Long-term interest rates have been rising in 2013.

Is this the beginning of the markets' taking away the printing presses in countries like the United States?

Further economic downturns from rising debt, falling demographic trends in spending, and implementation of government-sponsored austerity programs are likely to cause at least a short-term spike in longer-term interest rates. This is true even for safe-haven countries such as Switzerland, Germany, the United States, the United Kingdom, and Japan, due to deteriorating credit quality and ratings downgrades. Such a rising trend in government bond interest started in early 2013 and is likely to continue. It could peak by early to mid-2014, helping to trigger a stock crash around the world.

The key question for central bankers around the world should be: *Is the crisis so bad that we should be making such bold and unprecedented commitments to endless QE?* In the United States it is taking $1 trillion a year in QE and $1 trillion in fiscal deficits on average to keep the economy growing at a feeble 2 percent rate. What would we be facing without such stimulus? Obviously a major recession or depression! Would any investor or banker make that bet?

In Europe, even more than in the United States, the illusion prevails that, if the banking system is propped up by endless QE and bailouts, then the economy will return to normal at some point (Figure 9-3). Demographic trends alone argue that is not possible, and the unbearable debt burdens make it even less feasible. The Europeans are bailing out more with loans than with simple QE, which burdens the weaker countries and makes it impossible for them to come out of an ever-deepening downturn. Debt forgiveness, as with Greece, and debt failure and restructuring, as in Iceland and Estonia, are the only ways out longer-term.

Short-term loans also increasingly have been extended under the table, including TARGET2 loans and Emergency Liquidity Assistance (ELA). TARGET2 loans are trade payments from the weaker central banks that have not been paid to stronger ones like Germany's. TARGET2 loans have risen sharply to about $1.3 trillion. Almost $900 billion of that is owed to the central bank of Germany. That's another reason Germany keeps agreeing to bailouts that aren't apparently in its interest. Germany will get creamed in the short term if TARGET2 borrowers default. How long will Germany

Figure 9-3: Global Combined Balance Sheets

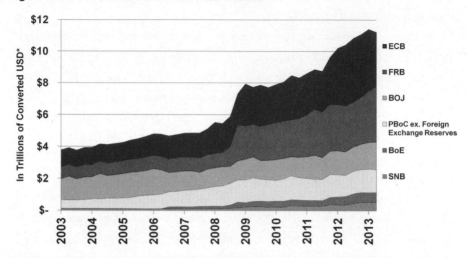

Data Source: Federal Reserve, People's Bank of China, Bank of England, European Central Bank, Swiss National Bank, Bank of Japan, Bloomberg, 2013; *Foreign Currency Amounts Converted in 7/2013

The combined balance sheets of the United States, ECB, China, Japan, Great Britain, and Switzerland as of the end of 2012 show $11.5 trillion in currency and bond holdings from QE policies, or 26 percent of combined GDP, and is only heading higher at this point. That's an unprecedented level of stimulus. Japan has committed to $900 billion a year in 2013 and 2014. Some level of additional stimulus is likely coming in the second half of 2013 from the ECB. Another $500 billion plus is coming from the Fed in the United States in the second half of 2013 as QE3 continues before it starts to taper.

keep holding this bad hand—especially with the fastest-aging society in Europe?

ELA loans have risen to $270 billion from the ECB to stem the run on deposits in Greece and Spain. This sudden and more recent rise in short-term loans, which, like TARGET2 loans, are in addition to declared QE, is what started increasingly setting off alarms for us. This has made us call for investors to get out of stocks in mid-January 2014, as the odds of a mini or major crash are growing.

The truth is simple: Europe, especially southern Europe, and even more so Spain, is not going to come out of a recession sustainably even with further stimulus and bailouts. At best, such support will keep the crisis at bay until Europe likely falls into a deeper demographic downturn or greater social unrest and triggers the next global crash.

The Perversion of QE

Quantitative easing or monetary stimulus certainly has it uses. For example, QE might offset a short-term, nonfundamental crisis in an economy, like the Japan tsunami and nuclear-plant meltdown in 2011, or provide short-term liquidity during the collapse of one or more major financial institutions. But government intervention over a long period of time perverts both markets and the economy's natural mechanisms for dealing with change and innovation, while creating an artificial atmosphere of low rates and low-risk perceptions. Such an atmosphere causes consumers, businesses, and governments not to deleverage debt substantially and instead to continue to overexpand and to misallocate resources and investments. The overexpansion creates market bubbles, which then have to burst again, and excessive capacity, which ultimately leads to price cutting, deflation, and falling profit margins and wages in the future.

QE and endless stimulus kill the "golden goose" of free-market capitalism!

Stock and investment markets, of course, love monetary stimulus and low interest rates. New money flows into the financial system, and low rates drive up the value of most financial assets. This creates market bubbles, which historically always burst and almost always go back to where they started, or a bit lower. Stocks have more than doubled in four and a half years—another bubble—more than they advanced from 2002 to 2007 in five years. Now economies worldwide are at an even higher level of debt, risk, and vulnerability! Stocks are likely to top around the time this book comes out in early 2014.

The recent artificial recovery that resulted from massive government stimulus programs has largely benefited the upper 1 percent to 20 percent of households in income. Individuals in the high-income group, who control over 90 percent of the financial assets that have bubbled in response to stimulus, have not as yet experienced high unemployment, due to workplace seniority and higher levels of education. Their unemployment rates are 3.5 percent! Higher-income households tend to peak in income and spending about four to seven years later than the average household; whereas most households peaked in spending in 2007, the higher-income group is expected to peak by 2014.

This high-income group, the only group still spending even as everyday households have languished, is already likely to spend a bit less with rising tax rates on the top 1 percent from 2013 forward. Demographically, the last kids are preparing to leave the nest among the higher-income households in the large Baby Boomer cohort between 2011 and 2014, causing spending naturally to trend downward. If the stock markets crash at the same time, then the economy in the United States could drop off faster than expected.

A lot of stock analysts would say that P/E (price to earnings) ratios and stocks valuations are not that high, but are more in the normal 15 range. Why would a crash in this stock bull market be inevitable? First, P/E ratios are similar to those that occurred when the last crash started in late 2007, and now risk levels are rising rapidly. Second, when you use inflation-adjusted ten-year average earnings instead of the most recent year, as Robert Shiller does, such P/E ratios are back in the danger zone of 25 and rising. And third and more important, these are not normal times: We have massive debt ratios and crises, civil wars in the Middle East, and slowing demographic trends. We are in the highest-risk economy since the 1930s. The risk level is higher than in the 1970s, plus the risks now are more global, which makes them harder to combat and control. In periods of slow growth and/or high risk from inflation or debt and deflation, stock valuations tend to fall to P/E ratios between 5 and 8 (as in the 1970s and 1930s). Such valuations would dictate a 40 percent to 60 percent drop in stocks even if earnings did not fall, as is very likely. Only the stimulus is keeping the economy going, the banks from collapsing, and lower P/E ratios from manifesting.

Recently in Myrtle Beach, I was in a roller-coaster simulator, one that rocks back and forth and projects a moving image. Even though I knew that this was not a real roller coaster, my brain and body reacted as though it were. Markets work that way as well. Everyone knows that the economy is fragile and high-risk right now. However, investors and businesses are reacting as if the economy were more solid, due to an artificial environment much like the roller-coaster simulator.

Do you know that about 40 percent of the earnings increase for stocks since 2009 in the United States has been the result of corporations buying back their own stocks and decreasing the number of shares? They can only do that because of artificially low long-term interest rates, as can hedge funds that leverage their investments up to fifty times. This whole recovery is built on BS and illusion.

Governments are buying their own bonds to lower interest rates and to cover their ever-rising debt and deficits; corporations are increasingly buying their own stocks given such artificially low interest rates to increase their earnings per share, while investment funds leverage up to fifty times. That amounts to a perversion of markets, not a sign of real and sustainable progress. The message from Mario Draghi, Ben Bernanke, and the leaders of other central banks and governments around the world is this: *We simply will not let another recession or stock crash happen!* Do you believe them? Are you willing to bet your financial assets that they can counter the greatest demographic decline and debt bubble in history?

Another consequence of QE is that investors and businesses continue to overinvest due to artificially low long-term interest rates, which suggest low risk during a high-risk period. It's not that businesses are going gangbusters in capital expenditures, but normally they would be retrenching and consolidating. Instead, businesses continue to invest and expand, albeit moderately. This adds to the excess capacity and excess stock and commodity valuations that were built up in the bubble boom. Excess capacity in a weak-growth environment causes discounting of prices to sell, resulting ultimately in price deflation and lower profit margins and wages.

Super-low short-term interest rates, set directly by the Fed and central banks, also have an effect. The Fed has pledged to keep near-zero rates into 2014 and is likely to extend that pledge into 2015 if there's an economic slowdown by 2014. Low short-term rates make speculation easy and affordable for hedge funds, investment banks, brokerage firms, and all investment-oriented institutions, but when these funds make a small mistake, as we've seen with firms like Long-Term Capital Management in 1998, AIG in 2008, and J.P. Morgan more recently, the Fed may think it has to intervene in the economy, as the winding down of such massive trades threatens market stability and the overall financial system. Why should this be allowed in the first place? Because the special interests of the financial sector lobby for it! The oil collapse from $147 to $32 between June and September 2008 was largely caused by hedge funds and leveraged investors' unwinding trades and meeting massive margin calls.

Hence, another consequence of QE is massive leverage in investment funds and institutions due to near-zero short-term interest rates held artificially low for long periods. Such high leverage only works with near-zero interest rates short-term to finance it. Way too many of our financial institutions have become leveraged hedge funds, in part or largely so. Speculation feeds bubbles, leading to their sudden collapse, and at extremes threaten the financial systems and markets. Most financial institutions have been intertwined since the Glass-Steagall Banking Act of 1933 was rescinded in the 1990s. Thus, a failure in one arm of a financial institution can bring down a commercial bank that was not supposed to be in the speculation business or can bring down an insurance company such as AIG. Such leverage should not be allowed, and short-term rates should not be held down indefinitely as that, in effect, incites such behavior.

Pension funds and investors moving toward retirement also get affected. Because short-term and long-term rates are low, investors can no longer get reasonable returns on low-risk fixed-income investments like government and corporate bonds and CDs. As aging Baby Boomers move from their fifties into their sixties in great numbers over the next several years, they should be choosing lower-risk and fixed-income investments, but government policies make that impossible. Hence, Boomers increasingly move into higher-yield bonds, stocks, and commodities, which feed the bubbles generated by an artificial recovery and monetary stimulus. Once those bubbles burst, investors will end up even worse off than if they had just settled for very low yields on safer investments.

Pension funds will have the most impact as they become even more underfunded; real contributions will have to be increased out of earnings, and investors will have to save more and spend less to supplement their retirement investments. In the United States, municipality pensions are $4 trillion underfunded and corporate pensions are $400 billion underfunded. These numbers are rising rapidly due to low returns as a result of government policies meant to save the banks at all costs.

Bill Gross of PIMCO recently stated that "the cult of equity," that is, high returns above inflation over time, has come to an end. He says the new reality for investors is 4 percent returns in stocks and 2 percent returns in bonds, or more like 3 percent in a diversified portfolio. This compares with most pension fund assumptions of 8 percent returns over time and individual investors who came to expect even more than that. Our forecast is even worse for stocks: 0 percent over the next decade on average, and perhaps 2 percent on bonds, or 1 percent on average.

As much as the media focus on our forecasts for a Dow as low as 3,300, the broader scenario is a very volatile sideways market (as in the 1970s and 1930s) with a downward bias for the next decade. The high end is likely to be 16,000 to 16,700 in late 2013 to early 2014, with a low end of 3,000 to 6,000 between early 2015 and early 2020—with stocks stuck more in the 7,000 to 10,000 range for most of the next decade.

This means zero average returns at best, probably a bit worse for investors and pension funds that stick to the old buy-and-hold philosophy that investors and pension fund managers tend to follow. As in the 1930s, stocks will likely be up for as many years as they are down. Your strategy personally has to be to sell when stocks are in the higher ranges and buy when they are lower (see chapter 7). The same will be true for most pension funds and investment funds—but they won't abandon their investment strategy of the past, so you have to choose to avoid them.

Another consequence of QE is higher-than-normal prices for food, gas, and other commodities, especially among emerging countries and everyday households in developed countries. Inflation rises in faster-growing emerging countries, which then have to slow their growth in response. QE in developed countries also pushes their currencies down against those of emerging countries, hurting their exports artificially. Hence, desperate developed countries end up killing the strongest global growth engines in the emerging world.

Still another consequence of QE is that governments encourage banks to lend more aggressively at lower interest rates and credit standards against increasingly overvalued real estate. Great losses follow. Now banks are being encouraged by low interest rates and monetary injections to buy overvalued government bonds and other, higher-yield financial assets that will generate losses down the road, including losses for central banks, the balance sheets of which have been flooded with overvalued sovereign and mortgage-backed bonds. This occurs especially when central banks start exiting their QE policies and interest rates rise on such bonds, causing their values to fall. After all, you don't get something for nothing.

Perhaps the simplest consequence of QE is that governments keep short-term and long-term interest rates artificially low to grow their debt and debt ratios beyond long-term, sustainable standards—like greater than 80 percent of GDP. When the spring season returns in the decades ahead and interest rates rise with natural inflation, government budgets will be overwhelmed with interest costs and governments will be forced finally to default on or restructure their debt, if they have not done so earlier in the economic crisis. Again, if you want to get a book that will make you sick from seeing how much and how long the U.S. government has manipulated the free market system and has corrupted capitalism, read *The Great Deformation*, by David Stockman.

Japan is the poster child for this dilemma. Any government that does not encourage and/or allow its massive private sector debt to deleverage and, instead, allows government debt to rise dramatically to ease the pain, will default once inflation and normal levels of interest rates return, as we expect will occur from 2023 forward.

The winter season is perhaps the most critical of all. It is a time when the bubble boom of the fall season is shaken down to eliminate excessive debt and asset bubbles. The sheep are separated from the goats, so to speak, concerning which new business models will accelerate out of a survival-of-the-fittest environment. Radically reduced debt loads, greater business consolidation and efficiency, reduced prices and cost of living, and radically new technologies and innovations will emerge. Thus, the stage is set for a new spring season and a new growth trajectory for decades, until the end of the next fall season and bubble boom (around the 2050s in the United States and the 2060s in the emerging world).

The largest and longest-term of the consequences of QE is that QE stops the economy's natural processes of detoxing and healing after a massive bubble boom that catapults new technologies and business models into the economy—again, it kills the golden goose, the invisible hand. Winter accelerates the new economy by weeding out the excesses in debt and capacity rapidly. Companies are forced into greater efficiency through consolidation and into the new business models and technologies that emerged to become mainstream in the fall season. The biggest illusion of economists, central bankers, and politicians is that the economy is a machine or inorganic process that can be set like a thermostat.

In fact, our economy is an organic learning and innovation process that requires booms and busts, inflation and deflation, new innovations, and the creative destruction of past ones. Those who rely on Keynesian economics will fail precisely because they proceed as if our economy is an inorganic, mindless machine, instead of a dynamic growth and evolutionary model.

Simple human greed and denial also come into play. The concept that you can allow debt and standards of living to advance beyond what people actually earned and produced, as happened from Europe to the United States to China, with no consequences or period of austerity to follow, is absolute delusion. Every period of history in which debts and financial assets have grown much faster than the economy has been followed by a decade of austerity, debt deleveraging, and low or negative growth to get back into balance. Lacy Hunt in the United States and Steve Keen in Australia are the best economic experts on debt deleveraging outside of my work.

Remember that the economy is not a thermostat: You can't set it on automatic. The U.S. government has tried to do this in many ways, among them by creating the Federal Reserve in 1913. In its early days the Fed did help iron out very volatile short-term cycles in interest rates, but the escalation of short-term stimulus by the Fed also helped to create a bubble in the

Roaring Twenties that led to the greatest depression in modern history in the 1930s! The lesson: not allowing the economy and markets to rebalance in the short term only leads to greater imbalances and greater crises down the road.

The ultimate consequence of QE is simply denial. Continuing to fuel an economy or bubble with more and more debt is immoral and unwise. The desperate and arrogant attempt by governments over nearly three decades to fight the natural consequences of excessive debt and greed by taking more of the same monetary drugs will only end badly. Everything we learn in our lives on all levels teaches us that lying, cheating, borrowing beyond our means, competing unfairly, and not interacting responsibly with others leads to dire consequences and to lessons that bring us and our actions back into balance.

As we have been saying for years now, there is no way that kicking this debt crisis down the road cannot end badly. The longer and harder we kick, the worse the crisis ultimately will be and the worse the consequences long term.

One final insight: The Greeks may be the luckiest people in the world! Oh, that sounds idealistic, given that they are in a depression currently and may have to exit the euro with grave short-term consequences. So why are they lucky? They were already a declining nation in productivity and competitiveness, but have been allowed to borrow at lower interest rates since 1998 due to the euro. They were able to buy exports like BMWs from Germany and other northern European nations at lower prices due to a lower euro for Germany, which made its exports more attractive. Now, after living beyond their means for over a decade, they got the first and largest bailouts to reduce their debt levels. The ECB and Europe will not be able to bail out all of the less-competitive nations to that degree. Greece does not have as high a level of debt in the private sector, as the Greeks live more simply in general.

Demographic trends in Greece are among the worst in Europe, but after this debt crisis it will emerge with one of the lowest total debt levels in Europe, both due to the deleveraging crisis Greece has been forced into and due to the many bailouts it has received. When the euro falls further, Greek exports will rise and tourism will flourish again. This will obviously occur even more if Greece exits the euro and devalues, as is increasingly likely. Iceland and Estonia have been forced to embrace austerity, with harsh short-term consequences, but the growth trends and unemployment numbers of these countries already are looking healthier than those of most nations in Europe.

Greece will not become a rich or great nation in the coming decades, and it may never be again. But it will end up better because of the euro experiment in the long run. That will not be the case for many nations in Europe, especially for the northern European nations, which first benefited from stronger exports due to a lower euro currency valuation, but then chose to bail out the southern European countries and got caught in a sinister debt trap. The more you lend and bail out, the greater your stake. The more the bailed-out countries fall, the more the rest of the EU loses ultimately, both in higher debt defaults and in falling exports down the line.

The ultimate economic law is just like in our personal or business lives. When you have a problem, blind spot, delusion, scandal, or deficiency, it is better to confront it and deal with it early on. It is better to go through the process of first acknowledging the issue and then transforming it rather than continuing in denial until it causes an ultimate breakdown, or what is called "hitting bottom" in addictions.

Germany and the ECB should have seen this crisis coming and admitted to the flaws and imbalances of the European Union. The EU should have forced a more sustainable debt restructuring, dealt with trade imbalances, and created a longer-term solution earlier on. One solution could have been breaking the euro zone into two divisions and currencies with the same open trade policies. Let the weaker countries devalue and stimulate more, and let the stronger revalue and lose some exports. Instead, Germany and the ECB have increased their bets on a bad hand; they will pay dearly for it. They should have folded their hand back in 2011 when Greece first defaulted and failed.

Spain and Italy were considered too big to bail out or to fail. The ECB has gone full in on its bad hand and has committed to bail out all countries and to do everything possible to preserve the euro. But now France is falling behind in competitiveness, and it is even larger. Germany keeps objecting at every step, but then caves at the last minute.

As with the four seasons in our annual weather and as in our technolog-ical and economic cycles, we start with innovation and hope, moving through stages of growth, through obstacles and further innovation to ultimate suc-cess, which leads to complacency, followed by denial and then by decline, failure, and acceptance—which leads back to restructuring, innovation, and renewal. The hope and growth come back. But the innovation and hope stage won't come back until we face reality.

The point is that we *cannot* afford to *not* fail here—that paradox is the real-ity that we most are avoiding! The United States had hope and moved to inno-vation again from 1933 forward after the Great Depression, which led to the creation of the greatest economy in the world in our lifetimes. We will see who emerges out of this crisis into greatness, in people, businesses, and countries!

Let's not screw up what Adam Smith and our economic forefathers began in the late 1700s. We can improve those models with better information and ever-increasing innovation. But let's not support the model that says we can grow in a straight line forever and never have to accept the consequences for our past excesses and mistakes—and never allow failure or learn and grow again.

A More Enlightened Approach to the Debt Crisis

In a mid-2013 debate with me on CNBC, Ron Insana called the Fed's poli-cies of endless QE "enlightened." I lost control and took his head off! Creat-ing money out of thin air to cover the symptoms of a massive crisis is *enlightened*? I call it a delusion and irresponsible, a cover-up . . . denial! An enlightened policy would be one that addresses the real causes of the great recession and that would enable us to deal with a very real challenge in a more civilized way than the total meltdown "orchestrated" in the 1930s by the free-market system. The invisible hand will find a new balance, rapidly and efficiently. But the process can be very brutal.

Our government is doing everything possible—TARP, massive loan guarantees, QE1, QE2, and QE3—to stave off an inevitable debt crisis that will on its own solve the record levels of debt, ever-rising health care and education costs, rising oil prices, growing inequalities in incomes and wealth, runaway unfunded entitlements, and a loss of competitiveness for the United States around the world.

In contrast to the United States, Germany has insisted on an austerity program in Europe that will lead Europe deeper into an already evolving recession (though hedging its bets with a stealth QE policy by the ECB). I think that austerity is the better policy, as it always comes in the winter season of the economy, only once in a lifetime. Austerity is likely to create massive long-term benefits for many decades to come, akin to the great U.S. and global expansion after the Great Depression and World War II. It is the long-term economic equivalent of "the pause that refreshes." You only get to a new expansive spring season by going through winter! Japan never did, and the United States and most of Europe have not thus far.

We must stop denying that we have become addicted to debt and stimulus. Government budget and trade deficits have continued since 1970 and seem endless. Private debt grew at 2.7 times economic growth since the U.S. boom from 1983 into 2008. Keynesian economics suggests that governments should run deficits in down periods (like the 1970s) to offset declines in the private economy, but only after running surpluses in good times. Yet we started borrowing in the down times of the 1970s, then kept borrowing at all levels in the boom that followed. The policies of the U.S. government will look unbelievably irresponsible decades from now.

Our recommendation to investors, families, businesses, and most of all to politicians is simply to understand and to cooperate with this inevitable winter season, rather than to fight it. A winter season (such as 1930–42) is the most challenging of the four economic seasons, but it also historically has been the most productive and opportune, especially for those who understand it. History proves this, as winter clears the decks for spring and for a new, expansive economic cycle, playing on the mass innovations of the fall bubble season, like 1914–29 and 1994–2008.

None of the 2012 presidential candidates had a clue about what actually caused this economic crisis and why there are no magic near-term solutions. Democrats such as President Obama and leading economists like Paul Krugman recommend adding more debt and stimulus to counter the debt crisis. Even Obama's latest plan to restructure more mortgages at lower interest rates does not restructure mortgages to fair market value. The plan simply protects the banks from writing down bad loans and does not allow the loans to fail.

Why not restructure the massive $42 trillion in private debt that peaked in 2008 back down to pre-bubble levels of $20 trillion? That debt more than doubled between 2000 and 2008 and dwarfs federal debt, even now at $17 trillion and rising. Seeing this like a massive Chapter 11 reorganization (as occurs all the time in businesses) with a government-orchestrated restructuring could eliminate $22 trillion in debt, free up cash flow for consumers and businesses, and save something like $1.5 trillion a year in interest and principal for years and decades forward. Why not do this rather than try to stimulate consumers to spend and to borrow when they are already too much in debt as demographic trends naturally slow? This situation is true to different degrees for all aging, developed nations, which collectively still control over 60 percent of world GDP and even more of the wealth.

Republicans such as presidential candidates Mitt Romney and Newt Gingrich recommended cutting individual and corporate taxes to stimulate investment in new capacity and jobs. However, something like $3.7 trillion in cash already sits on the balance sheets of U.S. businesses—the businesses simply aren't investing. U.S. businesses are facing the lowest corporate borrowing rates in history and are borrowing mostly to buy back their stock and artificially increase their earnings per share. Yet having expanded too much during the great boom into 2007, businesses remain too much in debt and with too much capacity. I don't see a sustainable recovery in consumer demand beyond the short-term stimulus plans—and where they see demand is overseas, not in the United States. Why would corporations invest just because they had lower tax rates on their profits?

Consumers also are facing record debt levels, at nearly 100 percent of GDP, twice that at the top of the 1929 bubble peak. These consumers are not buying houses as in the past, even given record-low mortgage rates and the greatest stimulus plan in history. Why? The answer, again, is in the demographics, as the Baby Boom generation has peaked in its twenty-five-year rising Spending Wave from 1983 to 2007 (a forty-six-year lag on births for the peak in spending) and will be saving more, spending less, and paying down debt for years to come. The next generation will not create higher spending and borrowing trends until the early 2020s forward, and even at their peak, the level of real spending will not be as high.

In the face of this inaction, we must still restructure the largest private debt and real estate bubble in history, along the lines of the American innovation of Chapter 11 bankruptcy—and restructure the unprecedented level of government entitlements in line with expanding life expectancies to include later retirement and means-tested, cost-effective benefits. The United States cannot afford for everyone to have twenty-two-plus years of retirement pay and unlimited health care benefits. It *is* that simple. Such benefits are not plausible given aging societies worldwide and a slowing world economy.

The United States alone has $66 trillion in unfunded obligations for health care and retirement benefits, a number that is rising. All the developed countries are aging and have exponentially rising entitlement obligations. When you add up our private, government, and unfunded entitlements, our debt totals more than $120 trillion, or *eight times* the collective GDP!

When a company is in trouble, the creditors tend to lay siege, forcing a fire sale of the company's assets, just like short sellers in the investment arena. They are like vultures descending on a corpse. Chapter 11 laws created a new environment, in which the courts would protect a struggling company for a period of time to allow it to sell off assets at a more reasonable price, cut costs, and renegotiate debt with creditors. The idea is that you can go to creditors and say, "If you will take a 50 percent cut in your debt, we can pay that out of this restructuring, but if you force us into Chapter 7 liquidation of our assets, you are likely to get only 10 percent." If the creditors agree, it is a win-win for everyone and the company reemerges into growth again with lower debts and expenses.

It isn't only the city of Detroit: most developed countries are heading toward bankruptcy to some degree, and this realistic and practical solution, which addresses the root causes of unprecedented debt and aging demographics, is the type of restructuring that we need in the developed countries. We do not need more fiscal Band-Aids and short-term stimulus, which will fade again and again, leaving us with more debt and more "bubbly" markets that will crash again.

The Twelve Benefits of a Deflationary Crisis

Recall that the most powerful and overarching eighty-year economic cycle evolves in a four-season pattern. The winter season is again the most challenging, but also the most powerful. Preventing it will damage developed countries' longer-term growth prospects, because the economy is not allowed to rebalance itself after a fall bubble boom.

So let's summarize the benefits of austerity and the winter season. The long-term payoffs or twelve benefits that will come from a deflationary crisis are:

1. *Housing prices, the greatest single cost of living, will come down.* Interest rates will come down, too. This cost reduction will lead to a higher standard of living for the next generation, in this case, the Echo Boomers! Escalating health care and education costs also rapidly will come down to reality.

2. *Commercial real estate costs will fall.* That means lowering costs for businesses even further, including those related to education and health care and governmental entities, which are real estate intensive.

3. *Massive amounts of private debt will be restructured.* In this case, I'm talking about $42 trillion in the United States, restructured to somewhere near pre-bubble levels, at $20 trillion. Debt restructuring will lower principal and interest costs by as much as $1.5 trillion per year for decades ahead. That is the ultimate stimulus plan, and it benefits the private sector directly.

4. *The toughest will survive.* The survival-of-the-fittest struggle in businesses will shift market share to the strongest businesses to give them greater scale and lower costs, which will be passed on to consumers for decades ahead as better products for lower cost. This happened, for example, with GM and GE from the 1930s forward. That's how we raise our standard of living.

5. *Long-term entitlements will be restructured.* The shift will reflect the reality of our longer life span, and workers will stay in the workforce at least ten years longer. Thus, consumers will earn, save, and spend more over their lifetimes, bolstering aging economies in the developed world. The peak in spending will still occur among consumers in their late forties in age as their kids leave the nest, but the slowdown to follow will not be as extreme and the next boom will be stronger as a result.

6. *Commodity prices will fall.* From food to energy to materials like copper, lower prices will help to lower the cost of living, especially in emerging countries that consume more commodities. Commodity exporters will be hurt at first, but there will be an even greater commodity boom to follow, from around 2023 to 2039, for them to benefit.

7. *Dictatorships, too, will fall in emerging countries.* This will put such countries on an economic path toward democracy and economic development. This is already happening and will continue, although it may take a decade and more for these struggles to come to fruition. Developed countries will see more transparency and a second democratic and network revolution in business as well, like during the 1770s forward in America. Edward Snowden may not look like a traitor in the end.

8. *Developed countries will be more eco-conscious.* Developed countries will realize, as their demographic trends continue to slow and their savings and wealth build naturally with aging, that they will most benefit from investing in infrastructure and cleaner energies in the emerging world, which will accelerate development of these countries and lower global pollution—a win-win situation.

9. *Restraints on global trade and immigration will diminish.* Natural restrictions on trade and immigration in the crisis at first will make the global downturn worse and ultimately cause more nations to realize that free global trade and immigration are for the best. Thus, globalization will accelerate and specialization of labor and trade will expand again in the spring season to follow.

10. *Developed countries will trend into higher-value customized products and services.* Developed countries will realize that they cannot compete in commodities and low-cost labor industries. These countries will be forced to move more rapidly into customized goods and services through network organizations that operate from the bottom up, not the top down. This trend will create a new, mass affluence in the developed world that will pass down over time into the emerging world, albeit to lesser degrees.

11. *Income inequality will decrease.* During the fall bubble boom, most of the benefits went to the 1 percent (top income earners), who were the innovators and financiers. In this crisis and beyond, the 1 percent will lose wealth and income on a relative basis as their innovations move mainstream and benefit the everyday worker, as from 1942 to 1972. The middle class will be restored at a higher level and will see greater gains in income and wealth than will the top 1 percent for decades ahead.

12. *New technology will be a driver.* Long-term innovations in technologies will emerge, including things like nanotechnologies that make goods out of thin air; robotics that take over everyday functions, high and low; biotechnologies that replace and regrow organs; cleaner, more affordable energies; and things we can't yet envision. If we could live to be 120 years old or older that would greatly extend our demographic cycles of learning/innovating, earning/spending, and changing society in our older, power years of wealth and influence. It could return growth and competitive advantages back to developed countries again.

There is another key issue here: The U.S. dollar has been the reserve currency since the English pound receded after World War II. As any country builds an empire its currency becomes the dominant reserve currency. This means its currency is used more for trade and becomes more valuable, allowing it to import more cheaply to support the growing costs of its empire and grow its standard of living through lower cost imports. But at some point, like the 1940s for England and now for the United States, it becomes too costly to extend and maintain such an empire. Such dominant countries buy more from the world and stimulate export industries around the world—which means they extend credit and create more of their reserve currency to facilitate world trade. The exporting countries then turn around and buy the government bonds of the importing or reserve currency nation. This is another form of stimulus or money and debt creation to facilitate more trade on more credit. This is another way of creating a bubble. But of course, all bubbles come to an end!

When the dominant countries like the United States today slow down and lose such dominance, they start importing less and that is like a contraction in credit on a global scale. The U.S. trade deficit has declined consistently since 2008 after expanding since 1970, and will shrink more or even turn into a surplus in the next great downturn. The United States is now increasingly becoming an exporter of oil and natural gas, and that will only add toward trade surpluses in the years and decades ahead. The reserve currency for global trade then contracts, just like the money supply or credit for a nation. This then tends to lead to global currency wars (or trade tariffs back in the early 1930s) that make the downturn worse. But that also means that the reserve currency tends to go up from lower trade deficits. I have also argued in Chapter 4 that the deleveraging of debt, more in U.S. dollars than any other currency, will destroy dollars and make them more valuable.

The global currency war is already accelerating after the United States accelerated its money printing with QE3 at a higher rate, followed by Japan going off the reservation and accelerating its money printing to a rate 2.5 times that of the United States when adjusted for the size of its economy. And China has accelerated as well with even greater plans for urbanization and money printing. Will Europe be next? Then what happens? I say "ka-boom" to world trade in the next few years, as in the early 1930s! But the end result is likely that other countries, like Japan, print more than the U.S. ahead, and the U.S. dollar goes up, not down, while its trade deficit continues to decline.

Everything I see from debt deleveraging to shrinking U.S. trade deficits suggests strongly that the U.S. dollar will rise in the years ahead, not fall, despite rising QE. And even QE may taper near term. The U.S. dollar and dollar-denominated assets are the safe haven for the years ahead, at least into 2016.

One of the largest shifts ahead for decades to come will be the restoration of the middle class (see the historical pattern in Figure 9-4). The top 1 percent of income earners controlled almost 20 percent of income in 1929, but only 8 percent of income by 1976. Their share of income rose back to 18 percent in 2007. The top 0.1 percent of income earners controlled in 1929 at their peak 10 percent of income; their share fell to 2 percent in 1976 and then rose again to 8 percent in 2007. Although the rich remained rich, the massive decline from 1929 to 1976 represented a big loss in economic dominance for the top 1 percent and the biggest rise in history for the middle class. This was true to a slightly lesser degree for the top 10 percent and 20 percent.

In the fall season, wealth shifts dramatically to the top 1 percent to as

Figure 9-4: Income of Top 0.1% and 1%, 1913-2011

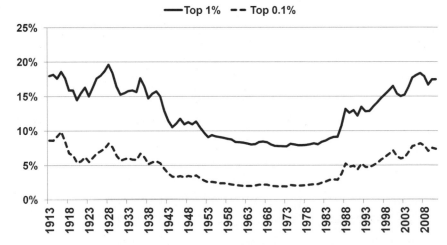

Data Source: Alvaredo, Facundo, Anthony B. Atkinson, Thomas Piketty and Emmanuel Saez, The World Top Incomes Database, http://g-mond.parisschoolofeconomics.eu/topincomes, 2013

high as 40 percent to 47 percent. When the bubbles deflate in the winter season, many of the financial assets and companies owned by the top earners decline sharply or fail, and the government raises taxes the most on those with the highest incomes. The cost of living comes down and new technologies become more mainstream and accessible, which helps the everyday household more than it does the top 1 percent to 10 percent.

We predict that incomes and wealth will rise faster for the average household than for the top 1 percent to 10 percent for at least three decades or more, restoring the middle class, as happened from the mid-1930s into the early 1970s.

I am certain that all four seasons of our economy have challenges and clear long-term benefits. All four seasons exist for a reason and occur in all human, technological, and natural cycles, both long- and short-term. The key is to understand such cycles—to take out your coats and snow skis and store your bathing suits and water skis in the winter season—and to prepare for, take advantage of, and benefit from this most severe and most opportune season. The businesses of the future and a new, more affluent middle class will emerge in the coming decades to generate productivity and higher standards of living, even in aging countries that are facing inevitable demographic slowdowns and/or slower growth in the future.

Restructuring Inflation in Education, Health Care, and Financial Services

The greatest liabilities in the future for our economy and government come in the largest and fastest-growing information-intensive service sectors: education, health care, and financial services. Education and health care have outstripped the Consumer Price Index (CPI) by a wide margin, especially private education (see Figure 9-5). Surprise, surprise! These two sectors are in a bubble.

Private education has seen the greatest inflation by far of any major consumer category, and for decades. The CPI has averaged 3.3 percent since 1980, health care 5.5 percent, while education has averaged a whopping

Figure 9-5: Education, Healthcare Costs vs. CPI

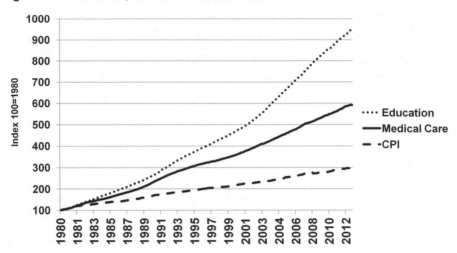

Data Source: Bureau of Labor Statistics, 2013

7.4 percent and has been accelerating more since 2001. This obviously is not sustainable.

How did this happen? Start with sharply rising demand from the many Baby Boom parents who value their kids' education above anything else. Then add limited supply of colleges, the high fixed costs for campuses, and the limited supply of professors and teachers. The education system has had us parents over a barrel and has simply raised costs dramatically in an information revolution where you would think costs of education would go down, not up, as has occurred in computers and software.

What causes bubbles to burst? When they get so high no one can afford them anymore, like the housing bubble that peaked in early 2006. It was not a falling economy that caused home prices to peak and begin to fall. Young new households that dominate the market simply could not afford to buy a home. Now fewer students believe they will get sufficient return on their (or their parents') investment.

One way we've kept the bubble going is by making college loans easier to get and more affordable. Now we have $1 trillion in a recent bubble of government loans to students, and that bubble is bursting as defaults are rising rapidly (see Figure 9-6).

Figure 9-6: Student Loan Bubble

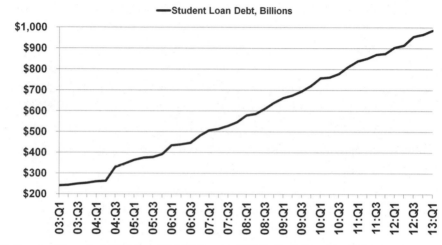

Data Source: Household Debt and Credit Report, N.Y. Federal Reserve, 2013

We're reaching the point in education where more students don't get a positive rate of return on a four-year degree. William Bennett, former secretary of education, just recently published a book called *Is College Worth It?* He says that only 150 of 3,500 colleges are worth attending, meaning that they have a positive return on investment.

The cost of high-end private colleges is something like $200,000 plus for four years. What if you just invested that money? Most kids would be millionaires within twenty to thirty years and be able to retire at age forty to fifty.

Bennett's top 10 schools out of the 3,500 tend to be Ivy League–level schools such as Stanford, Harvard, and Yale. I've always seen these schools as a screen for the brightest and most motivated young people; the fact that you got in and graduated puts you in the top tier for jobs whether the education is really that superior or not. I talked to someone who used to be on the board for deciding which applicants to accept at Harvard Business School, where I went. He told me, "We try to find people that are already going to succeed and then try not to interfere with that."

Bennett also believes that if you specialize in practical skills like engineering or applied science or business, a degree from a second-tier college or university can pay off. So, given soaring education costs, the best payoffs come from the best schools and the degrees that bring desired job skills, rather than philosophy or English literature.

Bennett reports that 46 percent of students who start college don't finish. In a difficult economy in which more college graduates are underemployed, the students who don't finish are at an even greater disadvantage. Among other things, how will they pay off their loans? Many will not. Won't that affect their ability to buy a house or get a mortgage loan? You bet it will!

The answer? Rising inflation is a natural economic process that stimulates investment for new innovations. The inflation of the 1970s produced the personal computer revolution and cell phones, among other things. The inflation in this low-inflation era is in education, health care, and financial services. That's where innovation is most needed.

The Next Decade Is a Revolution in Education

The first problem in education is tenure and the consequent high cost of teachers, who have insured their futures against the interests of parents and students. Tenure will have to be revamped to reward higher productivity and later retirement. As in health care where nurses provide more services at lower cost, more teachers will have to be allowed in more areas at lower degrees and salaries. This process has already begun with the advent of adjuncts at many colleges and universities.

The second problem is the huge fixed cost of real estate and facilities. In an Internet world, campuses may be reduced by half as students take some classes live and others online. That result will be a massive savings in costs. Colleges could sell off or lease facilities to businesses or research groups.

An even more significant benefit of Internet learning is that students can have access to the best professors and experts around the world, not just the professors on a particular campus. If a college or a network of universities offered me the opportunity to offer Internet real-time and/or recorded courses to tens or hundreds of thousands of students at a time, would I do that at a low per student cost (say, absurd as it sounds, 50 cents) in order to help our younger people navigate the future? You bet I would! It is not economical for me to go around and speak to individual student classes around the world. But it would be on Internet-delivered seminars with charts, Q&A, and everything else. I assume many experts would want to help students around the world at all levels.

Students should have a course and career concierge (or "browser," as I call it in chapter 8) that helps them identify their aptitudes and natural talents, and then tailors appropriate coursework to them in physical classrooms and on the Internet. The quality of education should increase through increasing personalization as the costs ultimately go down.

One of the essential needs (and opportunities) I see in education is helping students to understand their core strengths and weaknesses early on. The people who naturally get this early like Bill Gates, Michael Dell, or Steve Jobs seem to build the greatest learning curves and success. In fact, more often than not they have to leave the slow, plodding, standardized education system as they learn to focus more on their strengths and learn according to better and faster approaches.

I have seen a number of aptitude and personality tests that are very revealing and predictive. For example, in *The Creative Brain* (1998) Ned Herrmann talked about how we are different, depending upon how our brains are wired thanks to genetics and early childhood. He divides the brain's functions into four quadrants, and, after reading the book, I took a simple test to measure mine.

When his company sent back an analysis, it showed I was wired first in the upper right quadrant (creative/intuitive), second in the upper left (analytical and logical), third in the lower right (relational and communicative), and fourth in the lower left (details and administrative). My destiny and results were summarized in two simple phrases: financial forecasting and research and development—you couldn't peg me better than that. I wish I had had an educational counselor advising me to take a battery of such tests decades earlier; that would have allowed me to focus on what I was meant to do much earlier. There are many tests and seminars out there that can get people to realize their natural aptitudes (from the inside out) and even a new test from Sally Hogshead (at www.howtofascinate.com) that will tell you how others perceive you and how to position yourself in your business and relations to be more successful.

Guiding people to leverage their strengths in education is increasingly more important than educating them for the sake of education (although learning to learn is certainly crucial). How important is basic math when computers can do it in a nanosecond? For me, it is important to be able to do a lot of math in my head in both analysis and research and negotiations, but for many others, the computer can do it. I used to have a larger research staff until I realized I could just get an answer on Google faster than by deputizing a researcher to seek the information for me.

With education costs so high, this revolution is coming sooner rather than later. The failing economy will only accelerate this natural and inevitable process as the return on investment will only go down in a worsening jobs and economic environment. Suddenly schools and colleges will not have us over a barrel anymore. They will have to innovate and join the network revolution in organization, efficiency, and more personalized and customized service. We will say good-bye to tenure and massive campuses with endless statues and lush landscaping.

My stepdaughter made a great decision that we supported. She went to Long Island University and a program called Friends World College (now renamed LIU Global). She got to travel around the world and study in different countries and do real-life projects to help in those countries. We all need to become more international and educate our kids to be as well. We need hands-on learning, not just academic, and we need work-for-credit programs with businesses and nonprofit institutions. Learning key languages such as Spanish and Mandarin and Hindi will also bring major advantages in the future.

Again, the education system should be reorganized and personalized to suit individual aptitudes and the needs of the young and older student. It should leverage the Internet to deliver the best experts around the world, anytime, anywhere—at greater scale and lower costs. More education should be delivered real-time, outside of expensive classrooms, but there should still be live education and interaction in the sectors of education that require that, including apprenticeships with businesses and travel and experience of other cultures in an increasingly global world where emerging countries will soon dominate future growth.

The Revolution in Health Care and Retirement

Unfunded entitlements for Medicare, Medicaid, and Social Security are estimated at $66 trillion—that alone is over four times GDP, more than total private and government debt currently—and the costs are rising. This impending crisis will hit slowly but progressively over the next two to three decades, as Baby Boomers retire in unprecedented numbers as shown in Figure 9-7. The peak will be reached between 2025 and 2026 (or perhaps later, as more of us stay in the workforce longer). The unfortunate precedent is the Japanese, mired in their coma economy.

The average retirement age of sixty-three will need to rise in the coming decades, as Baby Boomers come to accept that they don't have the funds to retire in a worsening economy and the returns on their meager retirement funds are much lower than expected. There is no way that the entitlements can be paid for over the coming decades, as falling births and immigration will make the old-to-young ratio even higher than economists and world organizations are forecasting.

Citizens in all developed countries are in denial about their ability to collect upon retirement and health care promises made to them by governments and corporations during the greatest boom in history between 1983 and 2007. The next downturn will very likely be greater than the one in 2008–09 and will bring a greater crisis and sense of reality on everything—but especially our debt and our entitlements.

The simplest truths are that our life expectancies have been rising for

Figure 9-7: Retirement Wave, 63 – 65-year Lag on Immigration-adjusted Birth Index

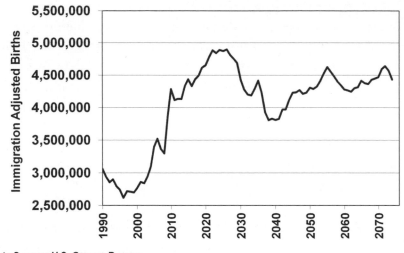

Data Source: U.S. Census Bureau

decades and we haven't adjusted our retirement age for that. We should be retiring at ages seventy-two to seventy-five, not sixty-two to sixty-five! Just adjusting Medicare/Medicaid and Social Security for our growing life expectancies would cure the largest part of our projected massive deficits and unfunded entitlements.

The reality today from life insurance actuaries is that if you live to age sixty-three, you are likely to live to age eighty-five, and that number rises one-year-plus per decade. If you do the math, you find the average person enters the workforce around ages twenty to twenty-one and works until age sixty-three, and then will live until age eighty-five (and most couples will have someone live until around age ninety, likely the woman). That translates to forty-two years of working and twenty-two years of retirement and health care benefits. It's simply absurd to think that we can work for two years for every one year of retirement. If there were a much bigger working generation to follow, like the Baby Boom that followed the Bob Hope generation, this might be remotely feasible, but only through subsidies from the larger generation. But the Echo Boom generation in most developed countries is not as large, and in countries with virtually no Echo Boom, there are declining workforce trends for decades to come.

Japan is the fastest-aging country (see chapter 2), but Germany is also a case I point to as its workforce, normally defined as ages twenty to sixty-four, will decline by 33 percent from 49.5 million in 2010 to 33 million by 2060, and 14 percent by 2030 (see Figure 9-8). Germany is one of the first countries to get real and increase its retirement age from sixty-five to sixty-seven. What if it kept doing that and raised it to seventy-four by 2030, sixteen years from now? Its workforce could rise from 49.5 to 54 million instead of falling to 43 million by 2030. That is a huge difference: 11 million workers, or 25.6 percent of the projected 2030 workforce.

Figure 9-8: Germany Workforce Growth Projections, age 20 – 64 vs. 20 – 74

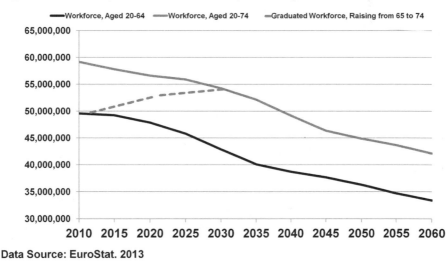

Data Source: EuroStat. 2013

All developed countries are going to have to raise their retirement rates, and a global crisis ahead will accelerate that process! This one change alone would eliminate most of the unfunded liabilities for national retirement and health care plans. This shift can't happen over several decades, as most Baby Boomers in developed countries will already be retired by 2025–30.

The most radical statement I can make here is this: *Retirement is bullshit!* It is a concept that has emerged since the 1940s and it just doesn't make sense.

Social Security was started in 1939 more as an early retirement program. In the 1930s, the older generation stayed in the workforce much later in a bad economy, and that crowded out jobs for the younger Bob Hope generation. Social Security was not meant to be a twenty-plus-year drop-out-and-play-shuffleboard program. People back then didn't live that far past their sixties. Now they do.

Equally important: Why would people want to drop out and do nothing? That doesn't make most people happy. They are more fulfilled when they are doing something for others—I've said this before, but it's true: It's what we humans were made for. It is more natural to keep working as long as your health is good. Work a bit less, maybe, and focus on more fulfilling contributions. But drop out altogether and play golf or sit at a pool? If you go to emerging countries, older people work until they die, and if they have health problems, the family largely takes care of them.

A more sensible approach is to target a retirement period of more like ten years to deal with aging and health challenges, not twenty-plus years. It makes sense to have people work longer to contribute more to government retirement (and health care) funding systems and draw money out of them for fewer years.

Another of my favorite mainstream economists is Bob McTeer, former Dallas Fed governor. He has endorsed my demographic leading indicators as "a way to see around the corners." He also characterizes most economists as "closet extrapolators." I couldn't agree more. For entitlement programs to work out in the longer term, overly rosy long-term forecasts of 4 percent plus growth and 1 percent to 2 percent inflation made by government economists must come true. This calculus fails to account for long-term downturns like 1930–42, 1969–82, and 2008–23. It relies upon greatly overstated forecasts for U.S. population growth, given that immigration slows dramatically in downturns and new births slow. Immigration slowed from the highest levels in U.S. history between 1907 and 1914 into the early 1930s to near zero! Births slowed from 1922 into 1933 and bottomed just after the greatest stock crash and depression in U.S. history—people have fewer kids when they wonder if they can support them. Who would migrate to a depressed economy with all of the risks and costs? Citizens also react by voting to restrict immigration when their jobs are threatened.

I've predicted in each of my books that immigration and births would decline substantially in the United States in the winter season of 2008–23. It's happening. Births for the Echo Boom saw a second peak in 2007 and have fallen ever since. Immigration, especially from Mexico, our greatest source by far, has plummeted much more so, since 2007.

Predictions for the rise in the ratio of over-sixty-five to working-age populations, as dire as they seem, are most likely *underestimating* the trend, as they are projecting about 60 million immigrants and births in the United States, which will not occur in a slowing economy.

The Bottom-Up Revolution in Health Care

I heard a story recently about an overwhelmed emergency room. Somebody came up with the idea of charging a $5 cash fee for registering at the ER. That simple, modest charge cut the flow by *60 percent*!

When end consumers think something is free, they are going to overuse and undervalue it. That may be the biggest problem with our overall health care system in the United States. No one is accountable, especially at the end-consumer level. Then there are all of the special interest groups that exploit the system.

We can't fix the present health care system any more than we can fix our tax code; special interests have been rigging them for decades and remain on hand today to defend their turf to the death. We need a radical restructuring and a revolution in health care. Such changes will only occur in a major crisis where we suddenly realize at all levels that the health care system (like the retirement system) is broken—and broke.

This is the genius of the winter season. Its primary purpose is to purge the system of debt, financial bubbles, inefficiencies, and special interests that naturally build up in a long boom through the spring, summer, and fall seasons. As we stated earlier in this chapter, our governments are keeping the fall bubble going and protecting banks, special interests, retirement systems, and a bloated health care system from a radical restructuring. A major crisis in the years ahead is the only hope for the United States and other developed countries to solve their long-term debt and entitlement imbalances. Thus far, doing it incrementally or diplomatically has proved politically incorrect and impossible.

I've talked about the network revolution in business (see chapter 8) and, earlier in this chapter, about such a revolution in education. Obviously, similar changes would benefit the health care system.

We need an insurance system that does not encourage unlimited use of medical services and equipment in an era when costs are skyrocketing here faster than any other sector outside of education (see Figure 9-5). I believe everyone should have catastrophic insurance with lower premiums, as in most health savings account (HSA) plans, and then have to pay for most of their normal health costs with the savings in premiums. That way people would be more sensitive to the relationship of costs to benefits. This is what I do, and I don't waste money on health care.

When more people pay for their week-to-week and month-to-month costs on their credit card, the bureaucracy will diminish, with fewer forms to fill out and co-pays to calculate. Again, I pay for most of my care with a credit card. End of story, no bureaucracy and extra paperwork.

In many European systems, medical education is subsidized. Doctors are a good investment and a scarce resource, and governments can borrow more cheaply than individuals. Then the physicians are given salaries in a government-driven system, which takes away the incentive to overprescribe tests, procedures, and drugs unless they are effective. Putting many basic services on a one-payer government-driven system also creates greater economies of scale in purchasing the most basic services.

My inclination is to favor the private sector in most industries, but this is not one of them. Our health care is too unaccountable, with perverse incentives across the board to overspend on things that don't work or treat only the symptoms rather than the cause, which can result in more long-term harm than good. An example? Prescribing painkillers and antibiotics for instant relief from everything and at costs covered largely by insurance policies so the patient doesn't feel the cost—except when your insurance premium keeps rising down the road. That's like punishing your kid a year after he does something wrong.

The United States has the highest health care costs by far and the poorest performance in health and life expectancy versus our peers in Europe, East Asia, and elsewhere, which typically spend half as much per person on health care. Things like bypass surgery can cost twice to four times as much or more here as in other developed countries. We need to have greater government involvement and consolidation in many areas and more private participation in others—like a single-payer government system for the most basic health care for everyone. Then the private system would cover more voluntary services and with HSA-like plans, not across-the-board coverage.

Finally, we need the new network model in this industry. General practitioners (GPs) should increasingly focus on very distinct segments ("browsers") of clients, from affluent, aging concierge medicine, to children and teenagers, to young adults, and so on. We need to focus on what each segment needs and what works best in their affordability range. The browsers will be referred to "servers" that focus on narrow expertise in everything from childhood infections to physical rehabilitation, from special surgeries to detox programs. It is the GP's job to get you the services you need and can afford when you need them. Specialists will work at a scale that brings more affordability (expensive equipment not used at high rates causes costs to go up dramatically).

Here's my commonsense view if you look at the best practices in health care around the world. There should be a government-driven one-payer system for the most basic health care services for all. That brings universal care and economies of scale and bargaining power to lower costs. Then everything above that is covered by private insurance but with government rules that you have to cover everyone regardless of prior conditions. What use is insurance if once you have a problem the cost goes up or you become uninsurable? Then governments should encourage high-deductible HSA-like plans that only cover more catastrophic expenses—not everyday health care, which people should cover themselves and be more accountable for.

Like the free-market system in business, we need rules that force the system to work for the benefit of the whole, not just the strongest. The greatest reality is that we cannot afford to extend highly expensive benefits beyond the basics to everyone as health care costs and potential solutions are only going up exponentially over time. We cannot afford to allow an expensive operation for someone who only has a short period of time to live, unless it is covered by private insurance or by the patient's family. Thirty to fifty percent of health care costs come in the last year or so of life by different studies and estimates. That is the greatest reality we simply have to face and come to grips with.

Restructuring Financial Services

Governments must also have a role in restructuring financial services. There are no substantial economies of scale in combining banks, investment banks, investment management firms, brokerage firms, and insurance firms. Ultimately each has a very different function, and it becomes a conflict of interest when a brokerage firm that is supposed to find the best investments for you is recommending the products of an affiliated investment management firm rather than taking an independent approach and truly representing you.

We've also seen banks and insurance firms with investment management arms that blew up after taking on massive leverage, threatening the viability and assets of the larger companies. In the case of AIG, for example, its insurance business didn't implode in 2008; it was a small investment division of the company that bet twice the market value of all of AIG on credit default swaps, a leveraged bet that real estate would keep going up.

One simple reform should be that no investment firm can leverage more than ten times, and even that should be for legitimate hedging, not speculation. Speculation only grows when allowed and encouraged by very low interest rates, and it never ends up benefiting the economy or investors. The Glass-Steagall Banking Act of 1933, a program instituted after the 1929 stock crash and bubble burst, was rescinded in 1996. By then, we had forgotten the earlier lessons. Why not let banks, investment banks, and brokerage firms merge and create greater entities with economies of scale and cross-marketing? The move helped bring on the same disaster the earlier generation had sought to prevent. We should separate these different arms of the financial services industry for greater integrity and safety, and at the same time reduce the too-big-to-fail paradigm that just keeps growing as governments protect large banks and financial institutions from failing—so they just get bigger.

You as a consumer or business need to choose financial firms that represent you, not their chain of partners. You need independent financial advisers, and banks that are not heavily laden with bad real estate loans and may not be able to make good on your deposit one day. Keep only the minimum balance needed for transactions in checking and savings deposits. Stow the rest in an investment account in your name, as banks cannot lend against that.

Finally, governments need to help their citizens do the right thing when it comes to savings. In the United States we have payroll taxes that go into a public program for Social Security, but this isn't the savings program it is touted to be as it takes today's contributions and pays them out to retired older people. When there is a larger generation to follow, this approach—it's really a sort of Ponzi scheme—can work. But the pyramid will fall in the decades ahead.

Australia has a system of forced savings into "superannuation" accounts in which workers and the self-employed have to save a certain amount of their income, but they get to invest it in their own account (like a 401[k]) for retirement. It's "super" because compound interest makes savings at an early age accumulate unbelievably. But most of us humans are wired to reach for the marshmallow today rather than three tomorrow. Governments need to enforce savings programs to combat our worst tendencies to not save and compound. Just a small percent per year from the early twenties forward will grow and make more people secure, both against unforeseen challenges and for retirement. And if retirement is pushed back into the seventies as I recommend, then the savings will compound even more.

It's no accident that Australia's government has the lowest debt in the developed world, and its citizens have some of the highest financial assets. Partly it's due to such strong real estate appreciation, but more to its forced savings policy.

The Advantage of Immigration

Over the course of the eighty-year economic cycle, immigration tends to be favored by the more individualistic generations, like the Baby Boom, which drive the summer season of innovation and the fall bubble boom. The two major peaks in net immigration into the United States over the last 120 years occurred in 1907 and 1991, 84 years apart. This is no accident as it follows the eighty-year, four-season economic cycle. The Henry Ford generation brought us cars, electricity, phones, and radios—and the largest relative immigration wave in history when compared with population. The Baby Boom then brought us the PC, cell phones, the Internet, and broadband—and the next-largest relative immigration wave in U.S. history.

Immigration slowed substantially from World War I into the Roaring Twenties (see Figure 9-9), then dropped to near zero in the early 1930s as the worst downturn in history both discouraged the entry of immigrants and their acceptance by jobless citizens. The more important trend was that

Figure 9-9: U.S. Immigration, 1820-2012

Data Source: Department of Homeland Security, 2013

immigration did not return to anywhere near the levels of 1907–14 in the next boom driven by the Bob Hope generation. These more civic and conformist generations are not as open to outside cultures invading their countries.

Today, we have a similar fall in immigration; the many people returning to Mexico have offset the immigrants from Mexico between 2005 and 2010 (see Figure 9-10). Our neighbor to the south was our largest source of immigrants in the past decades, but a lot of illegals who feel less and less welcome are going home now that our economy is not very good and Mexico's economy is doing better.

Figure 9-10: Net Immigration from Mexico

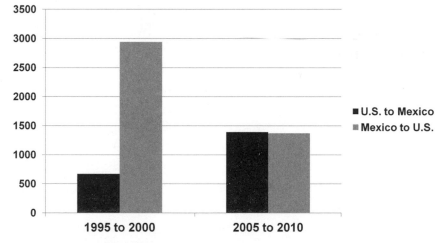

Data Source: Pew Research Hispanic Center, 2013

The Echo Boom, or millennial generation, is not likely to allow the strong immigration of the 1980s and 1990s, though they are more global and culturally diverse than the Bob Hope generation before them. The odds are that immigration will not return to the peak levels of the early 1990s in the decades ahead in the United States. That would be unfortunate, as immigrants bring diversity, innovation, and younger demographic trends to a country that is well suited to integrating them.

Immigration is also an advantage economically, rather like exports that leverage workers with higher-paying jobs and lower unemployment. There is an obvious price, of course: your culture gets diluted and changed. I can understand countries that don't encourage immigration for such social reasons, but that is a political choice. From an economic perspective, immigration is a positive factor. The difference between wealthy countries in East Asia and southern Europe versus the United States, Canada, Australia, and New Zealand is that the latter group is younger and more innovative due to immigration.

Given both the strong economic pluses and cultural challenges of immigration, the best policies come from countries like Canada, Australia, and Singapore, where immigration is strongly encouraged but the governments are selective in seeking skills and qualities in those who are admitted. There is less disparity in incomes and cultures between Australians and more educated Asians that they seek in comparison to the United States, where a high percentage of immigrants arrive illegally with lower educations and incomes. But those groups do fill critical jobs that U.S. citizens shun. Their incomes grow rapidly, and their kids learn English and integrate into the culture very effectively.

The United States is known both for attracting many of the best foreign students and for forcing many to return to their country due to quotas— even as hundreds of thousands of immigrants arrive each year via largely unprotected borders. This will change, likely in late 2013 or early 2014. Democrats and Republicans both want stronger borders—but such policies are being put in place at a time when immigration from Mexico is dropping like a rock. Why spend so much money there? Most of us also want to keep the higher-skill students. The difference comes in the path to citizenship for past illegals.

Where I come down on this issue is simple: if we did not enforce our borders for decades then we were sending a message that this is acceptable. I think every effort should be made to legalize the existing illegals, to give them a path to citizenship that requires some fines and efforts but is not onerous—we shouldn't be deporting parents and separating them from their kids or vice versa. The borders should be enforced and the illegality made clear in the future, but we should not overspend on physical barriers when immigration is already dropping because of natural economic trends.

All aging developed countries will be competing for the best students and immigrants in the future. The key is to target the skills and qualifications, high and low, that your country needs and to encourage such immigrants (as Australia, Singapore, and Canada do so well) to remain and buy real estate in a long-term slow market with excess capacity for decades to come. The countries that have English as their first language, or where it is commonly spoken, have an advantage here, as any immigrant would tend to want to learn English if they had to learn a second language—and that should be part of the citizenship qualifications to some degree. Countries like Japan, and eventually South Korea, need immigration badly and have great education systems, but the lack of broader English language is a major deterrent.

Maternity Benefits and Birth Rates

In the East Asian and European countries that are aging the fastest, there is a common denominator. These countries and regions are holding on to an old ethic that women do housework and are there to serve men. If an Italian woman has a baby, it's her baby, as men don't do housework or deal with kids. After getting that picture, women tend to have one child and then just don't get pregnant again.

In northern Europe, and especially in the Scandinavian countries where governments give and insure strong maternity benefits, a woman doesn't have to feel like having a baby is going to conflict with her job. In northern Europe, North America, Australia, and New Zealand, men have increasingly shared in household tasks and raising the kids.

Certainly it seemed natural enough to have a culture where women focus more on household tasks when they didn't have to work thirty to forty hours a week. But in an altered, two-career world, the woman of the household can hardly be expected to work full-time and do all of the household chores. If that's the standard, they will respond by having fewer and fewer babies—and your country and culture will commit slow suicide.

Governments will have to work through policies and cultural mandates and education that encourage more support for working women who have kids, and even tax rebates. Every country's future is at stake if they do not encourage better maternity policies and child-care assistance.

Slower Population Growth and Infrastructure

Fighting immigration is a natural impulse to protect jobs, but it's short-sighted—and it's going to happen naturally anyway.

I have been warning for decades that, during the winter season from 2008 to 2023, immigration will fall precipitously and births will decline substantially. This means the population estimates that our government and international agencies such as the UN make are far too optimistic. The government projects 420 million in population in the United States by 2060; I see 360 million. That's a huge difference.

I get the argument all the time that we are going to need more housing and infrastructures in the decades ahead. That I don't see. If there are going to be as many or more people dying than being born or entering the workforce, how could our population grow much—especially with growing anti-immigration sentiment in the United States and many other countries and falling immigration during downturns like this one?

The contrast between birth projections by the Census Bureau and my projections is instructive (see Figure 9-11). The gap between the more realistic scenario I paint and the government's typical straight-line extrapolation is huge, and, if anything, I am being a bit generous. If I am right about a depression ahead and an on-and-off weak economy over the coming decade, there is no question, based on historic precedents, that births will continue to fall substantially, as will immigration. Given an aging population and a slower economy even in growth periods, births are not likely to rise all the way back to the highs in 2007.

My projections versus the government's for immigration diverge in a similar fashion (see Figure 9-12). Notice that immigration dropped to near zero in the early 1930s and did not come back very fast in the spring boom to follow in the 1950s. The more collective and civic generations, like the Bob Hope

Figure 9-11: U.S. Births and Projections, Census Bureau vs. Dent Research

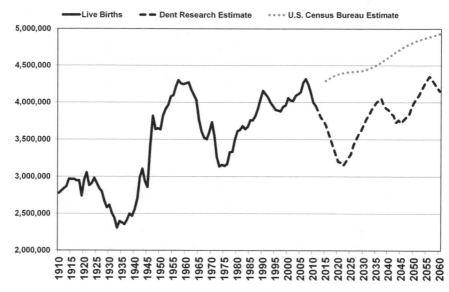

Data Source: U.S. Census Bureau

and Echo Boom, don't tend to be as open to immigrants. They also naturally react to the very strong immigration cycle that comes before and go the other way.

The difference between my estimates for births and immigration into 2060 and the government's population forecasts reveals a complicated picture (see Figure 9-13: 360 million in population by 2060 versus 420 million, and that is growing from 316 million in 2013). My calculations anticipate 44 million people added in forty-seven years, or 936,000 a year on average, or 0.27 percent growth. That comes to more like 20 million households or 425,000 per year. The government's forecasts foresee 104 million people and a growth rate of 0.6 percent, about 940,000 households a year.

One impact of a smaller number would be a workforce that starts shrinking (unless we retire much later); hence, the need for office space will be virtually nothing. Will we really need massive new infrastructures, homes, and offices? The decade ahead will continue to see the lowest long-term

Figure 9-12: U.S. Immigration and Projections, Census Bureau vs. Dent Research

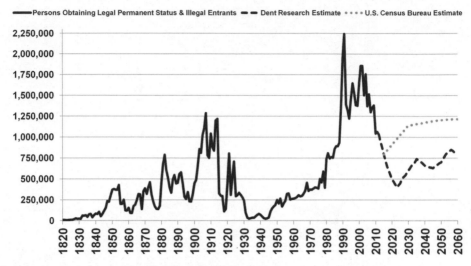

Data Source: Department of Homeland Security, 2013

interest rates of a lifetime, so it's a great time for governments to invest in long-term infrastructures. But what we really need is information systems that make us more productive, more than basic transportation, housing, and offices. Government needs to invest in things that will pay off the debt and create profits and productivity.

TO SUMMARIZE—In the coming years, governments need to:

1. Stop using short-term stimulus to fight a long-term structural challenge from high debt ratios and slowing demographics, as they are only perverting the very market systems that can allow us to rebalance and position for growth, efficiency, and innovation again.

2. Actively assist in restructuring and writing down private debt and only assist financial institutions to the degree that they write down debt for consumers and businesses. This will free up cash flow for the private sector in a down economy.

Figure 9-13: Population and Forecasts: Census Bureau vs. Dent Research

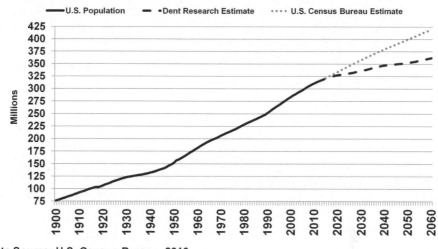

Data Source: U.S. Census Bureau, 2013

3. Encourage a more radical restructuring of education, health care, and financial services, to make them more consumer-centric, more accountable, less bureaucratic, and more bottom-up.

4. Transition rapidly to more realistic retirement ages (such as seventy-five) to save entitlement systems and put in place a means by which the age of retirement rises in the future to align with continued increases in life expectancy.

5. Attract immigrants (especially the higher-skilled), not repel them to defend jobs in the downturn. Create a path to citizenship for the illegal immigrants in the United States who are now leaving rapidly.

6. Ensure better maternity benefits for working women so fertility rates do not continue to fall. Target increased fertility rates in the coming decades.

7. Invest in select long-term infrastructures, like information systems that increase productivity given record low interest rates, or alternative energy, water, and wastewater systems that reduce pollution.

Avoid overestimating future needs for basic infrastructure given rapidly slowing births and immigration.

Governments have lost sight of the very dynamics that drive our progress and standard of living as they react to adverse debt and demographic trends. We need a wake-up call, and that is called the winter season!

There could not be a better time for revolutionary change in government, business, and lifestyles. In the closing pages of this book, I will talk about what I foresee in our near future: the first major political, business, and social revolution since the late 1700s.

A MAJOR REVOLUTION BREWS
EVERY 250 YEARS

Governments need to cooperate with the invisible hand of free-market capitalism, permitting the natural processes of progress and evolution to take their course. The miracle of democracy enables opposite principles to coexist in a dynamic interplay of growth and change, bringing the benefits to a broader base of people, not just the elite who naturally innovate and create most of the wealth. It's a simple fact that if more people participate in economic growth and innovation, the whole system and the most people benefit.

While I espouse free-market capitalism as much as anyone, every game needs rules and simple regulations to ensure competition and balance, to ensure that the benefits of innovation and growth reach more of the people and are not confined to mafias, monopolies, and established special interests looking to guarantee their continued success, whether deserved or not. But regulations have to be as simple and minimal as possible and not strangle the creative system.

That does not describe our system.

Today Washington, D.C., and Wall Street represent the epitome of power and manipulation in America—and they are obviously in cahoots! Only a major financial crisis they can't control will end this imbalance. That's why I welcome an economic crisis and transition: it is the only way out of the mess that has built up for many decades, with its endless debt and the special interest complications now written into our tax and business systems,

331

especially in health care and education. The progressive Demographic Cliff, with one country after the next falling off, will almost ensure such a crisis. Therefore, you should be prepared.

My first rule for the crisis ahead would be: *No lobbyists and special interest groups!*

There are countless examples past and present in which the powerful few take most of the gains, leaving the people poor. Think Iraq under Saddam Hussein and Kenya today. Most people were slaves even back in the Roman Empire, and things weren't so fair and equal back in the "enlightened" 1700s in its agricultural economy. The mafia always operates on fear and coercion to its benefit, making most people subservient. It is no different when governments in developed countries control the economy and make it into a mechanical machine—which it is not—perverting and handicapping the very invisible hand of innovation and progress.

I side clearly with the more conservative factions in politics when they argue against too much debt and too many regulations and fight against the degradation of the very free-market principles that have created our success for centuries. That's why my favorite book of 2013 was *Knowledge and Power* by George Gilder. Gilder sees radical entrepreneurs, new technologies, and free-market capitalism as the keys to the advancement of our standard of living. On the other hand, I don't agree with some among the supply-side faction when they oppose every social and political innovation that ultimately fosters progress at all levels. How strong would our economy have been if we hadn't established the equality of African Americans and women, and attracted immigrants and gave them a fair shot at the American Dream?

Even in the North, conservatives fought the emergence of the industrial economy (new technologies) and the abolition of slavery in the Civil War era. They opposed the emancipation of women and their voting rights in the late 1800s and early 1900s. They fought the civil rights movement in the 1960s. They didn't see the inherent contradiction: the same people who espoused free markets and democracy turned around and opposed much new technology and social change that drove progress. There is similar resistance among today's conservatives to fighting global warming, arguing it is a hoax when scientists are nearly unanimous in acknowledging the existence of climate change and its consequences. They are in as much denial as the liberals are about mushrooming debt. Such opposition is akin to the Catholic Church fighting Galileo about whether the earth revolves around the sun.

No, of course we shouldn't kill the golden goose of innovation just because our economy is slowing, even if that hurts some banks, businesses, and households. But how can people who call themselves "conservative" be against the conservation of our natural resources? On the other hand, we must look to new technologies to solve some of these issues, rather than, as some factions of the liberal side wish, to regress back to a simpler lifestyle. That's not going to happen!

One key solution I see is simply to factor the costs of pollution into what we make and sell. We know carbon-based energies have costly consequences: we need to identify those costs, add them to the pricing calculation, then let the free-market system find the best solutions—not the government. That is where government can make a contribution to the free-market system— account for costs that the free markets can't control. You can't expect companies to make environmentally sound decisions if that causes their costs to be higher than their competitors'. Put a tax on carbon and be done with it. Then it is a level playing field for all companies to compete and innovate.

In "Why Innovation Is Still Capitalism's Star," published in the *New York Times* on August 18, 2013, Robert Shiller argued that bottom-up innovation, from risk-taking entrepreneurs, is still the secret to our growth and success. He quoted a McKinsey study that said for every ten thousand real business ideas, one thousand are founded as businesses, one hundred get venture capital, twenty make it to an IPO or public offering, and two become market leaders. Radical innovation is a very hard and unpredictable process. I heard a venture capitalist a decade ago say that he makes money on one out of eleven investments, and he simply doesn't know which one it will be.

Governments should not determine which technologies are best; only entrepreneurs can do that after much trial and error. George Gilder believes future energy solutions will not likely be solar panels or wind technologies because they are not digital (though sun and wind may well be invaluable sources in more rural areas that don't have access to high technology and infrastructures). These technologies have not seen the dramatic decline in cost that semiconductor and other high technologies have. On the other hand, if we went back to living in the woods and burning firewood, we would have much higher pollution than today.

Those who argue that runaway debt is cheating the future for the benefit of today's prosperity must, in the same way, recognize that runaway pollution amounts to a parallel danger in the long term and likely a larger threat to the earth's future. What will happen if most of our coastal cities are flooded with rising oceans late in this century? Even if global warming does not cause all of the dire consequences predicted, pollution, like debt, is never a good thing when it exceeds natural growth rates. It's like dumping your wastes in your backyard. It's going to backfire on you one way or the other. Waste is natural but, when it is not recycled properly, it becomes toxic and kills.

The democratic paradigm holds that cooperation for the whole is the better way; it was in evidence from the Protestant Reformation in the early 1500s forward, and gained momentum in the American and French revolutions in the late eighteenth century. Human society evolved from small bands of hunters and gatherers to become communities of citizens in towns and cities. That has also meant that, as different clans lived together in cities, we subverted our individualistic interests to some degree to benefit the greater whole. Otherwise we would have nonstop violence and chaos. We need law and order, rules, and infrastructures that are commonly shared and initiated by government. And, yes, that means we need more government, too, and taxes to fund it all! George Gilder describes it as a more solid, orderly container from government that facilitates a dynamic private sector characterized by change and innovation. Capitalism cannot excel in a libertarian society or in chaos.

As I always stress, our economy is not like a machine; it is a dynamic system based on the interplay of opposites, in this case democracy/government and capitalism/innovation. The government brings stability, infrastructures, laws, and order. It should be as simple and predictable as possible, including our monetary system. The private sector, ultimately driven by entrepreneurs, brings the breakthroughs and innovations that create exponential S-curve growth, along with the cyclical setbacks. It should be as complex and dynamic as possible, and that's where my biggest criticism of liberal economists and politicians comes.

They want to turn the private sector and free-market capitalism more into a machinelike government. They want straight-line growth, more equality in incomes, no recessions, and complex and endless regulation to protect everyone against everything. But that's how you cage and eventually kill the golden goose. They don't appreciate that the capitalistic system has given us the luxury of trying to help the less fortunate and develop social safety nets. Up to a point, programs that deliver health care and social security and unemployment benefits are good, because people don't oversave for things that can be insured at lower costs and spread across society more efficiently.

On the other hand, the conservatives need to abandon the ideology that holds that we can still embrace the *Little House on the Prairie* paradigm. Wake up, please. On the frontier, our hearty pioneer ancestors needed little government and infrastructure. They hunted and grew their own food, educated their young, made and washed their own clothes, and even built their own houses, maybe with a little help from their friends. They didn't need much money as they bartered for the little else that they needed. Even in a latter-day place like Mayberry in the early to mid-1900s, small towns needed just Andy and Barney to run the town, along with a judge that came through once a month to resolve legal issues. And they had a lot of guns!

But most citizens of our world don't live in small towns or rural areas that thrive on less infrastructure, government, and fewer regulations. Those who do, by the way, tend to be in the poorest areas of developed countries and in emerging countries around the world. For better or for worse, we have to give up our old small-town values as the world continues to urbanize. We've accepted greater government and infrastructures—and we should focus on making them simpler, more efficient, and accountable rather than fighting them.

We can, however, subcontract as many of these services to the private sector as is possible. We need to identify what I call the "optimal minimum" of government services as we don't want to too much eclipse the greater innovation of the private sectors.

You can't run New York City on the same percentage of revenues as Mayberry. Larger cities are more complex and more productive, and they require higher cooperation and integration. They also require more dollars per GDP or per person to facilitate all the specialization and transactions. Progress is partly about younger people running from farms into cities to increase their job opportunities and enhance their lifestyle, even if they have to live in slums at first. (I covered the importance of urbanization in driving economic growth and progress in chapter 6.) Yet it is also true, even in this highly urbanized age, that government can get too large and complex, as it has in many ways. It's natural, after all, for a democratic society to vote in favor of more and more benefits and regulations with less and less accountability. So government must become more accountable and efficient in this winter season, just as businesses and households must do.

In larger and more concentrated urban economies, people can focus on what they do best and delegate what they don't to others. That means we earn more, but also spend more for many tasks. That means higher inflation, as it takes more money to drive such specialization, and many more transactions among people that benefit the whole. It means more government, common infrastructures, and regulations, but the result is greater choice in products, services, education, health care, and entertainment.

What I see from my own long-term research is ongoing, exponential technology innovations. Currently incubating, they will change the paradigm again and make today's current limitations in energy, urban congestion, pollution, and slowing demographics obsolete. I see younger people driving innovation in the economy, especially new college graduates. Rising numbers of younger new workers around the world (in the twenty-to-twenty-four age cohort; see Figure E-1) suggest a major innovation wave from the 1960s into the 2040s; then we are likely to see a slowdown in such innovation cycles and inflation trends given the correlation with young people entering the workforce and inflation. A lot could happen in the next three decades in new technologies, as Ray Kurzweil describes in *The Singularity Is Near* (2005).

The five-hundred-year cycle I've identified around mega-innovations in technologies (see Figure E-2) suggests we are still in the middle stages of an

Figure E-1: Global Innovation/Inflation Wave, 1955-2070

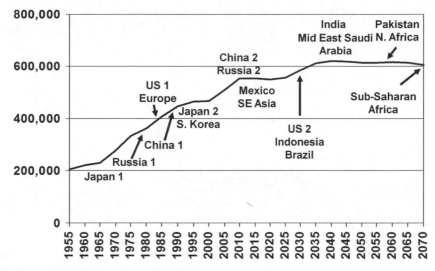

Data Source: United Nations Population Division

inflationary and innovative period that will be more like the late 1400s into the mid-1650s; it extends from the very late 1800s into around 2150. In the preceding innovative era, the greatest exponential demographic growth and technological progress started with mega-innovations like the printing press, tall ships, and gunpowder. In ours, we've seen an information revolution with TV, computers, and jet travel. There is a second information revolution ahead, rich in innovations in areas like biotech, robotics, nanotechnologies, and clean energies.

Suppose that biotechnology, robotics, and nanotechnologies prove not only able to fight pollution and global warming, but also to extend human lifetimes to 120 years plus in the coming decades? As usual, the advance would be seen first in the wealthiest countries (who will be able to afford it), but would ultimately spread to increasingly middle-class emerging countries. What if we entered the workforce later, at, say, ages 25 to 30, after even longer education, and then worked until we were 100 to 110, a work span of 75 to 85 years instead of 40 to 45 years as we do today? How much would that add to lifetime innovation, incomes, borrowing, spending, savings, and investment?

Figure E-2: 500-year Mega Innovation Cycle

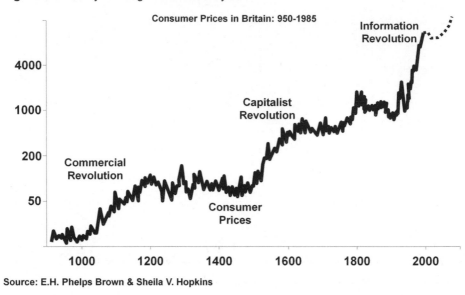

Source: E.H. Phelps Brown & Sheila V. Hopkins

A great extension in life expectancy would extend demographics trends and make them as impactful as in the last century, when our average life expectancy in the United States went from forty-seven years of age to seventy-nine today.

Robert J. Gordon, a professor of economics at Northwestern University, recently posed an interesting question: *What if U.S. growth is over?* He believes that the two big revolutions in industrial technologies since the late 1700s are not likely to repeat. We are already largely urbanized, which was the greatest benefit, and the Echo Boom is the first generation not to be better educated than their parents. He cites how long it took the standard of living to double in England, from 1400 to 1750—350 years! Was 1750–2007 just a freak time in history?

I think Gordon's is a very astute question, given all the slowing trends, the most essential of which may well be the Demographic Cliff with smaller generations following larger ones, first in developed countries from the 1990s into the 2020s and beyond. But I would counter with the exponential historical trends observed by many scientists and modern-day authors in business and technology, among them Gilder, Kurzweil, and me. It took a billion years for single-cell organisms to evolve into multicell. It took 2 million years for primitive man to advance from the first stone tools to harnessing fire. A small portion of the world was discovered after the first true human left Africa around eighty thousand years ago; that trend grew exponentially until the whole world was first inhabited between fifty thousand and ten thousand years ago. By way of summation, let it be said that our standard of living has advanced more in the last century than in the five thousand years before it.

All progress throughout history is exponential, but with cyclical setbacks when old technologies or advances mature and population surges slow. I maintain that it is those very setbacks that create the challenges that result in more radical innovations and reaccelerate the longer-term exponential growth trend. It doesn't matter whether you measure this from biblical times or all the way back to early life in scientific terms. It's always exponential and always cyclical.

I would also suggest that Gordon consider the 250-year revolution in political, social, and business organizations we are just starting to see from the information revolution, which can allow bottom-up organization around customers and citizens with little or no bureaucracy and management (see chapters 8 and 9). How much productivity and gain in living standards will that generate for decades to follow? The Demographic Cliff ahead will create a crisis that accelerates such innovations.

Combine an information- or network-based leap in productivity with rising life expectancies and you have another new paradigm of economic growth ahead. But it will take at least the next decade to see the first fruits of that next information revolution, and we will have to see the major breakthroughs in technology that the demographic wave of younger people in emerging countries would suggest is on the horizon.

Let's look at the chart that shows a 250-year cycle in social, business, and political revolutions (see Figure E-3). Here we see the Protestant Reformation in the early 1500s. The Catholic Church was the dominant force when Martin Luther and then John Calvin revolted; the revolution they started was fueled by the new printing press. Yes, social and political revolutions are

Figure E-3: 250-Year Revolutionary Cycle

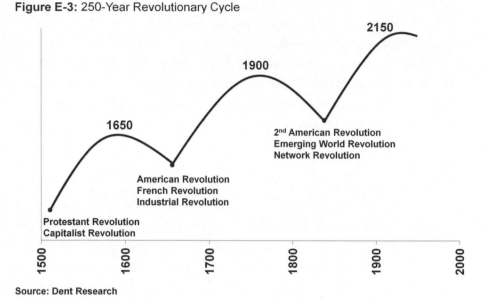

Source: Dent Research

built on revolutions in technologies for communication, travel, and production.

These change agents in the early 1500s facilitated a revolution away from
mass salvation to individualistic determination; a premium was put on working hard, even on saving and reinvesting. This was the birth of the Protestant
work ethic that, along with the new technologies, would transform the world
with the first Capitalist Revolution of the early 1400s, the beginning of a new
500-year Mega-Innovation cycle—that was joined by and corresponded
with this new 250-year Revolution cycle in the early 1500s for a powerful
advancement in economic progress in western Europe.

The Protestant Reformation also saw the beginnings of America, as people sought to escape domination from the Church of England and founded
Plymouth and Jamestown. Henry VIII was famous before that for creating
the Church of England, which converted England to the new Protestant
religion to escape the control of the Catholic Church (and also to allow him
to keep marrying prettier women who he hoped would produce a male heir).
The new branch of Christianity ultimately over many decades evolved into

a new ethic of self-reliance and hard work, not adherence to the establishment or blind faith in religion. That foreshadowed the even bigger revolution in democracy 250 years later.

The biggest bang of all came along when the Industrial Revolution met the Democratic Revolution in the late 1700s in the next 250-year Revolution cycle to follow the Protestant Reformation in the early 1500s. I don't need to say much more than I already have about how important that marriage of historic changes was to our economic progress—the resulting exponential growth of economies and stock markets speaks for itself (see Figure E-4).

Figure E-4: Stock Prices since 1700

Source: *Conquer the Crash* by Robert Prechter, with projection by Harry S. Dent, Jr.

Again, in the long term, growth is not only exponential but cyclical. Stocks saw a sixty-seven-year bear market from 1720 to 1787 after a long boom from around 1500, and then an exponential bull market from 1788 to 2013. That trend could move sideways in developed countries for many decades (possibly from 2008 to around 2080), while emerging countries continue to advance. But at some point we will see another global surge spurred by technological innovations and expanded life expectancy. That surge is likely to last into at least 2150—a long way out.

This next 250-year cycle in political, social, and business innovation hits in this decade forward; and we clearly are already in a revolution in communications with new computer, Internet, and social networking advances. This is likely to be more revolutionary than we think, as visionaries like George Gilder and Ray Kurzweil forecast.

We should see network models emerge for businesses and government. Dictators will fall around the world, unleashing progress in emerging countries, greater transparency in governments in developed countries, and breakthrough technologies. There are undoubtedly advances in clean and alternative energy and industrial processes ahead, along with advances in life expectancies. Travel technologies, too, will advance, as it is already projected that long-range jet travel time could be cut in half by 2030 and then more than that by 2050.

Currently, however, we stand at an impasse. The developed world is slowing due to aging trends. The emerging world is growing from demographics but is not likely to be nearly as rich as the developed world in this century and is facing a downward commodity cycle into the early 2020s. The growth after this crisis in the next decade is clearly likely to come more from the emerging world. But how much these countries can grow, compared with developed countries in the past, is not clear. After all, the best export markets for emerging countries are the richer countries like the United States and Europe. That said, emerging nations will certainly develop more robust domestic and consumer-oriented economies in the future, just as China is today as it recognizes the limits of export growth and infrastructure investments.

Recall that most emerging countries don't have the skills or infrastructures to compete in higher-end industries and information sectors, and, in any case, only so many countries can do that. That is, unless their younger, more innovative populations, who often get educated in the best developed countries, spark technological innovation. What if we in the United States and other developed countries continue to age and begin to lose our technological dominance? There are many technological changes that could shift the balance between developed and emerging countries. The odds do favor some shift toward emerging countries, which are growing faster and gaining technological strength, albeit slowly.

The key opportunity in the coming decades for wealthier and aging developed countries is to invest in the infrastructures and technologies that will accelerate the growing technologies, infrastructure, and middle-class households in emerging countries with lower environmental impacts. Even if they don't become as rich as we are, it would be a win-win with returns to our countries from such investments and higher exports to such growing emerging nations.

Isn't that what aging parents do for their kids? Such investments could also make such countries less polluted so their growth does not bring the whole world down, as China is threatening to do today with its unacceptably high pollution levels. If many emerging countries double their GDP per capita from around $5,000 to $10,000 in the coming decades, that will produce much global growth, but, again, there is the ominous specter of global pollution as the population balloons (see Figure E-5). If we don't come up with better technologies to fight pollution and climate change, demographic growth across the board may slow due to some ecological disasters. This has occurred in the past, and it won't be pretty if it happens.

Figure E-5: Global Population Growth

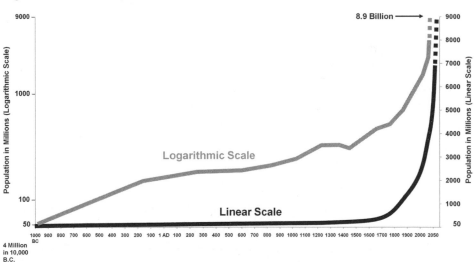

*Ratio scale shows constant percentage growth rate a straight, upward-sloping line; linear scale shows equal absolute increases, so steady percentage growth rate; to curve up;
Source: *Forbes,* January 25, 1999. pp 58-59.;Research: Edwin S. Rubenstein, research director, Hudson Institute, Indianapolis.
Source: Colin McEvedy and Richard Jones, *Atlas of World Population History;* U.N. Secretariat, World Population Prospects: The 1998 Revision: Census Bureau.

Which is the chicken and which is the egg? Do exponential technologies lead to exponential population growth or vice versa? And does one or the other lead to overexpansion, bubbles, and declines? The answer is that the process is a dynamic play of opposites, and both are essential.

While I regard myself as a demographic expert and analyst, I would have to agree a bit more with George Gilder, whose touchstone tends to be technology evolution. New technologies (which also tend, by the way, to come most from larger young new generations) are what allow populations to keep growing exponentially. There was a long period in human history from the end of the Dark Ages into the Industrial Revolution when the "Malthusian trap" applied. If population growth occurred due to higher prosperity, then there were simply more people to live on limited land resources and our standard of living went down, not up. Only better technologies allow us to produce more from that land and support more people, and so on—and that happened in spades after the Industrial Revolution.

We need exponential advances in technology to allow population growth amid limited present-day resources and pollution constraints—and we need exponential increases in populations and urbanization to create both greater opportunities for specialization of labor and more new young people and entrepreneurs who can continue to expand technology exponentially.

The human population has grown exponentially from its inception, despite intermittent mass declines due to ice ages, volcanic eruptions, plagues, and other events. But we've been able to map growth more accurately since the late 1700s. We can anticipate a projected peak around 9 billion plus between 2065 and 2070. Urbanization has grown along with population acceleration, starting in the late 1700s in Great Britain and western Europe, and now spreading through the emerging world into the 2060s.

All bubbles peak, and this bubble, too, will peak at some point, even if our population goes higher in the future after such an adjustment—which it almost certainly will unless we get wiped out altogether like the dinosaurs. What could cause such a dramatic decline in our population? Look back to the Black Death, which cut Europe's population in half in the late 1300s. The cause was an infection from Asia brought via the new trade routes, but what permitted its rapid spread were poor sewer systems, in which infected rats thrived. Europe had repopulated into cities after the fall of the Roman Empire, but people were still throwing their waste into the streets; that was simply easier and less costly. The infection may have seemed to come out of nowhere, but the truth was that it was a *pollution crisis*. Other events leading to a catastrophic loss of life include the near elimination of pre-Columbian American cultures when visited by western Europeans; those were more immediately the result of the spread of a disease. Other cultures have simply exhausted their natural resources and then died off as a result (see Jared Diamond's book *Collapse,* 2011 and his breakthrough book prior, *Guns, Germs, and Steel*). These include the inhabitants of Easter Island, as well as the great American civilizations of the Mayans and Anasazi, among others.

Although we human beings appear to be the most intelligent and most innovative species of all, we are also capable of being very stupid, short-sighted, and selfish. A hard history of survival in difficult environments has taught us to eat and survive today and worry about tomorrow later. In today's interdependent, highly populated, and global economy, that sort of "presentism" and isolationism won't cut it anymore. If we don't start to think and act more collectively and with due regard to future consequences, we could become damn near extinct.

I don't think that is likely to happen. But we do have to stop thinking we can borrow today and worry about paying it off later. We can't just eat today and worry about the consequences of weight gain later; we would do well to weigh carefully the choice between one marshmallow today versus three tomorrow. If we don't, we're suckers for every bubble that comes along and promises easy gains for less work and real investment and sacrifice. We can't just stand by and watch the rate of climate change increase, hoping that the ramifications won't amount to much. Even if the impact is slow in coming, it will be felt by our kids and grandkids. The truth is that such a trend is likely to be as exponential as everything else and to accelerate in the decades ahead, even though it has stalled a bit in the last decade. But technology will also continue to expand exponentially, and that is where we will find new solutions to these formidable challenges in population and pollution.

We have four major and clearly foreseeable challenges over the coming decades:

1. *Unprecedented private and public debt.* We must deleverage in the coming decade, against the determined efforts of banks and governments, or the debt will weigh us down for decades. As Thomas Friedman has recently said: "If we don't have a difficult decade, we will have a challenging century ahead." A difficult decade like the 1930s will deleverage massive amounts of debt, make companies and governments more efficient, and pay off with higher productivity and technological progress in the future, even if demographics continue to slow as presently forecast.

2. *Health care and retirement entitlements.* In societies that are both aging rapidly and living longer, there is no hope for these programs to be sustained. It is not politically acceptable to curb substantially benefits that have been promised for decades, so we need an economic crisis to bring citizens and governments back into reality and to accept benefits more in line with our life expectancies and the ability to pay for them. That will allow younger generations to have a shot at the American Dream (and the human dream altogether) and to grow and prosper.

3. *Authoritarian governance.* There are many dictators, tribal leaders, warlords, and mafias around the world who continue to suppress the progress of many emerging countries for their own power and wealth. They have got to go, by force if necessary. When they do, many more people will become middle class, at least at the lowest levels, and contribute more to world growth and to innovation.

4. *Environmental pollution.* There has been a mushrooming pollution crisis since the late 1800s as we defer cleanup costs at great harm to our environment. This could be the greatest threat to our global economy in the century ahead. It will take a new paradigm of technologies to combat such pollution and allow new growth without such impact; to go back to using little electricity or other resources would tend to slow human growth and innovation. If we don't innovate and price in the impacts of carbon-based and other technologies to allow

our free markets to innovate more effectively, pollution and global warming could end our population bubble for many decades and force human populations to levels that are more sustainable before they can grow again. That would not be pretty.

Despite the exponential growth for all of human history from any point in the past, there have been long periods of time when economic progress declined to allow for greater innovations to emerge—yes, that is why we need periods of sleep or slowing! With the Demographic Cliff that started with Japan in the 1990s and continues to hit almost all developed countries from 2014 into 2019, this certainly could be one of those times for the developed world, with a difficult decade (perhaps even multiple decades) during which emerging countries steal the show. But with the exponential rise in technologies, I don't see a Dark Age that lasts for five centuries or more, especially with the five-hundred-year cycle pointing up into around 2150. Major technological breakthroughs are likely in the years and decades ahead. I will be looking for them well in advance. But until then:

Steel yourself. If we don't have the guts and foresight to face and deal with these issues, then we deserve to see our unprecedented progress over the last two centuries—and the last two thousand years—fall, just as occurred with the Roman Empire. There are clear solutions to these problems, but all require that we face a harsh reality and employ foresight and our capacities for innovation, investment, and sacrifice.

Where is our Abraham Lincoln, FDR, or Winston Churchill? I think one or more will emerge in the next decade . . . but only in a major crisis.

You need to prepare for that crisis, which will occur between 2014 and 2023, with the worst likely starting in 2014 and continuing off and on into late 2019. Most if not all of the deflation and decline in stock prices I am predicting is likely to occur by late 2019. You can contribute to the solution by conserving your financial assets and reinvesting them after the crisis. Building that new business or nonprofit you're dreaming of will best serve the recovery and the new customized and network economy ahead.

I have given you the best of my long-term research, in simple terms that

I hope everyone can understand, and practical strategies at all levels from my thirty-plus years of real-life business experience. It's up to you to take advantage of this inevitable crisis, because government strategies to prevent it will fail in the coming years. The world will be your oyster if you understand the situation and act now.

Best of success to you and thanks for reading.

To keep in touch with what I am thinking and our new insights at Dent Research, go to www.harrydent.com and sign up for our free daily newsletter, *Survive & Prosper.*

ACKNOWLEDGMENTS

Thanks to: my literary agent, Susan Golomb; my partners at Dent Research, Rodney Johnson and Harry Cornelius; my research assistants, David Okenquist and Stephanie Gerardot; my newsletter publishers at Sovereign Society, Erika Nolan and Shannon Sands; my *Survive & Prosper* newsletter editor, Teresa van den Barselaar; my *Boom and Bust* newsletter editor, Mark Smith; the director of the Dent Network, Lance Gaitan; and its board members, Mike Robertson, Joe Clark, Don Creech, Daryl LePage, and Jim Lunney.

INDEX

Page numbers in *italics* refer to figures.